BICENTENNIAL
REX

By Michael Anthony Turpin

DEDICATION

To My Wife, Caroline: You are my Susie.

To My Brother, Miles: Yes, I admit it. I stole your rare coin collection and spent every silver dollar at the Little League field buying candy and hot dogs from Al's snack truck.

Plate 1

FUN NEL A TOR

Start with duct tape, 6 feet of surgical tubing and a plastic funnel. Next, tie the tube in a knot. Then attach funnel(use a lot of duct tape-just so it dosent break. Get two people to hold each end of the tubing, and a third to pull the funnel backwards. Place a water balloon or tennis ball in the funnel, and let it fly. Don't aim at people, animals, or babies- they get hurt.

WINTER

AMERICAN WINTER SPORTS.

CHAPTER 1

The Democrats seem to basically be...the kind of people who'd stop to help you change a flat, but would somehow manage to set your car on fire. The Republicans, on the other hand, would know how to fix your tire, but they wouldn't bother to stop because they'd want to be on time for Ugly Pants Night at the country club.

~Dave Barry

The town of Huntington Hills could have doubled for a Hollywood back lot of 1950's suburbia—a continuum of green-grass middle-class and upwardly mobile Californians who had built a bulwark against the urban sprawl of Los Angeles. It was a singular place—a pastoral refuge forged out of fire and earthquakes.

The San Andreas Fault ran along much of the eastern spine of Southern California—a serpentine fissure of geological tension that lay coiled like a spring, threatening at any moment to shake the foundations of those who settled to its west.

North and east of the San Andreas along the Walker Lane geologic trough rose California's most dramatic granite citadels: the Sierra Nevada. The collision of the Pacific and the North American Plates had also given birth to smaller fractures with names like Garlock, San Jacinto, Elsinore and Imperial - infant spider veins of geological capillaries that formed smaller peaks and foothills. The most prominent of these ranges, the San Gabriel and San Bernardino mountains, acted as broad shoulders protecting the region from the arid and dehydrating winds of the California high deserts.

Civilization ceased in these national forests and gave way to the nightly cries of coyotes, owls, and the stealthy scuttle of white-tailed deer that blended in with the dry chaparral, scrub pines, and tangled manzanita. Altadena rested at the base of Mount Wilson with its prominent radio towers feeding local television and radio stations. On a clear day, residents could see the idle Mount Lowe toll road as it zigzagged across Mount Wilson's purple and sienna edifice like a jagged scar.

The community measured three point six square miles and rested twenty-five miles east of the Pacific Ocean in a sheltered valley of palm trees, live oaks, and sycamores. Without fickle precipitation and irrigation by water stolen from Northern California, Huntington Hills would have been reduced to its original landscape of dry, dusty arroyos and brown, shrouded canyons. When it did rain, the suburban run-off was not conserved in reservoirs or ponds but instead coursed down copper gutters into underground French drains, spilling down well-designed sewage systems that eventually converged into the brackish polluted waterway that was the Los Angeles River.

In the summer, the valley formed a natural inversion layer that captured the urban Los Angeles carbon emissions, producing a noxious bowl of asphyxiating smog; in winter, the mountains served as a backstop, capturing northeastern-bound Pacific storm systems to greedily extract their moisture. This meteorological phenomenon produced February and March snow down to altitudes as low as two thousand feet and generated spectacular Chamber of Commerce photographs of sunny palms set against vistas of snow-capped peaks.

The town itself could be broken down into a vertical and horizontal axis, with each quadrant representing a nuanced socioeconomic profile. While the community was highly homogenous, it was impossible to generalize about any particular family. Each house acted as a kabuki mask for a range of circumstances. Wealth smoothed the edges of life's hard corners but could also stoke the fires of vanity and conceit. Each address was a serial with its own plot: old money, nouveau riche, broken homes, nuclear families, serenity, and chaos.

Huntington Hills' borders were subtle. Roads, homes, and landscaping served as unassuming lines of demarcation that separated residential and commercial, funded and underfunded, new and old, as well as white, brown, and black. For most middle-class families, a 91109 zip code simply meant a better funded school district and an improved quality of life for their children. It was a fair trade: the possibility of affluence and reassuring homogeneity in exchange for a tougher commute along the serpentine, traffic-choked Pasadena and Foothill freeways.

As in every town, there was a right and wrong side of the tracks; in the case of Huntington Hills, it was a gerrymandered economic dividing line that separated the community into the Hills and the Flats. One's net worth was less evident to children but easily detected by status conscious adults with the simple glance at an acquaintance's home address.

The higher up families moved economically, the more likely they were to live north toward Pasadena, in The Hills. Within these gently sloping multi-acre properties, they could rub elbows with the privileged of the Southern California business and entertainment communities.

The Flats was a five-mile stretch of modest properties that retreated southwest from the retail and commercial storefronts lining the main thoroughfare, Huntington Hills Drive. The residential grid was a simple triumph of suburban planning: a latticework of pleasant streetlamp-lined roads and wide, friendly sidewalks.

For most residents, sidewalks meant progress, access, and security; they were also the main thoroughfares for free-range kids, who walked, biked, and skateboarded great distances from their homes. The sidewalks were the primary arteries of a body that prized safety and unlimited movement.

To get to the home of Karl and Susie Patton and their four sons— Matthew, John, George, and Freddie—at 1828 Bedford Street, a kid would cut through a series of narrow alleys that knifed between the backsides of commercial buildings and the back yards of small Mediterranean-style starter homes. The Patton's two-story hacienda, built in 1928, was carefully constructed between cement and asphalt boundary lines: driveways, walkways, and a five-by-thirty-foot curbside greenbelt. It stood handsomely among red-tiled cottages and swarthy Spanish-style homes surrounded by gardens of rainbow-colored impatiens, citrus trees, bristling oleanders, lipstick-red bougainvillea and shaggy olive junipers. Casa Patton was fashioned out of stucco with a rich red adobe-tiled roof, wood beams, and wrought-iron window frames.

Change passed Bedford Street each day without stopping to say hello. The social, political, and racial fissures that were scratching away the veneer of America's magnanimous post-WWII infallibility were visible only on the front pages of newspapers. The town that curled like a cat at the foot of the purple San Gabriel Mountains slept quietly. But in December 1975, the community was on the crest of seminal events, all portending the dawn of a new era—America's 200th birthday and a presidential election.

"Teddy, what are we doing?"

"Dude, you're just stalling."

George Patton strained his eyes to peer out the drenched windshield of a chrome-blue Gremlin as the ancient wipers did little more than spread and even out the persistent drizzle of an unsettled December night. He and Teddy Galloway were parked in the Hills along Park Circle at the mouth of a long driveway that could have passed for a country road. A thin tributary of black asphalt flowed away from the street, passing silently beneath a menacing Cyclops of a mansion with its one illuminated upstairs window. Somewhere down the driveway near a pool and neglected tennis court was a guesthouse where a twenty-nine-year-old drug dealer named Ronnie Thomas waited.

"Last year, someone passed John a clove and it was laced with angel dust or something and he totally freaked out. What's this stuff supposed to do anyway? Make me a sex maniac?"

"You don't take them. She does. Spanish Flies make girls crazy *for* you. When Kelly Reed is drooling for you like you're Burt freakin' Reynolds, you'll be glad you met Ronnie. He's the only guy that has the flies. He was like a doctor in Vietnam and got them from some African dude who was a witch doctor and sells these things called Afro-dizzies.

"Georgie, she's a sophomore, a pep rep and a freak of nature with that body. You think she is going to just say to a freshman tool, 'take me you fool'? Hey that rhymes!"

"Oh, she's fast all right. I hear she's been to like fifteen Dead shows. Sheehy says she did it with one of the Allman Brothers. You know, the uglier guy, not the lead singer with the long blond hair. Actually all those dudes are gnarly."

Teddy had a soft face lacking the sharp contours that often accompanied puberty and maturation. He was a thick kid with wide chocolate eyes and a brawling thatch of brown hair that seemed freshly liberated from a baseball cap. He had a small mouth and a bubble-gum tongue that curled as he spoke. When he was nervous or excited, Teddy became verbally incontinent, and now he was hurling hyperbole and useless facts at George faster than the Sandy Koufax pitching machine at the El Monte batting cages.

George grimaced, unconvinced, and rolled his eyes. "So, if Kelly Reed's so easy and so into *gnarly* older dudes, why the flies and why me?"

Teddy leaned back in the driver's seat looking perplexed, "Dude, why she picked you to go to the dance when she could have a real man like *moi* will remain one of life's great mysteries. She musta heard the rumor I started that you're dying. This is strictly a mercy mission, or maybe, it's a *Befriend a Loser* service project for Omegas. Look, the flies are like buying insurance from your old man. You're just putting her in the right mood. Von was at this concert in Frisco where he saw some girl that had taken Spanish Flies and she was making out with everyone, including some Hell's Angel biker and I think, like a stop sign. Where am I when all this nymphomania is happening?"

George became annoyed. "I'll tell you where you are? You're home with Rosie. And for the millionth time, no one says 'Frisco'. Matthew says it's just called 'The City'. Anyway, Von is full crap. The last concert he went to was a Christmas assembly. You guys are lurkers, not lovers."

"Well, at least I will be alive at Christmas. I heard Java man, Timmy Irwin, was *really* pissed that she was going to the Christmas dance with you. I guess the missing link thinks he owns her. But, hey, you're right. Let's bag it and just go home. Your psychic freaking mother has probably already called my parents to find out that nobody's home."

"Galloway, you're fogging up the whole car."

All George could think about was what his father would do to him if he were ever caught with a drug dealer or Spanish Flies. He squinted through the windshield, wiping away precipitation with his shirtsleeve to peer at the sinister, shrouded windows in the distant guesthouse.

"What if there are undercover cops in there?"

"Everyone knows that if you ask a cop if he's a cop, he's gotta answer truthfully. It's in the Bill of Rights. We ask him if Mary Jane's home. If he says yes, we go in and then we ask him if he is a cop. If he says 'yes', we just leave and apologize saying we got the wrong address."

George stared into the darkness.

Teddy continued talking. "Although Van's brother, Scotty, did say Thomas was crazy in high school *even before* he went to Vietnam. He said Ronnie almost killed a kid from South Pass in a football game. Another time, he raped a substitute, but she was too scared to testify."

George aped Teddy's earnest expression and then made a patronizing stupid face. "Raped a teacher? The guy would be like, in San Quentin, you idiot."

He stopped and stared back into the night, thinking of his father again. "Old Karl says California's going to hell since we voted out the death penalty. No more gas chamber or electric chair means more murders."

Teddy started to shake like he was being electrocuted but saw that his friend was preoccupied with the dimly lit mansion. Teddy stopped flopping and punched George in the arm.

"Lighten up. Ronnie's sister, Joanie, is tight with Katie. They lived together when they went to PCC. Joanie still hangs at our house. She says her brother sounds crazy but it's like an act just to keep people away. If he was a psycho once, he's not anymore. He's like Boo Radley. He hides during the day, watches TV, and gets stoned. She says he got messed up during Tit in 'Nam. It was a huge battle where Chinese soldiers wasted like a million of our guys. Speaking of tits, Mister Rogers, can you say Mrs. Thomas? Oh my God! She is a total babe. Have you ever seen her? What I would not have given to be baby Ronnie. Anyway, I wouldn't worry. He's probably too stoned to stand up."

George gave a sardonic snort. "It's the *Tet* offensive, motor mouth. Chinese? They weren't even in Vietnam. You know, my Dad just missed going to Korea. He said they just kept coming and coming. His gunny was the only guy who survived in his whole platoon. By the way, how did you pass Party Marty's history class? A million guys did not die in Vietnam! So who's the real loser? At least I'm going to the freaking dance. You don't even have the guts to even ask a girl out. You will just sit home swatting to S.W.A.T."

George broke into a grin and started to croon Jackson Browne.

"Rosie, you're my friend. You wear my ring …"

Teddy had been one of George's best friends from the day George arrived at Crocker Elementary School in January of 1968. His old school, Stoneleigh, had found itself at capacity from an influx of new families, and George had been redistricted to a recently opened school closer to the Patton home on Bedford Street. The move was tough on him. New kids and new schools never seemed to mix – especially if you stood out for any reason.

Parents often referred to kids like George as "big boned" or "husky." To George, the term "husky" was cheap verbal primer thinly covering an even uglier undercoat: "fat." Just hearing "husky" made George want to punch someone. Having his two older brothers, Matthew and John, call him "fat boy" while they consumed 12,000 calories in a single sitting and appeared like extras in a POW movie made George even more self-conscious and left him wondering why he had been dealt the metabolic deuces in the Patton family. George took after his German great-grandmother who was built like a pallet of storage crates balanced on cement pipes. It was a miracle that anyone had actually married Omah. Apparently, there was a perfect match for everyone in the world. You just sometimes had to leave your country to find them.

George had hated Crocker Elementary—a name that sounded like a girl's cookbook. He despised the strange kids who stared at him; the long, sterile hallway that descended down to the adjacent middle school; and the massive sloping playground that would make an agoraphobic run for cover. He was already a big kid at seven years old, often mistaken for a third or fourth grader. He was desperately lonely for his old friends from the day he was shoved out of Karl's car and into Miss Stoner's second-grade class. No kid other than his older brothers had ever openly cast aspersions on his physiology, but it took less than minute at his first recess at Crocker for him to be tagged with a stinging epithet.

"Hey, Pumpkin Head!"

George had turned around amused, scanning the playground for the person who was the butt of this funny new word. He whirled to confront two elfin, tow-headed boys: identical twins dressed in white tee shirts, blue jeans and red cloth Keds. He felt a strange sensation of hot flashes and nausea as he realized he was the object of their ridicule. The twin tormentors weaved around him like Heckel and Jeckel, the annoying magpies in late-afternoon cartoons.

"Hey round mound, how come your head is so big?" asked David Camp, the two-minutes-older brother as he stared at his mirror image, Ed.

"It's the Great Pumpkin, Charlie Brown!"

Another kid wandered over as George turned five shades of crimson. Soon there was a crescent-shaped peanut gallery behind his two miniature provocateurs. Young George was unprepared and could only retaliate with a pathetic reference to their microscopic size. Years later, he would regret not coming up with something infinitely more cutting such as, "My dog takes craps bigger than you." However, it was always in retrospect that a bullied kid came up with his best retorts—sometimes as late as thirty years following a gut wrenching encounter.

"For a guy with such a big head, you're pretty dumb."

A group of kids gathered and laughed at George. He could not recall exactly which insult made him snap, but he distinctly remembered taking off after the Camp twins and ripping one of their shirts. Yet George was outclassed and confounded by the more nimble twin meerkats as they darted in opposite directions, mocking him and shouting, "Pumpkin Head."

A teacher intervened, and to his shock, six kids fingered George as the instigator.

Thus, on his first day at Crocker, George was marched to the principal, Miss Eloise Pratt. His shirt was also torn. He was fuming and despondent. Five minutes later, a short, stocky kid who could have been George's stunt double walked into the office with a hall pass. "I saw everything, Miss Pratt," Teddy said. "The Camps started teasing this new kid. He didn't do anything."

As was so often the case, Miss Pratt still felt compelled to chastise the boys. It seemed to George that when you were a kid, everything was your fault. If a dog bit you, an adult might thump you anyway, yelling, "What the hell did you do to make the damn dog bite your hand? Were you screwing around?" A kid was always guilty until proven innocent.

Yet on September 6, 1968, Teddy Galloway had come to George's rescue, and for seven years the boys had been inseparable.

By the early 1970s, George had grafted in well with his new school-mates. He was an empathetic kid with a big heart who could navigate his way through most challenges. He was a good student and, given his powerful squat build, everyone's pick for anchorman in tug-of-wars, offensive lineman, and cleanup hitter. He was the guy who lifted every-one else to safety but then got caught because he could not boost himself over the wall. He never completed a single pull-up in the President's fit-ness challenge and couldn't run a mile in less than twelve minutes.

As a bulky kid, his biggest challenge was clothing. The Pattons were of modest means, and George often wore hand-me-downs from his father, Matthew, and John. He did not recall ever having a waist size less than thirty-two inches and was perpetually popping buttons, rip-ping crotches, and tearing the seat of his brother-broken-in cotton and corduroy trousers. The introduction of denim prolonged his wardrobe but could not completely disarm his thunder thighs and U-Haul rear end. While these attributes made him a football coach's dream, he was a tailor's nightmare and an expensive line item in Susie's back-to-school budget.

His greatest fear was removing his shirt in public. His friends paraded like starving immigrants with washboard stomachs and adolescent hair in all the right places. George resembled alabaster Play-Doh fresh out of the canister. Each morning, he inventoried the annoying baby fat under his arms that seemed to over-accentuate his chest. John referred to this abundance of flesh as "man-boobs"—a term George did not care to ever hear.

Southern California was an island resting in a permanent jet stream of warm weather. Ubiquitous sunshine meant trips to the beach, pool parties, and sun bathing. He loathed his fast-metabolism friends and the V-shaped chlorine-green swimmers that wore speedos and looked for any reason to remove their shirts. Their abs resembled low rolling hills that climbed to broad shoulders. George was more like Antarctica—a wide, colorless landmass with no distinguishable terrain. He could not exactly isolate his biceps, abdominal muscles, or quadriceps, as they were all well insulated under a protective layer of permafrost baby fat. Further trauma would await him in middle school when boys' physical education class would invariably require him to run six-hundred-yard laps around the school perimeter or square off in basketball as either shirts or skins. To go "skin" in middle school PE was to advertise one's darkest fears to an audience of unforgiving, insensitive pinheaded boys. To further exacerbate the humiliation, a game might be held outside in full view of the girls who would be doing jumping jacks, playing dodge ball, or running the way girls who did not exercise often ran, in a sort of spastic headlong tumble as if they were falling downhill.

The gym teacher, Mr. Stephens, loathed George and his posse of languid irregulars for their creative efforts to avoid physical education. It had taken Stephens an entire quarter to figure out that George and his band of pudgy misfits were not completing the required weekly mile run. The boys would complete the first three hundred yards of the timed jog and then disappear into a Little League scorer's shack, crouching on dusty wooden plank floors while waiting for the final lap, when the thirty-boy class would be strung out across the entire course. They would leap back into the sweaty pack and sprint to the finish line in the required time of under eight minutes.

George's conscientious objection to any form of movement offended his gaunt PE teacher, who resembled an adult film star with his dolphin gym shorts, tight muscle shirt, blond sideburns and moustache. He looked at George and Teddy with sadistic disdain as he picked sides for basketball. "Patton, Galloway. Skins!" He might as well have said, "Patton. Naked!"

George removed his shirt and quickly crossed his arms, convinced from his brother Matthew's chiding that he had bigger breasts than Raquel Welch. Most of the girls were now circling the playground with their paroxysmal, awkward lunges. For the next thirty minutes, George moved in slow, self-conscious bursts, jiggling like a bowl of Jell-O as he rotated from one side of court to another. His only consolation was Galloway, who lent breathless comical color to their mutual humiliation.

"Psst! Georgie. We got bigger boobs than Sally Baines!"

George would laugh but also feel the ache of longing when he spied girls like Sally Baines, Karen Kelley, Tami Coultas and Kerry Figgins, lithe blonde and brunette goddesses who swirled like boiling suns at the center of his sexual universe. Even their names made them sound like swimsuit models. Yet, these Aphrodites were untouchable and perpetually insulated from guys like George, who comprised the flaky outer skin of their middle school social scallion. They were losers and wannabes who could never perforate the inner ring of popular boys who seemed blessed by better genetics, earlier puberty, family money, or a second home in Newport Beach. He was a tortured Cyrano to these untouchable Roxannes.

Now fifteen and approaching six feet in height, George had finally lost what his Irish mother lovingly referred to as his "famine insurance" and was eagerly entering the mysterious, jasmine-scented world of girls. Though objectively he was turning into a nice-looking kid with aqua-blue eyes and a kind smile, in his mind's eye the apprentice swan remained an ugly, chubby duckling. He felt the need to seek out every possible advantage with the opposite sex. His field accessories included Visine, English Leather cologne, "Gee, Your Hair Smells Terrific Shampoo" and spearmint flavored Binaca. Yet, his insecurity was dragging him further down a rabbit hole of desperation. He would now approach a psychotic Vietnam veteran drug dealer to buy an aphrodisiac for a school dance.

While most freshman girls were railroaded into home economics classes to learn to bake, maintain proper *Redbook* posture, and ultimately be hypnotized into believing that Prince Charming did actually exist and was out there wearing clean underwear, boys were forced into health class to learn the proper techniques for using deodorant, wearing a jock strap, avoiding women with venereal diseases, and abstaining from the use of drugs with names like bennies, uppers, downers, horse, and Mary Jane.

In the eighth grade, newly anointed teens like George and his friends were subjected to anti-drug movies to attempt to scare them straight. In the annals of anti-drug films, the 1970 *Pit of Despair* stood as a classic, converting the most impressionable among them into paranoid purists who would rather die of influenza than take any kind of medication. After viewing what older kids referred to as "The Pit", George was afraid to take so much as a Bayer aspirin for fear of running naked down the Santa Monica freeway pursued by a winged, severed goat's head.

Every anti-drug flick offered a similar plot featuring a normal suburban kid relenting to peer pressure and agreeing to attend a wild "tea" party with lava lamps, thirty-watt bulbs, beanbag chairs, sitar music, bell-bottomed girls, and drug dealers known as pushers. Against the backdrop of Three Dog Night's "Momma Told Me Not to Come," the all-American boy ends up with more holes in his arm than a cribbage board, and screaming as his party mates are no longer people but grotesque demons with narrow pink beaks. Instead of fleeing the den of iniquity, he takes a more direct route to the street, leaping out an open window shouting, "Look at me! I can fly!" Meanwhile, his emotionally dead friends look on in sociopathic indifference as a rag-doll dummy with flailing arms tumbles down to the sidewalk below.

Some kids were quick to dismiss the exaggerated melodrama of *Pit of Despair*, but George had been affected by the propaganda. He knew of people who occasionally smoked marijuana, but he was not interested in jumping off a tall building and becoming road kill. Someone might see him with his shirt off.

Drug use obviously was rampant, and if a kid sniffed, puffed or popped, he was likely to immediately grow long hair, quit taking baths, and barely manage a two-syllable response to any question. The best a druggie could muster was to walk around all day saying, "Solid, man." This wild-haired, drug-crazed gutter trash hung on the fringe of society like body snatchers waiting to co-opt good kids into a life of drugs, promiscuous sex, and crime—the trifecta of worthlessness, according to the Gospel of Karl Patton. John Lennon memorialized the quintessential hippie in the song, "Come Together." The Beatles were notorious for putting symbols and subliminal drug messages in songs like "Hey Jude," "Lucy in the Sky with Diamonds," and even "Yellow Submarine," extolling the virtues of expanding one's mind with opiates and hard narcotics.

While girls emerged from home economics with a new appreciation for the wonders of baking soda, George and his friends suddenly saw powdered sugar and flour as sinister accessories for pushers to further corrupt the poison they unleashed on Main Street.

But now George was about to make a deal with the devil. He was risking it all: his sanity, his freedom and the epidermis on his buttocks, to procure erotic Spanish Flies from a guy who was rumored to have killed a guy.

"What if he pulls a gun or a knife?" George was doing his checklist.

"Just fall on the ground, close your eyes, scream, and kick at the air. That's what Patrick does whenever I pound on him. It works. He kicked me in the nuts yesterday. It's sort of like what you do if you are attacked by a grizzly."

"That's the stupidest thing I have ever heard. How much money does he want?" George tried to change the subject.

"Forty bucks."

"Are you kidding me? I'd have to shine, like, eighty pairs of the Old Man's shoes to earn that kind of bread."

"Do you want them or not? Look, he does not sell tiny little dime bags. He is a big-time dealer and he is doing this as a favor because I know his little sister."

"Dime bags?" George turned, frowning toward Teddy.

"French Connection"

"Oh, I forgot. Well while you're sneaking into X-rated movies on Colorado Boulevard, we are scamming on real girls."

"French Connection was R-rated, butt-head, and I have my *own* girl-friend in Oregon. Besides, she'd get pissed if I screwed around on her."

"Of course, *right*…The thirty-year-old schoolteacher no one has ever seen that you bagged *last* summer. I forgot about her. What's her name? Cherry, Mary, or is it Larry?"

Teddy looked genuinely offended by his best friend's sarcasm. "It's Sharon. And she's like twenty-five."

"So what's a school teacher doing hanging out with a fifteen-year-old kid from Los Angeles?" George asked sarcastically, knowing that he was once again tearing at the one adolescent lie that stood between them.

Teddy opened his mouth to protest and George cut him off.

"Shut up. Never mind. Let's just do this."

The boys opened the door as a rush of cold wind and rain whipped across their faces. The main house was now dark. Someone had extinguished the light somewhere inside. The living room curtains were open and in the mist, it appeared to George that someone was standing near the window watching them.

George kept thinking about every little thing that could go wrong as he shuffled towards the guest house, which was tucked up against a covered kidney-shaped swimming pool. He could hear the thumping of bass, music and laughter.

His track record of breaking family rules and getting caught was pathetic, thanks to his clairvoyant mother, extortionist brothers, and a phone tree of women who seemed to pinch the truth out of every kid and report it to one another within days. The best he could hope for was to be caught by his mother. If his father ever found out, he would probably have to fake his own death like Tom Sawyer, eliciting just enough sympathy from the community that he might be spared some nuclear punishment.

"The Huntington Hills Bicentennial Steering Committee will come to order." A pudgy, bearded man in his late twenties stood at the dais. He wore penny loafers with no socks, red polished-cotton slacks, blue and red elastic belt, and a blue striped pinpoint. He slapped the lectern with a worn maple-stained gavel that looked as if it had been fashioned in seventh-grade woodshop.

After conducting the Pledge of Allegiance, the chairman turned to his left. "Our esteemed secretary, Miss Saunders, has shared copies of last month's minutes. Are there additions or corrections? Motion to approve the minutes?"

"So moved," muttered Karl Patton, as he glanced at his watch.

A bookish-looking spinster of indistinguishable chronology smiled and adjusted her horn-rimmed glasses, holding up a limp mimeographed paper with congested purple text. She broke into a two-pack-a-day, crooked grin that made Karl shudder.

"Seconded," someone shouted.

"Damn it, Malcolm. You don't second approvals. What are you, ignorant?"

"Fuck off, Freeman. I'll third and fourth the damn thing if you don't shut up."

"Gentleman, let's stay on track, shall we?" the chairman scolded. Karl Patton and three elderly men who could have been the chairman's grandfathers sat at attention in the small classroom. Only Len Downer, the mummified owner of the local nursery, remained silent. He looked incredulously at the two men and then at Karl. Malcolm MacDonald's arthritic hand slowly rose in the air and opened like a flower in time-lapse photography.

"I'd like to approve old business."

Freeman Dewitt, subcommittee chairman of the Rose Park fireworks, looked at MacDonald and winced. "Malcolm, you can't approve old business if there ain't no old business. Boy, I think an idiot slipped into your family gene pool when the lifeguard wasn't watching."

"Well, you're as dumb as a goddamn sack of sledge hammers. That's why you run a hardware store."

The chairman rolled his eyes, slightly annoyed at the two older men who were his father's golf partners. He smiled perfunctorily at his adoring tribe of mummified sycophants, acting more like the President of the United States than a man presiding over a five-person Fourth of July celebration subcommittee meeting. He was a pompous man, self-satisfied with his position, his physical fullness, and the complete control of his handpicked subcommittee chairs. The decrepit DeWitt beamed at the chairman, who could have passed for Sebastian Cabot or Orson Welles.

"Gentleman, let's move on. I believe we left off last month around the concessions for the Fourth of July picnic, but we needed to determine who should be in the procession, select nominees for the Grand Marshal, map out the exact route, and set the time for the fireworks. If we have time tonight, I'd like to make sure we get a complete update for next week's plenary session. I'd like to allow Karl Patton to update us on the parade logistics and his subcommittee's ideas for Grand Marshal."

The corpulent, *enfant* master sergeant of the Huntington Hills Bicentennial Steering Group was Ralph Hunt II, aka R2, son of Ralph Hunt, who owned and operated a chain of highly successful San Gabriel Valley grocery stores known as Hunt's Markets. Sixty-five-year-old Ralph Senior was a philanthropic and community legend in Huntington Hills, who had spent close to a half-century providing groceries to families, jobs for teenagers, and deep pockets to fund major town events such as the Fourth of July at Roses Park and the annual lighting of Christmas trees along Santa Anita Avenue.

In the past six months, Hunt Senior had suffered two strokes brought on by his prodigious weight and a case of uncontrolled diabetes. In the last year, he had lost half his foot to amputation but continued to work as if his chronic illness were nothing more than an annoying head cold. The second stroke had affected his mobility to the point where he was forced to pass the reins of his business to his eldest son, R2.

As Hunt Senior convalesced, R2 wasted no time assuming responsibility for his father's three markets and oversubscribed civic schedule, which included the Bicentennial celebration.

Karl sat in a classroom at Hills Junior High School, wedged into a desk that was intended for someone the size of his youngest son, Freddie, a ninety-five-pound sixth grader. At five feet nine, Karl was handsome and had little body fat because of his strict adherence to a daily early-morning routine of push-ups, sit-ups and ten miles on an exercise bicycle. At forty-five, he looked younger and infinitely more capable than the bloated blue blood who droned on about raising funds and building floats made out of swatches of American flags.

Why these damn meetings were not held in city hall or even at the local community center was beyond Karl's comprehension. He could hear the evening cleaning crew speaking Spanish and vacuuming a classroom through the wall as he shifted uncomfortably and inventoried his incredibly bad luck.

Susie's idea for Karl to join the hometown Bicentennial Steering Committee had seemed a stroke of genius at the time. He had been after Hunt's Markets as a client for more than two years. To work with the company's founder on his Bicentennial committee would give Karl the chance to demonstrate a range of skills and also meet some of the old man's business and social contacts, which were legendary in the San Gabriel Valley. Karl did not have much use for the younger Hunt, the red-nosed fraternity brat who drove a cherry SL Mercedes convertible and always seemed to be sporting a different bleached-blonde divorcee at restaurants or community events.

Everyone else called Ralph Jr. by the nickname "R2", but it made Karl feel physically ill to use the sobriquet. Just saying the words "R Two" made him feel like he was snapping a towel in the locker room with a bunch of mindless adolescents. Karl had close to fifteen years on R2, and the men had nothing in common. Karl was born into poverty, served in the military and worked his way into the middle class. He was fit, frenetic, and a father to four rambunctious teenage boys ranging from 19 years to 11 years old. Karl had been married to the love of his life, Susie O'Reilly Patton, for twenty years this June. She was the first woman he had met in California while staying one night at a San Francisco boarding house in 1949.

R2, on the other hand, was a creature of consumption. He wore the fact that he would inherit his family's fortune like a massive platinum medallion and was a fixture at local Pasadena and Los Angeles social clubs and watering holes: the prestigious San Gabriel Valley Equestrian Club, the haughty Bel-Air Golf Club, and the patrician Santa Monica Beach and Tennis Club. He was always swirling at the center of these social vortexes and held the title of champion of one sort or another— golf, beach club paddle, or consuming martinis.

Ralph Hunt II spent his working hours avoiding responsibility, polishing a sandbagger's ten-handicap and shuttling between his father's markets, where he was known to sit in the dairy refrigerator drinking imported beers or roaming the aisles looking for attractive women he might escort to their cars after he shoved aside the tip-hungry box boys.

In Karl's opinion, Hunt II was a shape-shifting, political windsock that had most likely protested the war but now professed to be a Republican. Hunt's greatest passion was spending his father's money.

For the past several weeks, the planning committee had been mired in petty squabbles over the logistics for a Fourth of July parade and had yet to pick a parade dignitary to represent the town—a tribute that R2 continued to privately advocate for himself. The only opposition to this idea was coming from Karl, who felt strongly that the Bicentennial Grand Marshal must be an individual who embodied the character, virtues and values that America had once found sacred enough to go to war. America was in a sorry state and this Bicentennial year was important to restore its citizens' faith in government and in its manifest destiny as a world democratic power. Somehow, R2 did not exemplify Karl's definition of a heroic ambassador, unless the future of world diplomacy involved hookers and five-hour workweeks.

Karl sighed and tried not to look as disgusted as he felt. It was December 16, a Tuesday night when he should have been at the office helping put to bed some of his client's January 1 insurance renewals. To be an insurance agent in December was to be at DEFCON 2 – one step from full thermonuclear war. Every client was on edge and potentially being entertained by a competitor. There were endless holiday dinners, holiday cards, Jürgenson's Bakery gift baskets to be sent, bonuses to be paid and an endless garland of business meetings. It was like pulling the holiday shift at Bullock's or working at the post office; it was a retailer's busiest time of the year.

In a span of three months, Karl had gone from building a strong business relationship with Ralph Senior that might have resulted in a lucrative new account for his agency to serving on a ship of fools captained by an incompetent buffoon angling to be the face of the nation's two hundredth birthday celebration in his town.

To Hunt's chagrin, Karl had organized his own independent sub-committee to manage the selection of the parade grand marshal. He wisely chose hard-nosed Russell Quintana, a smooth as Hermes silk investment banker who had built his fortune facilitating mergers and acquisitions in Southern California aerospace; Miles Myers, a commercial real estate broker; and his closest friend, Dominic DeSantis, a successful restaurant chain owner Karl jokingly called the "Father of Our Country" because of his thirteen children. Karl and Dom had done business together for many years, with DeSantis often referring Karl into his friends and suppliers—an impossible-to-penetrate, incestuous cabal of Italian businessmen.

Karl understood from the moment he was nominated by Hunt Senior that the seemingly innocuous parade committee planning could get thick with small-town politics. He wondered if Hunt had known that his only son would be petitioning so fiercely to be nominated as Grand Marshal. Karl had initially proposed that the Old Man be nominated. Hunt Senior was as important an institution to Huntington Hills as its infrastructure and city government. In a time when people longed to elect public officials who embodied integrity and heroism, the town needed to look no further than its own decorated WWII veteran and humanitarian.

R2 had caught wind of Karl's plan to approach Ralph Senior and had preyed on his father's humility and failing health to convince him that it would be too much of a physical strain to assume this role. After reporting back to Karl with feigned disappointment about his father's decision to decline the invitation, R2 had rammed through the plenary session this year's Bicentennial theme: "America: The Next Generation." He had then challenged Karl and his subcommittee to find someone who represented the future and not the past.

Karl was conflicted. R2 was the kind of guy who would horse trade. If Karl could land some more new business in the upcoming year, he would be the clear candidate to succeed Bob O'Brien as CEO of OB&T, a firm that had grown to be one of the largest private insurance brokerages in Southern California. In becoming CEO, he could declare his own independence from anyone and anything.

Yet the thought of potentially having Ralph Hunt II as a client offended Karl's sense of morality and community—and besides, he didn't like the way the plaid-panted Porky Pig with his spider veined snout leered at Susie when she occasionally shopped at Hunt's Market.

Compared to the bigger grocery chains like Ralph's and Market Basket, Hunt's was overpriced, selling a shopping experience to Huntington Hills housewives who craved handsome box boys, obsequious service and home delivery. Susie felt obligated to shop there because Matthew had worked at Hunt's his senior year and now John was earning money as a box boy. It was John who told his mother about R2's penchant to hide in the dairy case, drinking, smoking cigarettes, and even once passing out after inhaling nitrous oxide out of cans of Reddi-Wip whip cream.

The feckless owner's son worked hardest at currying favor with everyone, including the box boys, often tipping the teens with a free case of beer on the night of a dance or a prom. He would make a point to gather the boys in the back of the store and have them toss a full case of tall Coors into the trash bin behind the store.

"Gentlemen, that beer is flat. We'd better throw it out!" He would have them drop the case into the emerald green dumpster, wink at the boys, and then offer an off-color joke about bringing photographs of their adventures to work the following Monday. Despite her distaste for the younger Hunt, Susie tried to help Karl rationalize his personal objections to R2 and appreciate the bigger picture.

"Honey, R2 is a flawed young man. But look how involved he is with the community. He chairs the capital campaign at the community church. He's been President of Rotary twice and is a member of every club you need to be in to network and sell more new business. He is the future face of this town. If you can win him over, perhaps you could be a positive influence on him. It will help the boys to see their father engaged in civics. They're all at impressionable ages."

"Susie, don't call that piglet 'R Two'. The Hunt name got him into those clubs and on those committees and Old Man Hunt still has to work behind the scenes to ensure his kid stays out of trouble. If he is the future face of this town—a florid, country-club alcoholic who isn't fit to carry his father's jock strap—I'll take my chances living in Watts."

He had put down his newspaper and studied her as if she were an extraterrestrial who could not grasp the concept of what life was like on earth.

"As far as I'm concerned, you tricked me into taking this parade committee chairman's role." He felt himself losing control.

"I am so goddamned busy at work. And now, good old Bob has decided to hire some she-male from Alexander and Alexander to be part of our management team. He said if OB&T is going to play with the big boys, we need someone who has run with them. He also gave us some BS excuse about diversity and the fact that in the next decade over half of America's risk managers will be women.

"The guy has finally lost it. I am sure that loud-mouthed bitch is behind all of his affirmative action crap. She's probably got him attending NOW meetings or trying to find another 'grey feathered tit swallower' that needs protection under the goddamn Endangered Species Act. I don't know what happened to him. He gets remarried and it's like he lost his balls in an industrial accident. Good old Bob. He hasn't told any of us what the hiring of this new woman, Rebecca, means for his or our succession planning. I *now* need to spend even *more* time at that office before Connie O'Brien, the tree-hugging, trophy bitch and our new butch head of risk management convince Bob to carry on with his socialist hiring binge and we become the goddamn United Nations!"

Susie sighed. His nightly invectives rose like orange cinders swirling above a hell-fire blaze of old-school dogmata. She glanced into the living room, where Freddie was doing his homework.

"Karl, not every single woman over thirty years old is gay."

"Well, aren't they?" Karl said, smirking.

The week before, he had become unglued over the state of the Republican Party and "that idiot Gerald Ford." Karl could not understand why Ford was off visiting China when he should be home working on his reelection and helping heal America's deep resentment about the political fiascos of Vietnam and Watergate. Pardoning Nixon had not helped matters. Now there were rumors of the CIA violating civil liberties and prosecuting a shadow war of assassinations and coups in other countries. Whatever it is was doing, the damn CIA was not being covert enough about it. America was now slowly waking up to NY Times and Washington Post stories of Langley's spooks, unsanctioned shadow wars, and double standards of foreign policy. America did not get it. Any sovereign nation that cared a shit about its national security and world power needed an army of shadow warriors and black operation teams to do the messy stuff that the Constitution did not contemplate. Any ex-military man knew this. Yet, for God's sake, if you are going to bump off the bad guys, don't leave a blood trail.

Everyone, including many in the GOP, was questioning the government's credibility. People wanted change, which always caused the political pendulum to swing in the opposition's direction. Just how far was anyone's guess. It was usually the party in power, in this case, the GOP, that would take it on the chin. He pointed to a picture in the paper of the Democratic contenders. The Georgia senator, Carter, was kissing his wife at some Southern holiday soiree under a fist of mistletoe.

"Honey, did you know that mistletoe is actually parasitic? Just like the Democrats. They all belong in the fucking Parasite House at the Zoo. The ticks, the bloodsuckers – they're all on the Reds' payroll." He held up the *Los Angeles Tribune*.

"Here, look. George Wallace could pass as Brezhnev's long lost brother, for God's sake."

Susie did have to admit that the similarities were striking.

Freddie Patton had stopped writing his book report on *The Bermuda Triangle* and was now eavesdropping as his father lit into the state of American politics. The youngest Patton was a strange mixture of intellect and self-centered fear. He had accepted his father's view that Democrats were passive-aggressive anarchists determined to sell America the rope with which it would ultimately hang itself. Freddie was intrigued by Karl's latest rant regarding liberals as bloodsuckers. He had been to Griffith Park and the Los Angeles Zoo, but had not seen the Parasite House. Yet, seeing wasn't necessary for believing. He had never seen a tapeworm, either, but had suspected that he had one last summer. He shuddered and unconsciously felt his bottom like a man who periodically pats his back pocket to make certain his wallet is still there.

Freddie was rewriting his homework. He had not been allowed by his mother to submit his first book review on the recent bestseller *Helter Skelter* by Vincent Bugliosi. He had found the crime thriller about the Manson murders in John's room and devoured its contents over a wide-eyed several days and was now rereading it for hidden messages. He had not slept in his own bed for a week, choosing instead to doze at the foot of Susie and Karl's bed, where it was less likely that any Manson family members would be looking for him.

The previous night he had tried playing Revolution Number Nine from the Beatles *White Album* backwards on the family turntable. In the blackened living room, Freddie was certain he had heard the hidden message that had prompted the Tate and La Bianca slayings. Producer Alan Parsons was rumored to have inserted a satanic skeleton key into the lyrics by engineering the hidden message "Turn me on, dead man. Turn me on, dead man …" – a dark missive that could only be received when listening to "Number Nine, Number Nine" in reverse direction. While the actual lyric sounded something more akin to "Mon-yon-min-man, Mon-yon-min-man", Freddie was convinced he was communicating with the dead.

Banished back to his own bed by Karl after having the pluck to ask his father to stop snoring, Freddie had become so panicked at the notion of walking down a dark hallway to use the toilet, he had begun urinating in the corner of his closet and out the window of his bedroom onto the driveway.

Freddie spied into the dining room and watched as his mother patiently waited for his father to conclude his nightly diatribe. She smiled at Freddie and trundled her eyes. Susie loved her youngest son, calling him the "oldest youngest man I've ever meet." Freddie was abnormally fascinated with money, power, and the paranormal. He was a pyromaniac, a hypochondriac, and a mathematical genius—a mongrel complexity of family attributes often ascribed to the ultra successful or the criminally insane. He loved to read the business section of the *Tribune* and had taken to following stocks with Susie, who had decided that it was time for women to develop more financial independence by playing the market.

Susie loved her time spent with Freddie as they pored over stock prices, EPS graphs, and leading indicator reports on the economy and industry.

"That kid is a strange little bastard," Karl remarked to Susie one day as he observed his son turning the television's UHF dial to Channel 22 to watch a grainy cable channel called *Charting the Market*. Hosted by ancient stock trader, Gene Morgan, Freddie would track the Dow's weekly progress and urge his parents to speculate on stocks.

"This is the kind of crap pin-headed accountant's watch. It's not normal. Why doesn't he watch *The Three Stooges* like George?"

Susie smirked. "Dear, we are all complex instruments that come off the same assembly line but with different features. Our son possesses a sophisticated antenna that seems to pick up only horror and business stations. He's either going to grow up to own the world or terrorize it—or both."

She was a beautiful woman with midnight-black hair, wide crystal-blue eyes and a mouth that seemed perpetually curled at its sides out of sympathy. At forty-two, she was still striking—tall and slender with broad shoulders and a narrow waist. She sighed and tried to look engaged as an increasingly truculent Karl moved on from his son to an allegory comparing the United States to Rome and Ford to Nero fiddling while the empire burned to the ground.

"The goddamn guy took one too many hits to the head at Michigan."

"He got us out of Vietnam, Karl," Susie gently responded.

"Yeah after that bastard Johnson got us deeper in Asian monkey doo-doo. I'm sure the word withdrawal sounds really good right about now to all the boys who lost arms, legs, and lives. Shit, we could have won that war with one arm if we had just dropped a few nukes on Hanoi, especially while Jane Fonda was up there visiting Ho Chi Minh learning how to shoot anti-aircraft guns at our A-6's. Now Laos has fallen. What's next? The liberal media wants us to forgive and forget about all those sneaky little pacifists who went to Canada. If I were goddamn President, I'd be like the Wizard of Oz and make them bring me back the drapes from the US embassy in Saigon before I let them back in this country."

"Honey, calm down. If this pageant committee thing is really too unbearable, just resign and explain to Ralph Senior that business issues came up. He'd understand. I'm sure Ralph Jr. can't mess things up too bad. It's not like it's the Rose Parade."

Karl rubbed his forehead and then softened into a knowing smile.

"Nah, I'd be letting the old man down. You know they cut off part of his foot last week. Poor bastard. He's a hell of a businessman and a true conservative. He built his business, never took a handout from anyone and won the Silver Star, for god's sake, in the Hürtgen Forest. God must have been having a shitty day at the office to give a patriot like that such a jellyfish for a kid."

Susie smiled. "Any father's love is supposed to be unconditional. My guess Ralph sees his son more for what he might still become than what he is. Perhaps that's why he likes you so much. Maybe you're the man he hopes R2 could become."

"You always use the same tricks to twist things into making me feel guilty." Karl laughed and reached out to hold his wife's hand. She patted the top of his arm and turned, catching her youngest son watching them from the living room. She winked at the boy.

Freddie was comforted by the sense of warmth and validation that surged through him every time his mother cast a glance his way. Her hyacinth-blue eyes seemed to always guarantee that things were going to be better. He felt protected and secure in the shadows cast by his parents and three older brothers. Sighing, he returned to what his English teacher would later tell his mother was a brilliant but disturbing book report about the mysterious vortex in the Atlantic that swallowed up cargo ships, airplanes, and small pleasure craft without so much as a trace. Freddy's thesis was that satanic Haitian pirates financed by the Cubans and Baby Doc Duvalier were secretly behind the unexplained phenomena in the place that author Charles Berlitz had dubbed *The Devil's Triangle*.

Karl looked at his watch. Freeman Dewitt was still wheezing on and on like a balloon with a slow leak. The guy was so old he looked like mottled blue cheese. Karl's stomach groaned in hungry protest at the thought of a Hamburger Hamlet cheeseburger with a side salad slathered in blue cheese dressing. Miss Saunders looked up at Karl and smiled before returning to her animated shorthand.

It was becoming increasingly hard to disguise his contempt for this constipated process they called a steering committee. The group had been meeting for six months on the second Tuesday of each month. Instead of feeling closer to his hometown, he was now convinced that two of the elderly storeowners were senile and a danger to themselves and possibly the community. He also suspected that Miss Saunders might actually be a man. He found himself staring at her massive hands and wondering if she was Huntington Hill's version of Christine Jorgenson.

Karl was not sure what disgusted him more – transsexuals or the woman's liberation movement. The feminist revolution's spiritual leader, "Mizz" Steinem, was trying to reengineer the American family into the Addam's Family. Pretty soon, he mused, he would be ironing his own shirts and asking Susie what time she was going to be home for dinner. Susie admired and respected Steinem's wit and wisdom and reminded Karl that traditional American values did not include any form of suppression—economic, social, or domestic.

His mind wandered as the stuffy classroom tugged at his eyelids. Karl needed a soda to wake up. Soft drinks or coffee could keep him alert until the wee hours of the morning but they also gave him massive heartburn. The end of day caffeine burn was already smoldering in his chest after twelve hours of client problems and a six-pack of his favorite beverage, Mountain Dew.

The meeting ground on, and R2, their Henry VIII chairman, did not seem to care. Karl could almost see the guy dressed in a king-sized codpiece, overskirt, and kirtle while physicians attended to his gout. In spite of the fact that R2 was a Pillsbury doughboy abomination, Karl had come to the conclusion that he owed it to Susie, Hunt Senior, and OB&T to get along with him and try to win his business. But he'd be damned if he was going to name him Grand Marshal of the Bicentennial Parade.

"Karl, do you want to bring us up to speed on ideas for the Grand Marshal?" R2 offered a crocodile grin that did not alter his eyes.

Sobered out of self-reflection, Karl began with a protracted and prosaic description of the parade route from city hall down Huntington Hills Drive with its conclusion at Roses Park, the site of the town's annual Fourth of July celebration. He did not mention his committee's preferences for the Grand Marshal - only that they were still discussing candidates and it would be premature to announce anything yet.

"Okay. Let's hope we have a tad more progress next month." Scarcely concealing his disappointment, R2 concluded the meeting without giving anyone else a chance to speak.

"Any other business? Good. Move to adjourn."

Almost everyone in the room clamored to second the motion. While the elderly attendees struggled to extract themselves from their school-desk prisons, R2 darted over to Karl.

"Karl, you much of a golfer?"

"Well, with four kids, Ralph, golf's the first thing that goes overboard. The next is your masculinity."

"R2, please! Jesus, all that domestication sounds awful. I'm glad I haven't gotten pinned to the ground by a female and a gaggle of little brats. Most of these gals I date just want to dip their hands in the family treasure chest. I usually get to their chests before they get to mine." He gave a porcine wink that made Karl's stomach churn.

"We're getting a foursome together this week at LACC and we could use a fourth. Care to join us? We could talk about some of the proposals you and dad have been kicking around and also discuss your ideas on the parade."

Karl felt the trap close behind him.

A police siren wailed in the distance, followed by another. Everyone looked out the window of the classroom facing Huntington Hills Drive. Blue and orange strobe lights splashed across the asphalt as the squad cars raced through a red light.

Karl sidled toward the door. "Damn, Susie mentioned something about Freddie and some kind of holiday cotillion I'm expected to chaperone. Her goddamn relatives are coming into town. Can we take a rain check and maybe meet for lunch next week?"

Hunt frowned. "Just give me a call next week. It's the busiest time of year for all of us. But guys like us have to sneak away now and then."

Karl waved and walked out to his brown Ford Granada, muttering to himself. "Busy, my ass. You'll be sitting in a goddamn dairy refrigerator drinking eggnog and sucking on cans of Reddi-Wip."

CHAPTER 2

By 1975, it was clear that drug use was increasing, that the gains of prior years were being lost, that in human terms, narcotics had become a national tragedy. Today, drug abuse constitutes a clear and present threat to the health and future of our Nation. The time has come to launch a new and more aggressive campaign to reverse the trend of increasing drug abuse in America. And this time we must be prepared to stick with the task for as long as necessary.

~Gerald Ford speech to Congress April 1976

Seventeen-year-old John Patton exited the shower, dried himself and thoughtlessly tossed his towel on to the hallway carpet. A filthy dog resembling an industrial mop with brown, dreadlocked hair picked up the discarded laundry and trotted several feet to the base of a bedroom door, where he proceeded to drop the damp towel, rolling all over it, grunting with pleasure.

"Good boy, Maxie," John said, rubbing the dog's stomach with his foot. He opened his bedroom door to a sudden surge of Bruce Springsteen's *Born to Run*. Closing the door to prevent the imminent paternal scream to "shut that crap off," he crouched over his beloved stereo. An audiophile, John was meticulous about his music. His albums were categorized and protected in plastic sleeves. Music moved him. Lyrics were life lessons from oracles that understood what it was like to be a teen—

the confusion and the restless need to be anywhere other than where you were at that exact moment.

John's stereo system was a technological work of art and a critical accessory to his daily life. He spent hours with friends in stereo stores evaluating Pioneer, Kenwood, Infinity, Sony, Dolby, and Harmon Kardon components. His best friend, Brooks Wagner, the acoustical savant had introduced John to the expensive and seductive world of high fidelity. Brooks' Marantz 2440b receiver, Thorens turntable, Frazier speakers, and Akai GX reel-to-reel tape deck constituted the more-modern binaural equivalent of an Apollo spaceship. To the untrained eye, Wagner's stereo system could have passed as a workstation at Pasadena's Jet Propulsion Laboratory.

In every high school across America, teens engaged in an arms race of stereo components building bigger and more complex combinations of sound in an effort to claim the high ground of high fidelity. Lacking Wagner's lucrative allowance, John meticulously saved his money, so he might continue to augment his system with new modules. His most recent purchase had become a source of tension with his father. He had bought not one, but two, amplifiers, including a fifty-pound monster Power amp that cranked out 250 watts per channel and could knock down a lawn jockey at fifty yards.

With its slim arms and a stylus that jumped nervously if someone spoke too loud, his Pioneer turntable was as sensitive as a spy novel polygraph. The SG Equalizer with its silver faceplate had 12 slider controls and allowed him to produce a signal-to-noise ratio of 120 decibels. His father had no idea what any of this meant. All Karl knew was that each evening it sounded like two Sumo wrestlers were upstairs mating.

John moved the amplifier's sliders with dexterity. The dials gave its owner the impression that he was a genius capable of bending sound waves and creating never-heard-before combinations of bass and treble. Now, the treble climbed to accentuate the shrill of Clarence Clemons on the saxophone. The album had been released only a few months ago, but its title song was already John's anthem to escaping his seemingly preordained life. Although he was only a sophomore in high school, John was already bored with his friends, his family, and his town. He had bigger plans and had decided his trajectory in life included seeing the world that pulsed unseen beyond mountains and across burning western deserts. His emotional compass seemed perpetually directed to all points east. He was George Bailey forever attempting to escape Bedford Falls.

He was a straight-A honors student and the most dutiful of the Patton boys. His obedience afforded him privileges that only his elder brother, Matthew, a freshman at Cal, also enjoyed. He had no curfew, but since it was basketball season and he had finally succeeded in making the junior varsity team, he was determined to lead a monastic life of studies and practice. While many of his friends were attending the dance that weekend, John had eschewed three separate invitations to don a tuxedo and celebrate the holidays at the annual Christmas Ball. On this night, he would play Prince Charming to a special person, a Sleeping Beauty that needed to be rescued from the dragon of a loveless relationship.

Susie suspected her son had ulterior motives for skipping his high school's holiday gala. He had already set up a sleepover at his friend Seth Erickson's house. Susie knew Kitty Erickson and was fond of her refreshing honesty and deliciously cutting Southern iconoclasm. Susie was not inclined to approve of sleepovers in high school, but she trusted John and understood her son's attraction to the libertine household of Erickson, one of the more "progressive" families in Huntington Hills.

Despite being the object of countless female classmates' fantasies, John had never expressed much interest in girls his age or the parties that seemed to flare suddenly on any given weekend when the cocktail and country club circuit parents left their teenagers in charge. John had less time for the dances, formals, and other rituals of his comfortable, aristocratic suburb. He wanted something more substantial, deeper, and more mature.

Standing in front of the mirror, rolling his stomach muscles and flexing his biceps, John was a striking, lanky teen stretching to six-feet-two with arms that were laced with veins and muscles beginning to offer the outline of a man. He had soft brown eyes that matched his hair, which he combed back and to the right side. He chose to wear his hair shorter than Matthew, who had straight black hair to the middle of his shoulder blades. Long hair was an offense to his father, and John did not consider the social statement worth the goodwill he would burn with his dad. His modus operandi was always the same: work hard to build a surfeit of trust you could spend like golden coins for privileges at critical moments.

John thought about what he would say and how he might broach the subject. Just thinking about her pushed a surge of adrenaline through his chest that made him want to go outside and shoot free throws under the glow of the outdoor garage light.

She could have been Julie Christie's twin sister with her thick, voluptuous lips and her massive kaleidoscope blue-gray eyes. He had heard enough from Seth in the last few months to know that she was unhappy. He also knew that he had an extraordinary mind and would someday excel in the world of men. Dealing with his friend would be tricky, but in time he would come to understand. He had heard Seth remark a thousand times how he hated his old man. Seth Erickson clearly admired John, often following him around campus and seeking him out at lunch, pep rallies, study hall, and parties. The big question was whether Seth could accept John not as a friend but as a father.

Susie did not take kindly to poisonous suburban gossip or the snarky housewives who undermined newcomers and unconventional families like white bloods cells attacking a foreign pathogen. Susie had grown up on the other side of disapproving stares from neighbors and pious, church-going families in Northern California. Her wild uncles and brothers were routinely in trouble with authority figures. It was not uncommon to see an O'Reilly male arrested or in hot water for provoking the privileged that ran the community. Susie had learned from her mother to protect your own. She perambulated through the lives of her husband and boys like an Irish beat cop, scanning the alleys and shadows for anything that might lead them astray or unfairly impugn their character. Privacy and reputation were family heirlooms to be treasured and preserved. She had no tolerance for people who might attempt to discuss her personal business.

When Susie moved to Huntington Hills, she made a habit of lecturing her boys about thinking for themselves and rising above other people's preoccupations with scandal and speculation. Susie was a huge fan of Eleanor Roosevelt and often quoted her when coaching her sons on the finer points of small towns and gossip. "Boys, great minds discuss ideas, average minds discuss events, and small minds discuss other people."

She was also fond of telling her children that no one could make them feel inferior without their consent, another Roosevelt maxim. She practiced what she preached and was a trusted confidante to a growing legion of women who were discovering that they had choices and power. Liberated housewives no longer needed to lead lives of quiet desperation or derive their self-esteem from their husband's accomplishments.

Susie had a wide range of friends that included a new breed of independent women - divorcees, widows, opinionated mothers, and working moms. She was a reliable nexus for information and freely shared what she had learned about men as she managed her own den of thoughtless troglodytes.

Because Susie listened attentively to all her friends and could disarm anyone into sharing her most intimate secrets, Karl had nicknamed her "sodium pentothal." Like the Red Cross, she was a first responder, always lending a hand to families in crisis, gravitating toward real people and avoiding those who spent their energies trying to safeguard a veneer of perfection.

Susie hated the fact that children often were forced to bear the scarlet letter of dysfunction for the sins of their parents. To her, a broken home was not a transgression or a sign of social leprosy, but a human tragedy. Because kids were clearly more at risk in single parent households, Susie took it upon herself to open her home to friends of her boys who otherwise might be stigmatized simply because they were the products of divorced or alcoholic homes. She was not naïve and certainly regulated access to a subset of kids she referred to as "Lampwicks"—life's trouble-seekers and lower companions. But she gave every kid a chance and saw it as her responsibility to afford some structure to kids who had done nothing wrong besides "drawing the short straw in the cabbage patch."

Susie admired divorced women who had the guts to kick out a philandering husband or remove themselves from a bad marriage. She noted that a small town often turned its back on single moms and that some women considered recent divorcees as a threat to their own marriages or perhaps a sign of a character weakness: "You know, she just couldn't keep her man from straying."

If she knew anything, Susie knew men and she regarded most of them as egomaniacs with inferiority complexes. As middle age brought crow's feet to their eyes and pounds to their waists, insipid men sometimes sought solace and fleeting self-esteem in the arms of secretaries and cocktail waitresses. The really dim-witted ones cheated right in their hometown.

She sensed that Kitty was having marital problems. She could smell it the first time she met Garrett Erickson. His eyes had lingered on Susie for a millisecond too long and his half-smile suggested that they had met before. In her past life working as a maid in her parent's boarding house, she had crossed paths with plenty of guys like Garrett. They were charming scavengers and restless souls asymptomatically ill with the malignancy of self-centered need. Rumor had it that Garrett was carrying on with another woman who lived in town. Susie was waiting for the moment when Kitty might take her into her confidence.

Garrett Erickson was the hip creative director at an up-and-coming West Los Angeles advertising agency. He had obsidian black hair that fell to his shoulders and mutton chop sideburns. He drove a Porsche and on weekends would ride around Huntington Hills on a Harley, breaking eardrums, turning heads, and spraying dirt and gravel on the road adjacent to the local baseball diamond. In his Johnny Cash black-leather chaps, Garrett was a workingman's alter ego and every housewife's fantasy bad boy. He was the road less taken, the riskier option, the life that you could have had if you just had the nerve to jump into the deep end of the pool.

Karl, too, had heard the rumors that Garrett was a gambler, womanizer and shameless self-promoter. While hip was in, Karl knew that too much hip made you an ass and could lead to a dislocation from the things that matter most: your wife, family and community. *You go to one of those advertising agency Christmas parties and you wake up the next day with a Xerox copy of your secretary, Miss Wannamaker's rear end, and no recollection past your first puff on a marijuana cigarette. Three months later you walk in the front door to find pregnant Miss Wannamaker holding hands with your wife and her new divorce lawyer. No thank you!*

Karl didn't care for the Erickson family, and though he preferred not having kids from "screwed up homes" at his house, Susie made the blond, soft-spoken teen feel welcome and went out of her way to befriend Kitty. Karl did not approve. "That woman is more liberal than a goddamn bordello madam," he groused.

Susie smiled defiantly and confirmed that John was indeed spending the night of the Christmas prom at the Ericksons. Karl continued to nitpick. "John should be dating girls and living it up a little. He's always skulking around the house—up in his room, listening to music. The kid's too sensitive. A night in that house and he is going to come home wanting to join the Black Panthers and protest Hunt's for their poor record on box boy civil rights."

"And what's wrong with that? Karl, if you can just stop for five minutes trying to shape that boy into what you want him to be, you might be able to see who he already has become. And I love Kitty. She's educated, articulate and does not suffer fools. Yes, she's a bit of a hippie, but she's also smart and can see through many of these so-called pillars of society that anchor our community. She's clearly misplaced among new money pretense. I think she's a remarkable combination of self-confidence, candor, and beauty. You married me and I am one hundred percent Black Irish."

John had listened to his parents' exchange through the wall heater that separated the family room from Karl's home office, just as he often eavesdropped on his mother's phone calls and would sometimes hear her defending Kitty to other friends.

He smiled. He would get to see her after all.

From the first day John walked into the Erickson house, his senses were bombarded by Chinese sandalwood joss sticks and the exotic sitar music of George Harrison's *Wonderwall Music*. The living room was padded with throw pillows and settees, while doorways were threaded with beads.

Two massive Irish wolfhound dogs wandered the house like Lion Country Safari wildlife leaving chairs and couches covered in a fine patina of gray hair. Garrett's "gentleman's" magazines lay brazenly on his office coffee table. The Ericksons even had a hot tub, and Seth and his twelve-year-old sister, Candy, were allowed a glass of wine or beer at dinner. Any adolescent boy would have paid his hard-earned allowance to spend the night at the home of such French-thinking people. And John had been invited as a guest. Best of all, it was the home of the most stunning mother in the entire San Gabriel Valley.

Kitty was a cool breeze of bell-bottomed pantsuits, flowing floral blouses and earrings that fell in great hoops, like rings at the playground. A Southern dervish of hair, diamonds, and fingernails, she often entered the room followed by a stream of smoke and strong perfume while holding a Virginia Slims.

John had adored Kitty for the entire autumn of 1975. At times, he could barely hide his crush.

"Why, young man, you are getting more handsome with each hour. I suppose every debutante in Pasadena is holding her breath hoping you might be on the other end of a ringing phone."

"Mrs. Erickson."

"Jonathon Patton, you may call me Kitty. Your mother and I are dear friends."

John blushed and felt his chest clutch as he gazed into the sea-green irises of the Southern beauty. "Kitty, did you ever see *Doctor Zhivago*? You look just like Julie Christie."

"Why, Jonathon, that's the kindest compliment anyone has shared with me in years." She leaned over to kiss him on the forehead. Her fragrance poured down over his closed eyes and lifted his nose and mouth toward the vacant space she left behind as she breezed into another room.

Kitty never lost her cool or civility. When Seth and John had been caught lying about shooting bottle rockets off the Erickson's roof, she admonished the boys by calling them "mendicants and rascals." John had returned home that night and had looked up the definition of the words and started calling his friends "mendicants". He found himself obsessing about his friend's mother day and night.

Yet fantasy would eventually collide headlong into adolescent guilt. Karl's compulsory Protestant church Sundays added to John's sexual confusion, whiplashing him against the rocks of remorse and lust. He divined enough from Pastor Mather's sermons in church to know it was inappropriate to have impure thoughts about his friend's mother. He tried to deconstruct his fantasy - imagining her mangled in a car wreck. He considered her with bad teeth and facial hair at one hundred years old. He tried to envision her sitting on the toilet. Nothing worked. How could Mr. Erickson go to work in the morning and tolerate being apart from such a beautiful Alabama belle?

Befuddled and bewitched, he did the math of all young men, calculating that in 1981 when he was twenty-two, she would be fifty-one. When he turned fifty, she would be a youthful seventy-nine. He decided this particular Saturday night would be his time to proclaim his love to Kitty and to propose dropping out of high school to get a job worthy of supporting the love of his young life.

George and Teddy knocked on the door of the pool house several times before hearing someone yell, "Turn that fucking stereo down, you dumb spick!"

It sounded as if people were moving quickly inside the bungalow, shuffling chairs, opening and closing drawers.

"Who the hell is it?"

"It's, um, Ted Galloway. My sister Katie's friends with Joanie. She said you'd be home."

"Enter!"

Ted and George walked into the low light and smoke of a neglected pool house that had been converted into one-bedroom studio apartment. They adjusted their eyes to colored lampshades and the pungent stink of marijuana and stale beer. Two of the windows and the sofa were covered with sheets. The faded and torn blue and white striped wallpaper had been covered with posters of Jim Morrison, a massive marijuana leaf, a peace sign, and an *Easy Rider* movie poster of Dennis Hopper giving the bird from his Harley.

"So what do you weenies want? How do I know you, anyway?" The low harsh voice came from behind them and they turned to see a tattooed, lanky shirtless man in his mid-to-late twenties hiding behind the door. He emerged from the shadows holding a four-foot, feathered bamboo peace pipe.

"Katie and Joanie, they …"

"Cool it, Oscar Meyer. I just wanted to be sure you weren't pigs. The Old Lady in the house and I don't get along and her way of dealing with it is to call the cops."

Teddy turned to George and whispered, "That's his mom. But she's not that old."

George rolled his eyes Teddy and furrowed his brow. "Really?" he said.

Ronnie Thomas looked like he should be the lead guitarist in a rock band with his farmer's tan, heavily veined neck and arms and long hair tied into a single ponytail. A brown horseshoe mustache fell over a Cupid's bow mouth to a narrow cleft chin. He considered the boys with the lazy, burned-out eyes of someone who had seen too many things too soon in life. *These suburban soft-palms are probably good for fifty bucks.*

George stared at Ronnie's leather necklace with its metallic peace sign the size of a Kennedy half-dollar. The veteran wore baggy camouflage pants and his rough hands were covered in dried paint. On his right forearm was a montage of tattoos including one large black eight ball with the word "Hue" written in blood-red ink.

A Hispanic-looking youth also covered in paint and wearing dark glasses, wore a head bandanna and rested on the ancient cloth sofa. He laughed at the adolescents in their jeans, sweaters, and boat shoes. "Doc Ronnie, these jokers look like they fell out of some fag fashion catalog, man."

"We wanted to buy some Spanish Flies from you," George blurted out.

Ronnie made a strange face. "You want what?"

Teddy jumped in. "Your sister, you know. She said you had a friend who was a doctor and had Spanish Flies. You know, African Desiacs. We need some. We have, like, forty bucks."

"Well, you get right to the point, don't you, dickweed? And if I had some Spanish … Flies, I am pretty certain you weenies can't afford 'em. You got fifty bucks? They're ten bucks apiece."

George frowned and glanced at Teddy. "We only got forty bucks. That's what Joanie told us … you know … that it would cost for the flies."

"Joanie, huh? Where'd you see my sister?" Ronnie softened, his lips upturned into a genuine smile.

"She's friends with my older sister, Katie. She hangs at our pool all the time. They went to PCC and lived together up in that apartment on El Marengo."

Ronnie gazed vacantly across the room toward a picture of he and his sister when they were small children. "Yeah. I remember Katie. That's your sister? Huh. Yeah, she's a sweetie. She still dating that dude? What the hell's his name? You know, his old man owns all those car dealerships?

"Brantley ...Harper."

"Yeah, that's it. *Harper Toyota, Harper Toyota. San Bernardino freeway at San Gabriel Boulevard ...*" Ronnie hummed the Harper dealership radio jingle and then whirled to address Gonzales lying on the couch.

"Gonzo, who gives a kid a handle like *Brantley*? I'll tell you. Some rich asshole like my old man. Harper probably thought of the name while he was buying suits at Brooks Brothers – that's after he bugged out on his first family like my dad to marry some country club bimbo. Dude most likely sends his kids to some stuck up Pasadena private school so they don't have to mingle with the local trash like us."

"No, they don't," said Teddy, getting uncomfortable with Ronnie's growing agitation.

"They don't what?" barked Ronnie.

"They don't go out anymore. Katie is dating some guy named Steve Diggins that she met at Cal State Northridge. They're getting married next year. I think your sister's in the wedding."

The shadow passed from Ronnie's face. "Man, that's cool. Good for her, man. Baby Joanie in a goddamn wedding. What a trip. That's something I would pay to see."

"I can get you into the wedding." Teddy blurted, immediately regretting his over-enthusiasm.

Ronnie laughed. "Yeah, that'd be a fucking good one, kid. Although, I would like to see my little sis. If you catch her, tell her I said 'Bucky is cool.'" He turned up the song *Oye Como Va* on the stereo.

Ronnie nodded toward the man resting on the sofa. "My homeboy spick loves Santana. Where are my manners, Gonzo? So, grunts, this is PFC Arturo Gonzales. He is my business partner and was one of my main men from a broken group of Phu Bai bad boys."

"Claro, mi amigo!" gasped Gonzales as he exhaled a plume of smoke.

George was not certain what to do. He waited. Teddy appeared to be overwhelmed and was inching back toward the door.

Gonzales spoke more clearly. "Amigos, you know my man Doc Ronnie killed five gooks up near Phu Bai and then another two at the Perfume River in Hue. Doc Ronnie hace lo que le sale de los cojones."

George could not recall much of his Spanish II vocabulary but he did remember "cojones" meant "balls."

Ronnie broke into a slow, intoxicated knowing grin. "Gonzales, here was my B-A-R man. Company F, Ninth fucking Battalion, Second fucking Marines. Gonzo is a chee-cah-noh from East L.A. He is moo-ey bue-no with a Browning, but he got in trouble for taking some sou-ven-'ears.' "

"*Solamente ocho orejas, hermano.*"

George again caught just the two words, "ears" and "brother." He was now ready to commit to going to church every day for the next twenty years if God would just intervene and evacuate him out from this drugged out war movie.

Gonzales got up and lifted his sunglasses revealing glazed, red marbles. "How old were you in 1968, you little wiener? Still sucking on your mama's teat, I bet."

George suddenly forgot his birthday. He could not think straight. The words came out of his mouth while his brain pondered whether Gonzales still preferred to take ears from his victims. "Let's see, I was born in, um, 1961, so I was like..."

The room erupted in laughter. Gonzales approached George. "Shit, amigo. You need a hit off this jag. You can't even remember how old you are."

He handed George the shriveled rolled cigarette that was half-wet with saliva. George gagged as he pulled pungent smoke inside his mouth but did not inhale. He was not about to go schizophrenic before doing his homework. He handed the joint back to Gonzales.

Ronnie rose from a chair, opened a dark briefcase, and took out a plastic scale. "Leave them alone, G. These boys are bona fide gold-collar Huntington Hills juveniles. A few years ago, they mighta been our CO's. Besides, if you scare them, they might pee on my clean floor.

"Spanish Flies? Hmm. I don't know if we have..."

He made a face at Gonzo and raised his eyebrows and shrugged as he was trying to decipher their cryptic request. Suddenly, his eyes beamed with understanding and he turned back to Teddy and George.

"…any left over from the last batch. Actually, you know what? I just remembered I do have some flies. I am giving you the last of a very special batch. Wait here."

Reaching under the couch, Ronnie grabbed a plastic baggie and opened a door that led into the pool house bathroom. The boys watched as the dealer returned from the toilet with a small plastic bag full of what appeared to be dead houseflies.

Ronnie's tone became serious. "Now listen, assholes. I'm a goddamn medic and I am telling you these things are incredibly potent. Take one in between your forefinger and thumb and mash them into powder and put them in at least eight ounces of liquid. They're tasteless, so no one should notice. If you give the girl too much, she could go 'dee dee mao'. You don't want to know what a woman can do when they're on this stuff.

"It is for a girl, isn't it? I mean you guys aren't fags, are you?" Ronnie began to draw the bag back away from the boys as if he was having second thoughts.

Snorting back a laugh, Gonzales spit out some of his beer.

Teddy snapped the bag from his hand. "No way, dude. This is for a cheerleader. So, what happens if a girl takes too much of this stuff?"

"It ain't funny man. She becomes like, man what's the word, like a… humpasaurus. I tell you flies are dangerous medicine. *Muy malo.* You're playing with fire and nature."

Teddy held up the baggie and studied the flies while George handed Ronnie forty dollars.

"Look, I gave you ten of them," Ronnie said. "That's worth at least a hundred, but because you know Joanie and all. Now don't go getting busted and narc on me. This stuff's illegal in at least one hundred countries. Don't fuck me over or I'll send Gonzales here to crawl up on your roof some night with his knife. You'll never hear him, and your momma won't know what happened until after your ears are gone."

"Look," sputtered George. "We don't really need to buy ten …"

"Well, then just sell what you don't use! Make a profit. I don't care." Ronnie looked offended. "Do you think this is a 7-11?" He laughed again without any emotion. "You see us selling slurpees, Gonzo?"

"Doc Ronnie, I only see some fruits shaking!" He burst out laughing at his own joke and then slowly lost interest returning to watch a muted television.

Ronnie plopped back down on the couch and took out a leather wallet. As he slipped the two twenty-dollar bills alongside a thick wad of cash, he stopped and held up his hand, listening.

They all could hear the sirens now. The windows flickered blue and white raindrops.

"Goddamn it," Ronnie yelled. "My old lady called the cops again. She musta saw you little fuckers walking down the driveway."

He pointed to George and Ted. "Get in the bathroom and crawl out that window. If you run down the hill and cross West Virginia road, you can cut into Roses Park. The cops can't find you there unless you are complete idiots."

Ronnie pushed open a space in the roof of his bathroom and shoved a suitcase and pillowcase in the opening before replacing the ceiling tile.

"Get the fuck out of here, and if you get caught, keep your mouths shut or one of us will come looking for you."

Teddy and George tumbled out the window into wet ivy and plunged down the wooded hillside, tripping over tree limbs and branches. They waited in a thicket of oleanders while a police car raced by them accelerating up West Virginia Road. Once the street had darkened to silence and wet asphalt, they darted into Roses Park.

"Dude, what about my car?"

"I can't believe you got me into this." George said, gasping for air. "The Mexican dude cuts off people's ears for fun." His heart was pumping and his face was flushed. "Screw your car."

The boys waited for twenty minutes at the base of the hill below the Thomas mansion. They could see flashing blue across the branches of the wet oak trees at the crest of the hill. The boys scurried across the road and melted into a thicket of dark, wet bottlebrush. A downpour of water showered them as they shook the moisture free from the bushes. As they worked their way through the tree line that buttressed the commons, George felt the thin baggie of flies in his pocket. The adrenaline rush of their escape had sharpened his senses. He peered into the sea of purple night and the empty park and suddenly felt invigorated by this adventure.

I wonder if this is what it was like in Vietnam.

CHAPTER 3

December was the time of year that fatigued Karl most. It was a brakeless, high-speed joy ride down a boulevard of excess: the profligate purchasing of gifts, a succession of business and neighborhood parties, a month-long festoon of decorations, and sheer exhaustion that weighed a man down like lard-laden fruitcake. Add in the bi-annual home invasion from the Susie's Northern California Celtic relatives, sprinkle it with alcohol, and simmer over a week of close quarters for a Christmas pudding guaranteed to be full of profanity and secular surprises.

Susie was busy removing last year's unused Christmas wrapping paper from a secret storage space in the basement when she heard Karl's familiar cursing as he dropped the ancient family Lionel train set on the living room floor and his big toe.

"Jesus, son of a bitch…"

"That's a nice way to usher in Christ's birthday." Susie yelled from the basement. "Be sure to wipe that thing off!"

After eleven months in the basement, it would remain her responsibility to properly inspect the papier mâché train diorama for black widows and rodent feces. As she climbed to the top of the groaning stairs, she startled running headlong into a six-foot plastic Santa that was soon to be placed on the roof next to the chimney. To those passing by the Pattons' house at night during the Christmas holidays, the colossal illuminated rooftop Santa appeared to be an extraterrestrial hell-bent on breaking in to abduct the inhabitants.

Two weeks earlier, the Sears Christmas Catalog had arrived, heralding the first day of an Advent season brimming with material wants. Any hope that Karl might have of creating a deeply spiritual holiday experience for his boys was defiled by what he considered the "Dictionary of Debt." Susie merely called it "The Encyclopedia of Elves."

From the moment the Patton family laid their fingers on the Sears Christmas consumer tome, they fell under its mistletoe spell. Each section was laden with adult gumdrop modern conveniences and sugar plum children's gifts, each sweeter and more contemporary than the next.

It was an age of wondrous inventions and innovation. In suburban America, Sears offered Susie an adult primer on how to materially improve one's circumstances, and with each purchase a family burrowed deeper into a cocoon of creature comfort. To the Patton children, it was literally an inventory of every item warehoused within St Nicholas' bag.

Susie would assign each son a different-colored pen with instructions to circle items in the catalog that he felt might best capture Santa's imagination. The yuletide registry shamelessly hawked everything from gabardines to garden hoses. Sears even sold elevated pools that could be filled with water straight out of a garden hose. Karl dismissed the pools as "tacky." The Patton boys could not have disagreed more.

Each year, Matthew would use his precious first-draft selection by circling the same $800 10' by 20' plastic monstrosity, replete with its heavy-duty, micro-resin safety ladder and pool skimmer. The children playing inside the pool seemed to be having so much fun. They were not attempting to drown one another or disable a pool skimmer by tying its flickering tail into knots. They were playing with a bright, overblown beach ball—the kind of ball a real kid might be able to enjoy for perhaps a total of twelve seconds—before it was bitten by a hyperactive dog or exploded under the weight of a pile of boys. Matthew had argued that Huntington Hills was in the heart of Southern California—the Mecca of swimming pools. December temperatures could reach into the low eighties, heated by the restless Santa Ana winds. This was not a question of *wanting* something; a pool was a social and personal necessity.

Besides the catalog, early December also brought a tidal wave of other forms of yuletide commercialism. Glowing televisions barraged teens and children with images of toys and games.

"I want that for Christmas, I want that for Christmas," Freddie would repeat mindlessly as he watched Saturday morning television. Between Tom & Jerry, Land of the Lost, Scooby Doo and Bugs Bunny cartoons, Hasbro, Milton Bradley and Mattel streamed images of toy ovens making real chocolate cakes, board games and rockets that would fire a thousand feet into the air and float harmlessly—avoiding every tree branch—to land safely back in a kid's postage-stamp garden. This year he had set his sights on an Evil Knievel Stunt World Play Case for $12.95. According to the commercial, a kid could help Evil complete his ill-fated attempt to jump the Snake River Gorge on the X-2 Skycycle. Freddie slid off the couch and wrote down the name of the toy as the announcer chided him. "With your help, Evil might finally succeed".

Huntington Hills was drunk on adolescent avarice and holiday cheer. Cherry-red garlands stretched across city streets while residential pines, magnolias and oaks were transformed into colorful midnight beacons that whispered to every living person: "Buy, buy, buy..." Department stores dominated the retail landscape of nearby Pasadena and were the epicenters of consumer spending that competed for the hearts and minds of suburban parents.

Susie knew that moms got the short end of the candy cane, having to purchase the shirts, socks, sweaters, and practical items that were opened and rapidly discarded into mounds of paper and boxes. She also was responsible for consolidating the myriad irrational requests into a practical Santa list that would guarantee surprises but not sink the S.S. Patton into the dark waters of consumer debt. Armed with the catalog, Susie outfitted Karl with the requisite shopping list and shoved him out the front door into the confused mayhem of Sears, J.C. Penney, or Bullock's—or all three. For Karl, the "big shop" weekend before Christmas was like a prostate exam.

Sears remained ground zero for all Patton retail activity. The massive warehouse store in East Pasadena had no windows and seemed to devour shoppers once they entered its massive doors. To Karl, discount stores were like Las Vegas casinos —designed to suck him in, pull him through, and spit him out into the parking lot wearing only his underwear and pushing a cart full of bullshit. The Chicago merchants that had once sold mail-order buggies and horse feeders were now focused on bricks and mortar wholesaling, and in a time of economic uncertainty, the store was overrun with bargain hunters.

Karl loathed shopping of any kind. He was made to make money, not spend it. It was if God himself were testing him. His normal shopping outings were a frantic race against invisible combatants. He felt naked in large stores as he competed to purchase items and return to the safety of his neighborhood. Anyone working in retail was stupid. He would race to fill his list of items – always to be purchased on sale - and then produce a confusion of coupons and dated newspaper ads that would confound the dim-witted part-time teen working at the checkout counter. If a line of impatient shoppers began to build behind him in his checkout line, he would merely turn and growl.

On this day, he made a beeline for an open counter, only to be cut off by an ancient do-it-yourself handyman who could not understand why the nice young lady at the bedding register could not help him find a number six Allen wrench.

"Excuse me. I'm looking for a wrench." The kindly old gentleman peered up at the young retail clerk through Coke-bottle glasses.

"Sir, this is linens and bath supplies. You'll want the hardware section on the Floor Two."

"And where is that?" said the old man staring at an escalator jammed with people and bags.

Karl stood behind the elderly do-it-yourselfer and twitched with annoyance. He had been waiting to make his purchase, some pink hand towels for Susie. The boys were getting restless. Freddie had slipped out of his hand and was now bouncing on an adjacent bed. George and John had disappeared into a rack of clothes. There was a crack and a yelp as Matthew had snapped a towel too close to Freddie leaving him with a red welt and tears in his eyes. Karl came unglued and hissed, "Everyone stop your goddamn grab-assing."

Grab-ass was a part of Karl's unique lexicon describing any antisocial behavior worthy of punishment. Grab-ass was punishable by the spanking of the grab-asser's ass, which was not a pleasant experience. In the

1960s and early '70s, Karl and other T-Rex fathers could still get away with publically whacking their children. An alpha father might observe another patriarch meting out punishment and congratulate him on his forehand technique. However, the nuclear option of spanking in public also meant a howling child, which invited derision from liberal, Dr. Spock mothers. To avoid this inconvenient disapproval, Karl had perfected a new method of pain—a fingernail squeeze of the inner arm. Known as The Vise, the torturous grip sent a firm message to any potential grab-asser that the episode of disobedience was now coming to an abrupt end. Often, the vise grip left behind small bruises the size of dimes that were dismissed by a mother as normal playground scuffs and scratches.

The holiday cash registers were crowded like airline counters after a flight cancellation. Karl was anxious to leave but needed to buy Susie's final Christmas presents. He was too proud to ask for help but too imprisoned in the world of men to exhibit a clue to her interests and fashion preferences. He was an ex-soldier, pragmatic and utilitarian. He did not realize that many of his gifts reinforced the notion of female indentured servitude. The state-of-the-art GE vacuum, the fancy Australian dust mop, European measuring cups, German Krupp knives and hand woven Egyptian cotton towels might as well have come with a ball and chain.

It would take Karl decades to discover that the only thing that Susie wanted was time—precious moments to be left alone with a good book or an old movie. This was unfortunately not for sale at Sears. It was not in Karl's DNA to understand that women hailed from a different galaxy and tended to attach equal value to the smallest of gestures and the grandest of gifts. They especially did not shiver with excitement at the sight of a new oak rolling pin.

It was the Saturday before Christmas week, the implicit community deadline for all holiday lights to have been hung. While Karl would have preferred to resist the annual pagan ritual to save on electricity, he did as Susie instructed him, faithfully tracing the eaves of their home. Every one, including the dog, avoided Karl on Susie's "honey do" afternoons. He was an unstable rocket fueled with caffeine and angry self-pity.

"Shit! Goddamn it!" Karl yelled as he sucked his thumb after smashing it with the hammer. He was loud enough for Mr. Hardy across the street to laugh and yell. "You need a taller ladder, Karl. And where are those boys of yours? Make them hold the nail."

Karl waved and muttered something about Hardy under his breath.

Inside the house, Susie was transforming the interior into a Christmas wonderland. Huge plastic bags filled with garlands lay at the foot of the stairs. A tree stand and golden tree skirt rested near the living room stairs.

A hair dryer blared behind a closed door as George readied for his Christmas date with Kelly Reed. Holed up in the bathroom for more than two hours waging war against his acne, he was now trying to pop and disguise a pimple that had risen through his skin like an unwelcome lava dome one day before the biggest date of his life.

John had been waiting impatiently to shower and prepare for his evening over at Seth Erickson's house. "Get out of the goddamn bathroom, pizza face. You're not going to get any better-looking by picking that zit."

The door to the bathroom locked. John immediately yelled downstairs, "Mom! Zit boy won't get out of the bathroom."

In the hall, John heard George's muffled shout above the hair dryer. "I'd rather be pizza face than a pussy that always locks the door when he's taking a shower. What do you need to shower for anyway? You're only going over to Seth's house."

Too infused with Christmas spirit to be distracted, Susie yelled back up upstairs, "John, use our bathroom, hon. Please, don't be like Freddie and wipe your bottom with my nice towels. Hang them up when you're done and use your own razor, not your Dad's. He always seems to know when you kids touch his stuff."

George sat in the bathroom staring at what appeared to be a third eye in the middle of his forehead. As he administered his mother's tan pancake makeup to dull the inflamed edges of his acne, he heard his father curse outside again.

"Son of a bitch, motherfu…"

Each year Karl blasphemed his way through the holiday light decoration process. The gods seemed to despise his impious embrace of the Christmas season and were once again tormenting him as he plugged the thread of colorful bulbs into the outside electrical socket. Having secretly climbed the magnolia tree in front of the house, Freddie loved watching his father wrestle with the green serpent string of bulbs and swear each time he produced a half-illuminated strand.

Karl considered these half-assed outages a challenge to his American ingenuity and resolve. His Christmas lights were like small banana republics. If one bulb fell into communistic darkness, a domino effect of failures would follow, resulting in the entire house's yielding to yuletide ignominy. A house with dead bulbs whispered that the owner was a slacker and unable to provide for his family. Karl's battles with extension cords, burned-out fuses, and blacked-out gaps of lights were the stuff of Patton family legend and were always punctuated by his unholy eruptions. Karl gritted his teeth and tried to remove a broken bulb with needle nosed pliers. He silently hissed his favorite word.

"Mother-fucker!"

A beat-up Ford Woodie station wagon with two surfboards on the roof rack passed slowly by the house, pulled a U turn, and then scraped against the curb. Freddie dropped out of the tree.

Karl looked over at his youngest son who had been avoiding his chores and spying on him. "You sneaky little shit, have you been watching me this whole time and not helping?"

"It's Matthew. He's home!"

From the back of the wagon, Matthew Patton lifted his duffel bag, while another teen with bleached blond hair handed him his surf board, gave him a soul brother handshake, and then smiled at Freddie.

"It's the little dude. Hey, Mister P!"

"Hey Judd!" Freddie yelled as he ran up to the two young men.

Matthew dropped his bag and punched his younger brother softly on the shoulder. "Is the man who lives in Daddy's mouth saying bad words again?"

Freddie grinned at his older brother with a look of sheer adoration and laughed.

"Dad had some good ones today. There was one about a pig fu …"

"That's enough, Freddie. Good to see you Judd." Karl said sharply.

"Matthew, good to see you're finally home. I thought school ended, what, Tuesday and it's now Saturday?" He flipped the back of Matthew's hair with his hand. "And I see it's still hard to find a barber in the Soviet Union."

Matthew lost his smile. "That's a new record, Dad. I was wondering how long it would take for you to mention Communists, my hair, or the Socialist Republic of Berkeley."

Karl smiled, choosing to ignore the comment. He gave his eldest son a hug. He could feel Matthew stiffen.

"Better get inside. Your mother wants to see you. How did your exams go?"

Matt looked annoyed. "Jesus, I just got here and you already want to know how I did. Can't you just say 'good to see you'? Why is everything about measurements and grades with you?"

"Can't improve what you can't measure, son."

"Well, Dad. Maybe I measure myself against a different standard."

Karl looked at his son and felt his blood pressure rising. "Freddie," he said, "get your ass over here and help me figure out which of these god-damn bulbs is bad."

When the defective lights were finally bested, the colored light strands ran along in analog confusion—two reds, a blue, two greens followed by a white, and then two more reds. Karl was close to exploding. Freddie was about to offer something constructive, but thought better of it and offered his unequivocal support. "It looks cool, Dad."

Across the Mason-Dixon financial dividing line of Huntington Hills Drive, wealthy Santa Anita Road homeowners were skillfully stringing alternating red and green lights across roofs and around each dormer window. Their hundred-foot pine trees were brilliantly lit with a palette of perfectly numbered lights that flickered like a thousand roman candles, while the Patton roofline and single hibiscus plant looked like a cheap Tijuana cantina.

Inside the home that Karl had christened "The House That Hugs," Susie had just hung the Advent calendar. Each son had, at some point, proclaimed that the cartoonish calendar was now too juvenile to appreciate. Yet there was something irresistibly magical about this talisman with kitsch artwork and its fragile pre-cut doors. It elicited overwhelming curiosity from each kid, especially Freddie after Matthew told him that the Catholics used these calendars to pass messages to one another during the Inquisition. The calendar might very well contain the secrets of Fatima. By December 20, Susie knew that a kid would risk eternal damnation for the opportunity to secretly open a window and try to decipher its odd illustrations.

"Hey, Mom!"

"Matthew, you're home!" Susie hugged and kissed her son on the cheek and then looked him in the eyes. "Was that you and your father arguing our front?"

"He is such a dick. I am here two seconds and he wants to see my grades."

Susie walked over and began to remove figurines from a box that held her prized nativity scene. "First of all, I do not want that language in my house. Secondly, he has a right to ask you for your grades since he is paying your tuition. Third, he's my husband. I love him and if you love me that means you love him. Euclid's law! My enemy's enemy is my friend … or something like that. Enough of your militant college behavior! You're home. You need food and a chore list."

"I literally just got home."

"Matthew, finals ended three days ago. I know you and Judd surfed for two days at Hollister and at Bixby. I talked to Martha Quinn, so it will do no good to lie. I can see the sand in your hair and you smell like the ocean. God knows how you can surf after seeing *Jaws*. I can't take a bath without being able to see the bottom of the tub."

"Sharks eat seals, Mom, not people."

"Here, grab this manger and follow your mother. We need to set up the crèche for baby Jesus." She spoke as if she were talking to an infant.

Matthew watched as his mother faithfully arranged wise men, shepherds, and the supporting cast of animals, all the while humming *The Little Drummer Boy*. The sacred nativity eventually would be mischievously reconfigured into a highly inappropriate conga-line orgy of animals and figurines where all participants and its principal choreographer, Freddie Patton, were surely going to hell. Soon after, baby Jesus would disappear and miraculously appear three days later in the dog's mouth as he lay on the floor chewing on what Susie thought was a bone.

Arthur Fiedler and the Boston Pops were playing "Sleigh Ride" on the living room stereo. The air was cooling outside, and Matthew felt himself relax in the familiar smells and comforts of home.

"Well, Matthew, it looks like it is just you, your father, and I tonight." Susie smiled and hugged her eldest son. He grimaced at the mention of his father.

"I made a pot roast in your honor and I think we might even get the Christmas tree. John's spending the night at the Ericksons. George has a very important date with the Reed girl, who is a cheerleader I might add, and Freddie ..." Susie smiled wistfully and looked as if she were going to cry, "Freddie is going to his first holiday cotillion."

Matthew laughed. "Is he going to do the box step with the Captain and Mrs. Mac?"

Freddie frowned. "I've got a stomach ache. I can't go to this stupid dance with all those dumb girls and idiot boys."

Susie smiled lovingly and went onto the back porch to retrieve a blue sports jacket, slacks, and tie.

"Oh, yes. He will be the last Patton boy to learn the box step, fox trot, and waltz."

Matthew smiled and winked at his younger brother, "It's not as bad as you think, buddy." He turned and opened the refrigerator. "It's worse." He laughed and continued. "Where's Georgie? I got to warn him about Tim Irwin. He's been stalking that Reed girl since last year when she was a freshman. He punched out Buddy Little last year just for talking to her at a party. His oars are not all in the water. Probably ate too many paint chips as a kid. If I were George, I'd get a lower risk date or buy some brass knuckles. The guy is a complete dick."

"Can we please stop using that word?" Susie admonished as she moved to check the pot roast. When Matthew left the room to find George, she was still frowning.

CHAPTER 4

Teenage boys, goaded by their surging hormones run in packs like the primal horde. They have only a brief season of exhilarating liberty between control by their mothers and control by their wives.

~Camille Paglia

It was the uniform of the condemned: the hand-me-down blue blazer, striped tie knotted with a baseball-sized double Windsor, a starched white pinpoint, and itchy gray wool slacks with razor-edged military creases. Freddie chafed at his collar and yelled downstairs to his mother. "Mom, I just barfed. I'm sick."

"I'll be up in a minute to look at your throw-up."

"Too late, I flushed it. There was so much. It was gross."

"You're going Freddie."

"No I'm not. I think I have cholera. There was lots of blood in the vomit."

Karl lofted a verbal grenade up the stairs as he waited impatiently for the parade of boys to assemble. "If you're not downstairs in five seconds, I'll cholera your ass!"

Freddie was going to the first of what promised to be several humiliating cotillion classes. He did not know what a kid did at cotillion, but judging from the wry smile on his older brother's face, he was not going to like it. Susie had hoped that the etiquette and dance academy would transform her young heathens into gentrified aesthetes whose table manners were exceeded only by their ability to do the cha-cha. Like most parents, she secretly held hopes that this rigorous social sandpapering would prepare one of her boys to someday become the U.S. cultural attaché to some exotic European country.

The dance macabre was held at the Huntington Hills Community Center and was hosted by the imperious Captain and Mrs. McManus. Captain Mac was an ex-Navy officer and a rigid cardboard cut-out who feared no man except his spouse and dance partner, a Joan Crawford stunt double complete with hyperthyroid eyes and a fearsome tire-skid unibrow. Her toxic perfume could have emptied an entire trench line in WWI. Most boys suspected that life with Mrs. McManus was the equivalent of going to war: long periods of boredom punctuated by episodes of sheer terror.

After dropping John off at the Ericksons, Karl pulled up to the community center. Susie got out of the car and turned Freddie toward her. "Now let me take a look at you."

She smiled and put one hand on her chest as if she were ready to cry—again. Freddie was about to cry, too, but for a different reason. Susie leaned down and straightened his black watch Scottish tartan tie. She walked him to an illuminated foyer where a woman she didn't recognize was welcoming the children and writing nametags. Slipping back into the dark, she watched as Freddie firmly shook the woman's hand and told her his name.

Plopping into the passenger side of car, she turned to Karl and smiled, "Our baby boy is growing up."

Karl scoffed. "He was never a child. He came out of your womb reading a *Wall Street Journal*."

Inside, a tight knot of restless and irritable sixth-grade boys hugged the walls, pushing and shoving one another toward the demilitarized zone of ballroom floor that separated the Y chromosomes from the mysterious tangle of Cinderella X's, with their perfumed, bowed hair and polished glass slippers.

"Heel, toe, heel, toe, slide, slide, slide," shrilled with mind numbing repetition through an ancient loudspeaker. For the young attendees, the experience was as close as they might come to a political reeducation camp in Cambodia. For Mrs. Mac, each Saturday evening brought the chance to transform into a dreamy Blanche Dubois reliving a time when Tommy Dorsey music floated on the cool autumn air and young men lined up to fill her dance card. When the first few notes of *Blue Danube* fell like a soft silk veil, the McManuses roamed the floor in a nostalgic blackout looking for partners.

A silent rosary could be heard from the mouths of every child. "Please, God, do not have her pick me. Please God, please, please."

An alabaster claw clutched Freddie's arm. "Come with me, Master…" She glanced at his nametag. "Patton. Let's show this ballroom how to waltz!"

Nervous snickers and total humiliation swirled around Freddie as Mrs. Mac proceeded to break him like a green colt. After Freddie had endured the waltz and box step with the skeleton lady, the music mercifully stopped. He shuffled back to the fray of cowlicks and tight collars, emasculated and reeking of cheap perfume.

"Hello? Seth? Kitty?" John, noting the front door had been left ajar, entered the house and peered into the living room. The wolfhounds, Callum and Kitty, were milling outside on the back yard patio, which was unusual since the strange beasts were normally draped over the couch or wandering aimlessly through the house.

The stereo was skipping, the stylus stuck in a groove. John could see the cover of Carole King's *Tapestry* tossed on the sofa. A thin kite string of smoke rose from a lit cigarette resting in an ashtray. He heard the faint hum of singing from the kitchen, not unlike the sound he used to make as a child playing alone in his room.

John yelled again. "Hello?"

Still the humming but no sign of Seth or the rest of the family.

John walked down a narrow hallway, tastefully adorned with artistic black and white photographs of the Erickson family. Each photo of Kitty, Seth, Mr. Erickson, and Candy was posed and perfect. This was in sharp contrast to the Pattons' photo albums filled with grainy Polaroid pictures from distant motel parking lots, theme parks and run-down beach-house apartments. Invariably, there was always one kid crying in a Patton photograph. Looking closely, one usually could see Karl's hand curled or digging into the arm of the offending grab-asser as he grinned and hissed, "Smile, or I will give you something to really cry over."

John edged cautiously out of the shadowed hallway toward the kitchen light, where he could now see Kitty sitting at the country table with an open bottle of wine and a white book that appeared to be full of photos.

"Kitty?"

Kitty did not turn her back, but moved to dab her eyes with a napkin.

"Why, Jonathon, you are twenty minutes early. I don't abide well with surprises. You've caught me in such a state."

"Yeah, I'm sorry. I got dropped off first and came inside when no one answered. The front door was open." He surveyed the sink filled with dirty dishes and the stained pans still resting on the stove.

"Where's Seth?"

"Oh, he's on a short errand in my car. He'll be back soon. Come and sit down and behold the glorious days of Camelot and great expectations."

"Excuse me?"

"Oh, Sugar, I was just lookin' at my wedding album. It seems like a million lives ago when I was Eva Marie Saint in *Raintree County*." She started to sing softly. "…For the brave who dare, there's a Raintree ev'rywhere. We who dreamed found it so, long ago…" She hesitated and then lifted her hand to straighten her hair.

"Come to think about it, your mother is the Irish twin of Elizabeth Taylor."

John was uncertain whether she was drunk, but he could sense pain and raw vulnerability. He pulled up a chair and pointed to the bridesmaids.

"Who are the girls?"

Kitty turned to John and into the light. He moved back, startled at the sight of her red and puffy eyes streaked with mascara. "Goodness, I must look like the horrors of Mr. Poe," she sniffed. "Running mascara is emblematic of all that is Southern and sentimental. We are susceptible to great tempests of emotion."

He glanced at sepia photos of attractive teenaged women with beehive hairdos and pink satin dresses, all grinning like identical Pan American flight attendants on some TV commercial.

"These are my sisters from Chi Omega. They are my truest and best of friends. This one married a senator and is now living in Mobile. This charming creature married the star running back on the Crimson Tide, but he ended up leaving her. It's rather odd how we come into this life sent from heaven only to all end up on the road to perdition."

Kitty picked up the wine glass and stared vacantly into its contents before draining it. "It's much easier to run from storms than to try to navigate through them. John, you should remember that integrity is earned and not simply granted with age. My mother always used to say that we must finish what we start in this life so we can earn the chance to improve ourselves in the next one."

She was talking to no one in particular. John noted that the wine bottle was three-quarters empty, with the broken cork still impaled on the screw and both discarded in the sink.

John hesitated, overwhelmed with the scent of her hair, the tears, and the moment.

"I'd never leave you."

Kitty looked up and smiled faintly at John. "You're sweet, darling. That is the nicest thing I have heard since you told me that I looked like …"

Kitty suddenly understood that the handsome seventeen-year-old was soliciting her. She felt herself being transported into another made-for-TV melodrama. She slowly inched her face away from John who had eased to within six inches of her chair. In a sudden twitch, he struck like a cobra, moving to kiss her. Anticipating his awkward offensive, she shifted and turned away from him, sending her shoulder blade crashing into his nose, striking him with such force that he fell off his chair and his nose started to bleed.

"Oh, my God! John, are you all right?" She rushed to get a towel and started to laugh in nervous bursts.

"I love you," John said nasally, as he sat pinching the bridge of his hemorrhaging nose.

She quickly handed him a towel with ice. "Oh, my dear boy. I'm flattered but I'm old enough to be your mother."

John tilted his head backwards. "It doesn't matter. I can take care of you. I can get a job. I have over a thousand dollars saved. We can go to Alabama."

"Oh, Lord," she laughed sarcastically. "That is definitely *not* an option for this jezebel. Son, you have your entire life ahead of you." She leaned over to put her hand on his shoulder.

The back door opened and Seth burst breathlessly into the kitchen. "Mom, I couldn't see Dad's Harley anywhere…What happened?"

Seth's eyes narrowed, settling on John, who was holding a bloody cloth over his nose, and then darting quickly to his mother, who had an odd look of guilt and trepidation on her face. "What's going on?"

"We need to tell Seth," John said, speaking into the blood-spattered towel.

"Tell me what?"

"Nothing, darling. It's a tempest in a teapot. John's upset because we are upset."

"No. I'm upset because I want to be with her."

Seth seemed incredulous, ready to laugh at what was likely a bad joke, but he felt John's earnest resolve and he darkened. In an explosion of raw emotion, he hurled himself at John, knocking him on to the floor, striking him several times in the face. Kitty shoved and kicked her son to one side.

"Seth, that is quite enough! Stop it this instant! Your friend was confused and felt sorry for us because of what happened."

John rolled over and looked up from the floor, his left eye swelling. "What do you mean, what happened?"

"You asshole!" Seth raged. "It's none of your goddamn business. Now get the hell out of our house."

John lifted himself from the linoleum floor and glanced down at Seth. John towered over him and could easily have destroyed him in a fistfight.

"You need to go, John," Kitty said. "I can give you a ride or we can call your parents and tell them you and Seth got into a little tiff."

John lingered as if he wanted to say something more, but then swallowed his words. His fantasy had been nothing but a seductive lie. "I'm gonna walk home. I feel like such an asshole."

"That's 'cause you *are* an asshole!" screamed Seth, trying to pull away from his mother. In the other room, the wolfhounds began to bark.

"Seth Forrest Erickson! You remove yourself to the other room."

She turned to John, who was now walking to the front door. "My dear friend, 'Love is never lost. If not reciprocated, it will flow back and soften and purify the heart.' Washington Irving wrote those words two hundred years ago."

John stood in the doorway, a lonely silhouette facing a dark December night.

"Yeah, maybe in two hundred years, I'll understand what the hell just happened."

He moved out toward the street lamplight and shut the front door. Outside Kitty could hear John talking to himself.

"I'm such a dick!"

George was having an epic time. The band was playing *Shining Star* by Earth, Wind and Fire. The Allendale Country Club had been transformed into a Christmas wonderland of red-and-gold tablecloths, magnificently decorated trees, and fresh pine boughs that looped around great wooden beams crisscrossing the interior roof. Under each entrance and doorway dangled fist-sized sprigs of mistletoe. Several teens were necking underneath the holiday decorations, while adult chaperones glanced at their watches and looked bored. Perhaps the greatest miracle of this nascent Christmas season was the fact that George was actually on the dance floor.

George understood that girls liked to dance and that asking the opposite sex on to the dance floor could improve the odds of an amorous encounter. High school dances were one of the gardenia-scented rites of passage compulsory to a young man's journey.

The annual Huntington Hills Christmas dance was a restive current of social posturing and unrestrained hormones. Each year, an uneven skyline of boys and girls adorned the country club's walls and tables watching the vortex of motion with envy and contempt.

The eye of this anxious adolescent tornado was an evolving social order of post-pubescent royalty. The dancing was free form, with boys confined to safe, unimaginative jerking from side to side with the occasional overbite and riff of an air guitar. The girls were infinitely more expressive, swaying like Moroccan belly dancers in an eddying hot wind, their arms above their heads. And then there were the mavericks, the individualistic kids who dared to dance outside the safety zone, using moves borrowed from *American Bandstand* or *Soul Train* to challenge the social hierarchy and dance with the most popular girls.

After enduring the trauma of cotillion, George often sat with friends, mocking and badgering the counter-cultural souls and swingers from the safety of the shadows. Yet, as he moved around Kelly Reed and watched the sheer grace of her body—her muscles, hair, and attractive smile, he realized he had been the real loser for not having the guts to attempt to dance.

In the eighth grade, George tried to break ranks with his inept brethren by practicing moves in front of the mirror weeks before a dance. However, there was no sequence of steps or motions that did not make him look as if he were on the cusp of an epileptic seizure.

Karl was no help. The man, who had grown up in a time with great dance steps like the Jitterbug and the Lindy Hop, had one series of moves that the Patton brothers referred to as "the hydroplane." He would sway side to side like a Rodeo Drive palm tree while moving his hands parallel to the ground. He appeared to be a tragic Prometheus forever condemned to administer Pledge wax to an imaginary tabletop.

Matthew and John were no help, as they were equally challenged on the parquet. His last hope, Susie, could not stop giggling each time they privately attempted to do a popular version of the cha-cha-cha. George was the dancing bear in the circus.

He had almost forgotten about the baggie of flies in his pocket. He was not sure when to sprinkle the powdered love potion into his date's drink. He was uncertain that he even wanted to use them. She seemed to be giving him all the signals that she wanted to be with him. He was hot and sweaty from dancing, but otherwise, he was having a great time.

"Hey, you want to go outside?" he said.

"Yeah, it's so hot in here," Kelly said as she adjusted her top.

George looked handsome in his blue Atkinson's blazer, red foulard tie, and gray slacks. For once, Susie had been forced to buy George his own clothes. He no longer could fit into the John and Matthew's hand-me-down clothes. The new coat and tie did not have the punitive feel of church clothes, but instead fitted him like a military officer's uniform. He was becoming his own man.

Kelly wore a low-cut green silk gown, pearls, and diamond earrings. In the weak balcony light, her entire face appeared to be glowing. Fairy lights sparkled in the trees and the distant rhythmic bass was tracking with the beat of his heart. Teddy Galloway was full of crap and really did not know anything about her. George had fantasized about this moment and about what their first kiss might feel like.

He did not have to wait long. "Hey!" Kelly said, smiling and laughing at George. "You're zoning out on me."

"Oh, I am? Are you ticklish?" He grabbed her waist, and she screamed.

"No, oh, my God! Stop. I am *so* ticklish."

As she bent to one side, she grabbed his wrists, stopped squirming and stared invitingly. It was the moment John had told him would happen. He could hear his brother's words:

"…after the tickling, she'll turn and move her face closer if she wants to be kissed. Then you plant one on her."

George moved toward her and tilted his face. She closed her eyes and their lips met. She tasted like cherries and warm moist dough. She put her arms around his neck and pulled him closer. She smelled like the perfume section at Bullock's. He was in love.

Kelly opened her mouth wider and inserted her tongue into George's mouth. His brother had failed to mention wandering tongues. George had a sensitive gag reflex and was not excited about this slippery probe.

He broke off the kiss and gazed at Kelly. "Do you want to get out of here and go to Bert's?"

Kelly looked surprised and a bit annoyed. "There'll probably be just a bunch of loadies there. Partying just makes me sleepy. Besides, we don't need to be stoned to have a good time."

George was confused. The kiss had been nice. The dance was fun. The tongue was a definite curve ball, but he was willing to get back into the batter's box. But it appeared that the locker room scouting report of nymphomania had been wildly overstated.

George persisted. "C'mon. Let's just go. His parents aren't home and we could use their room."

Kelly stopped smiling. "For what? Did someone tell you that this dance is like the Prom and whoever you go with has to sleep with you?"

She studied his expression. "Judging from your clueless face, you've probably been listening to stories about me sleeping with some guy I've never heard of, or about me making it with some famous black 'SC football player. Are you that stupid that you believe all the crap made up by hard up guys about girls that *won't* sleep with them?"

George looked at her in disbelief and recovered into a sympathetic half smile. "If it's any consolation, I hadn't heard about the black football player."

Kelly shook her head in disgust. "Oh yeah, I feel a lot better now. George, I had you all wrong. I thought maybe because you were younger, you might just be up for a nice time with someone who liked you. I should have known that a freshman couldn't think for himself."

She stormed off toward the terrace door that led on to the dance floor. As she wheeled back, her eyes were blazing with hurt and disappointment.

"Don't bother with getting us a ride home. I'll find my own way home."

She turned to walk away and wheeled around in anger. "You know, Bobby Shea asked me to go out with him tonight, but I said I was going to the dance with you. I told him I had a date. I should have told him that I had to babysit."

"Hey, I'm an idiot. I admit it!" George suddenly remembered the baggie of Spanish flies in his pocket and yelled behind her. "Do you at least want a Coke before you go?"

Karl was the son of a German immigrant and was orthodox regarding the purchase of the Christmas tree. Der Weihnachtsbaum would be procured no earlier than ten days before Christmas Day. The tree must be at least a seven-foot-tall blue spruce. The only hitch was that it must be purchased at the local YMCA tree lot. Susie was loyal to the YMCA for keeping boys occupied and out of jail.

Karl's fleeting holiday nostalgia always melted under the fading glow of the Y tree lot's sparkling lights, with its army of clueless volunteers who could not be fired because they were, in fact, volunteers. It was the equivalent of being forced to attend a village idiots' convention. He never referenced the tree lot by name, but instead chose to refer to is as "Cretin Central."

Fifteen minutes after Karl purchased the tree, five "elves" were still rubbing their chins and walking around the Pattons' station wagon.

"How you want to put this baby up on the wagon, Ray?" asked an overweight, ruddy-faced fellow wearing a Santa's helper hat and holding a hand axe.

"I got an idea," shouted a tall, dour mortician of a man. "Let's swing it across the back and push it forward."

Matthew glanced at his dad and knew this was not going to end well, and that once again Matthew would be embarrassed. It was bad enough that he was home from school for an entire month under the thumb of Il Duce, but he was now reliving all the reasons why he had wanted to move out.

Karl was beside himself as he watched the "Christmas Cretins" trying to lift the massive blue-grey spruce onto his roof rack. He could take no more and finally interrupted. "Gents, I think my son and I better do this before you scratch all the goddamn paint off the Impala."

The men, already sensing Karl's distain for their logistical retardation, melted away, mumbling something to the effect, "It's all yours, asshole." Matthew noted that for as long as he could remember, Christmas was a time when everyone swore. After heaving the evergreen onto the car and enduring an excruciating snail's pace drive across town, Matthew sighed as the Impala eased into the driveway of their home on Bedford Street.

While Matthew and Karl unloaded the tree, Susie drove to the community center to pick up a sullen and defeated Freddie. Solemn in the car, he yielded only monosyllabic answers to Susie's cheery questions. Once home, he raced upstairs to shed his humiliation and his cotillion clothes. A few minutes later, he bounced downstairs, his mood visibly improved by the Christmas music and the smell of a fresh evergreen in the living room. The Patton family, sans John and George, began the time-honored process of trimming the tree, adorning it with white lights and ancient ornaments.

As Sandler and Young sang *Mr. Sandman,* Freddie started to throw silver tinsel on the tree. Matthew sighed out of boredom at the entire scene. What was once a treasured Currier & Ives tradition now seemed to him to be a sham, a capitalist invention to pick the pockets of working people by turning the winter solstice into to a massive orgy of consumerism.

In the entry hall that rested a few steps above the living room, the mongrel Max studied the activity and surveyed his new target—the tree.

"Don't you even think about it, you scraggly pile of crap," Karl snarled as he looked over at the family dog.

"Dad," Freddie pleaded, "don't talk to Maxie that way." The boy ran over and hugged the tangled mop with a tail. A tongue appeared from a thicket of hair licking Freddie on the face.

Karl, who prided himself on being a workingman and master provider, saw the dog as representative of all that was wrong with the country. Max was the consummate freeloader. He had no job, ate other people's handouts, did not bathe, slept all day, procreated with every female dog in the neighborhood, and had the undeserved sympathy of everyone in the house. "That animal is the ultimate Democrat," Karl told anyone who would listen.

The Christmas tree was positioned in the far corner of the living room, where the dog would be least likely to urinate on it. The tree stand that supported the evergreen was a wobbly family heirloom that caused the tree to lean like the famous Italian campanile of Pisa. The perpetual tilt of the holiday blue spruce was an emotional hemorrhoid to Karl, leading him to constantly manipulate its position with primitive joists of newspaper and magazines. This, in turn, would guarantee its continued instability until the inevitable day arrived, when a door would slam, a person might raise his voice, or the wind would blow outside, and the tree, on cue, would crash to the ground with a shatter of ornaments and light bulbs.

George squatted in a bathroom stall for the final hour of the dance – listening to inaudible music and a parade of over-stimulated teenage boys who raced in and out of the men's room, discussing their carnal aspirations for the night. He once again patted the Spanish flies in his pocket and sighed.

The toilet seat in his stall was broken and creaked in protest each time George shifted his legs to prevent his feet from falling asleep. At around 11pm, two parent chaperones entered the restroom, congratulating one another on making it through the event. He recognized one of the men's voices as his former Pop Warner football coach Van Reynolds.

"All the animals accounted for, Jay?"

The deep baritone voice of Van Reynolds bounced off the walls and fell into George's hiding place like an avalanche of bad memories.

If there had been a Guinness world record for the most times one individual threw up during a single football practice on one smoggy Southern California afternoon, it would be George Patton playing junior midget football under Coach Reynolds. Reynolds favorite expressions were, "Man up!" and "Walk it off, dawg" – two highly sympathetic responses to limping, bloodletting, vomit or a mild compound fracture. The Georgia native was a former college football player and a disciple of Alabama's Bear Bryant who was infamous for his Marine Corps gridiron practice methods.

Vomiting was a sign of toughness to youth football coaches and the ability to puke and play revealed much about a young man's character. To George, any injury should qualify as a million dollar wound worthy of light duty, time off from running and a perhaps a chance to offer the coaches a few plays that he had designed during afternoon Social Studies class. George loved football but he loathed running and despised certain parent coaches who were desperate to recapture some ancient moment at the expense of 14-year-old boys and the contents of their stomachs.

"Jesus, Van. I need a stiff scotch. Is it just me or did you see what some of those little girls were wearing tonight? They're all beginning to look like south of Spring Street hookers?"

"Jay, I think it's us. You ought to see what my Mimi considers an acceptable outfit. The damn mini skirt should come with its own street lamp!"

The men laughed and with the splash of water and slap of the door, George was alone again. He stood up on the creaking seat like a WWII cartoon Kilroy, peering over the bathroom stall. Seeing only empty sinks, he exited his cell and moved into a hallway bustling with waiters and caterers cleaning up the main dining room.

George had lost his ride. Kelly had left the party an hour earlier with two sophomore girls who had also ditched their freshman escorts. He would now have to call a taxi or home and risk waking up his father. This would lead to getting picked up by his older brother, Matthew, only compounding his humiliation.

He walked out the double doors that marked the entrance to the club and surveyed a near empty parking lot. It was too far to walk home.

"Lose your date, Patton?"

George turned and looked up at a smirking Bobby Dennison, a slow-moving brontosaurus of a football player who lived in the Hills. He stood waiting for his car with his date, Annie Todd, a stout, thick-ankle girl who smiled sympathetically at George. Apparently word must have leaked that Kelly had dumped George. *This is what I get for dancing outside the safety zone.*

"Actually, my date lost me."

Dennison seemed stupefied by George's admission as a young parking attendant pulled up in front of them in a ruby-red BMW. The silver-spooned lineman descended the stairs and plopped into the driver's side of the car, oblivious to his girlfriend who waited until the valet opened her door. As he closed the door, Dennison looked up at the car valet who had scooted back to the driver's side window. Once the young parking attendant realized a gratuity was not forthcoming, he shook his head and ascended the stairs to the country club. Dennison revved the engine and popped the clutch, lurching forward with a cough of exhaust that fell over George.

"Perfect." George mused.

A familiar voice suddenly perforated George's bubble of self-pity. "Georgie?"

He turned to see Mikey DeSantis, his neighbor from nearby St Francis High. Mikey was the fifth of eight DeSantis boys. His father was Karl Patton's closest friend. Dom catered many of San Gabriel Valley's non-profit and community events. Like Karl, Dom DeSantis did not believe in child labor laws, which meant that each venue featured at least six DeSantis family members who would be working the bar, food, kitchen or tables.

The DeSantis sprawling ranch-style home rested diagonal to the Patton's backyard. The boys had cut a not-so-secret passage through the ivy fence that separated their properties. The "Days" boys were welcome extensions to the Patton family. They were third generation Sicilians – hard working, reliable and hairy. To George, the DeSantis male mafia was the hairiest group of men that he had ever seen. Most DeSantis adolescents had a five o'clock shadow by the third grade. Not a bully in the bunch, they were a friendly tribe of Big Feet that enforced neighborhood rubrics and faithfully appeared each Sunday at Mass along with their five sisters to be forgiven for transgressions committed during the previous six days.

Each son was conscripted as a minimum wage worker to bus tables or cook in their father's restaurants. By the time a DeSantis boy graduated high school, he had usually financed the purchase of his own car and mastered the balance of work and school. Karl Patton considered the DeSantis boys the poster children for responsible adolescence.

"Hey, Georgie. What the hell are you doin'?

George looked relieved to see a familiar face.

"Long story. I'm looking for a ride."

"If you don't mind a munchie run. I've been dreamin' all night of a double double. The old man doesn't let us eat anything from the buffet. He makes Larry drive any leftovers down to skid row. The old man gives homeless drunks free calzone but he won't feed his own kids!"

George jumped in the cab of Mikey's truck and was impressed at the customized interior. He felt his own stomach growl and knew that food would help to dull the edges of his disappointment, although this time, the sharp ache was going to be hard to eradicate because George knew it was self-inflicted.

After rolling through the drive through window, the boys found a dark corner of the parking lot and turned on KMET. Jim Ladd, the station's emphatic rock jock ruled the evening airwaves, and tonight he was on a Pink Floyd and Led Zeppelin kick. Sunday night radio would be even better when Ladd handed off the microphone to the strange and twisted Dr. Demento. 94.7 KMET was the center of every teen's radio universe.

"I love freaking Jim Ladd!" Mikey coughed with a mouth full of double-double cheeseburger.

Tonight Ladd seemed to be speaking directly to George. He did not want him wimping out listening to soft rock like James Taylor's *Fire and*

Rain. Ladd's music and militancy made it clear that no woman was worth it. He dared you to crank Led Zeppelin, open your windows, and with the help of Jimmy Page and Robert Plant, put every female on notice that you were destined for a higher calling.

Mikey had invested a large percentage of his working capital into his Chevy K-10 truck and its customized Blaupunkt audio system. With the amplifier, the speakers could crank 150 watts per channel – which, in the confines of a truck cab, sounded like you were seated three rows from the stage at an Aerosmith concert.

George made a sudden happy grunt while drinking his shake as his favorite song *Kashmir* began. Jimmy Page's signature guitar riff soon melted into a wild collision of musical influences from the Far East and North Africa. George began to feel better as he spied a station wagon full of east parking lot stoners drive up to order food.

"Crank this song, Mikey!"

George watched the car with amusement. With eyes leveled just above the dashboard, he smiled as the red-eyed potheads stopped short of the ordering kiosk, debating who could maintain their composure long enough to order eight cheeseburgers, six shakes, and four fries. He watched as they broke into a game of rock, paper, and scissors, to determine who would face the pimple-faced teen in the illuminated drive-through window. Several cars began to back up behind them. A car filled with girls honked in protest. It was a typical Saturday night in Pasadena.

After satisfying their stomachs, the boys pushed silently home, listening to music all the way. As Mikey turned on to Bedford Street, he turned down the stereo and slowed a few houses before the Pattons.

"You know, the only guy that scares me more than my old man, is your old man."

As the Chevy rumbled off, Mikey beeped his horn gently and yelled back through the rear window, "Don't worry, Georgie, you won't be a freshman forever."

George stared at the taillights as they illuminated briefly at the intersection. He hated being a freshman. He was the lowest life form on the food chain. The world of girls and women was a complex topography and there were no reliable maps. A greenhorn trying to cross a great wilderness, he felt overmatched and underequipped. He walked down the driveway toward the back door that was always left unlocked.

"Where the hell are you going?" A voice came out of the black from the corner of the house.

George jumped and fell backwards into the ivy.

"Who's there?" he hissed.

"It's me, numb nuts," John whispered. "What are you doing home? I thought you were all set up for your 'sure thing.'"

George sat down and shared his tale of woe. He took the baggy out of his pocket and showed his brother. "I am such an asshole. I mean this girl is a babe and she liked me."

John looked at the bag of flies. "Dude, I think you got ripped off. These look like a bunch of dead houseflies. Spanish Fly is like a liquid or something. Ronnie Thomas probably went into his bathroom and picked a bunch of dead flies from the window sill." He laughed out loud.

Softening, he held up the bag. "I might be able to get rid of these for you and get your money back. But I just have to find someone dumber than you, which may take a while. Georgie, just remember the golden rule of the locker room: every guy lies. All those boneheads who told you crap about Kelly Reed probably have never done it with a girl. Everyone lies about doing it. I mean it. Everyone lies."

"So why are you sitting out here?" George peered into John's darkened face.

"I hit on Seth Erickson's mom and he punched me."

"No way! Oh-my-God! Do you think she is going to tell Mom and Dad?" George was now being very loud, and when he heard his own voice he covered his mouth.

"Nope. But I think I need to avoid Seth and Mr. Erickson for a few months."

"I don't feel so bad anymore."

"Well," John said, "I'm glad something good came out of my nightmare."

In his upstairs bedroom, Freddie was trapped in a bad dream. He had fallen asleep reading *Helter Skelter* and had a vision that Leslie Van Houten and Tex Watson were breaking into his home with sharpened knives and forks. He was awake now, listening carefully, and he could swear that he heard the devil worshippers talking in hushed tones in the driveway. He froze, holding his breath to be certain his own heartbeat did not diffuse the noise of the imminent home invasion.

He had been fighting the need to urinate but was not about to navigate the five feet of hallway to the bathroom where Charles Manson might be hiding in the shower. He could not pee in the closet or in the corner behind his door. He had made a resolution to find a new makeshift urinal in the event cult members might be lurking in the stairwell adjacent to the hallway.

Freddie tiptoed to the window, keeping an eye on his bedroom door for any signs of the serial killers. He pushed the window open and began to pee sideways.

John was the first to hear the splatter, and then the spray hit him. He looked up at the same time that George peered toward the deep purple sky. A splash of urine whipped across their faces.

"Shit," said George. "It's starting to rain."

"It stinks. It smells like rotten eggs," John said, running toward the back door.

"Gross. You think it's acid rain?" George said, as he caught up with John.

CHAPTER 5

This is no simple reform. It really is a revolution. Sex and race, because they are easy and visible differences, have been the primary ways of organizing human beings into superior and inferior groups and into the cheap labor on which this system still depends. We are talking about a society in which there will be no roles other than those chosen or those earned. We are really talking about humanism.

~Gloria Steinem, Speech to the
National Women's Political Caucus

Karl arrived early at the office to assist two account managers as they struggled to negotiate the final pieces of a complex January liability renewal. The agency's founder and CEO, Bob O'Brien, was a Caltech engineer who had worked in aerospace as a risk manager and had been a fixture in the LA insurance community for better part of thirty-five years. He had recently bought out his original partner, Phil Taft, and was now the sole shareholder of the firm. At fifty-seven, O'Brien was striking, with snow-white hair and an unusual olive complexion— a genetic anomaly for an Irishman.

Bob had cashed in on his brains and *Guiding Light* good looks and applied his talents to the insurance business—an industry that seemed to reward those who could develop relationships and understand the nature of risk. As they gained more success, O'Brien & Taft added people and clients, with Phil assuming the role of operations and Bob playing the part of new business and client leader.

Bob became involved with Southern California centers of influence, local politicians, business associations and charities. At fifty, he met Connie Flannery, a thirty-one-year-old political activist at a fundraiser for George McGovern. Bob's kids were now grown, and he decided that his marriage had become stale. Two years into a predictable mid-life crisis, Bob divorced Margie, his wife of thirty years, and Connie Flannery became the new Mrs. O'Brien.

Sporting a young, dynamic wife and a "do-over" life, Bob attacked his work with a renewed vigor that led to even more success. His ability to combine intellect and charm distinguished O'Brien & Taft from larger insurance brokerage firms. OB&T attracted clients to the agency with a value proposition that promised intimate service and immediate access to highly qualified experts and technical professionals such as claims and industry risk specialist Karl Patton.

Karl had graduated Phi Beta Kappa from Santa Clara and while he was one of a handful of Protestants at the Jesuit University, he had developed a strong set of friendships and contacts in the Southern and Northern California Catholic communities. After five years working as a financial analyst for San Francisco-based Fireman's Fund, Karl met Bob O'Brien and the two men hit it off.

The Pattons and O'Briens met when Bob was still married to Margie. With similarly aged kids and a compatible outlook on business and politics, the families were close and spent countless hours together. Susie had never forgiven Bob for walking out on his first wife. Yet Bob had been good to Karl, promoting him rapidly and giving him all the clients with odd or complex risks that did not fit traditional insurance company appetites.

OB&T was organized around specific industry verticals such as agriculture, aerospace, construction, entertainment and hospitality, five business segments that dominated the California marketplace. Karl became the industry expert, developing creative methods of risk coverage and finance with groups like Lloyd's of London, where underwriting syndicates funded by rich widows and individual investors would be more open to insuring exotic exposures. Karl had learned over the years that everything could be purchased for a price. He could literally insure a burning building if the policyholder was willing to pay the premium.

Karl became Bob O'Brien's most trusted lieutenant. In a fifteen-year period, the firm had grown from less than five million dollars in revenues to more than thirty million. Nonetheless, OB&T Risk Services was not well regarded by everyone. They were a splinter under the saddles of major insurance brokers such as Marsh & McLennan, Frank B. Hall, Alexander & Alexander, and Johnson & Higgins, the bigger players who could not understand how a smaller firm with such a limited footprint could so successfully handle multinational and Fortune 1000 firms.

Karl and Susie entertained regularly and anchored a range of the agency's C-Suite relationships from the brilliant West Los Angeles Jewish community, who ran many financial, entertainment and professional service firms, to tough, blue-collar Italians who had built their construction and hospitality businesses one brick at a time. Susie was Karl's social antenna, forging strong personal bonds with the owners' spouses and in doing so, gathering useful insights about their personal circumstances—vacation interests, family backgrounds, and political orientation—all valuable intelligence that allowed Karl to better understand the personalities and foibles of each customer.

Client entertainment was occasionally tricky when Karl and Bob shared host duties at a charity dinner. Susie still held a grudge against Bob over his abandonment of Margie. She was cool to Connie and protested the younger woman by ignoring her. This suited Karl fine because he loathed Connie's politics and resented her militant feminism.

At a recent Risk and Insurance Management Society dinner, Connie had been goading Karl when she suggested that Jimmy Carter, the governor of Georgia would be the best candidate for President in the upcoming election.

"He's leading the Iowa caucus, Karl. He is not an insider," Connie yelled over the din of dinner conversations. "Besides, the man is a saint. Goes to church, loves his mother, and has probably screwed only one woman—his wife—and that was after a hell of a lot of begging." Connie cackled at her own crassness. Karl made a face at Susie.

"My God, Susie. I think your neoconservative, Nixon-loving storm trooper is turning blue!" Connie laughed, and then slowly lost her smile.

Karl had been so upset by Connie's opinions that he had breathed in when he should have swallowed. His tri-tip steak was lodged in his windpipe. "Jesus Christ, Connie," shouted Bob. "Look what you've done. He's having a heart attack."

Noticing that Karl was holding his throat, Susie was up in an instant. "Someone help him!"

A large man from an adjacent table pushed over and hit Karl hard in the back. He fell forward on the table and knocked two glasses to the ground. He grabbed his throat and then fell backwards into the man's arms.

Connie screamed at the interloper. "Jesus, what are you doing?"

Another slighter man pushed the stranger aside and grabbed Karl's midsection in a great bear hug and hoisted him off the ground.

"I'm a doctor." He grunted. "We have to push up under his rib cage, fast,"

The small physician hoisted Karl twice and slowed when he heard Karl give a huge congested cough and gasp, clearing his windpipe. The restaurant erupted in applause and Susie was crying, hugging the man who had practically ruptured Karl's spleen administering a new emergency response technique he had learned at UCLA called Heimlich.

Though his eyes were watering and he was still unable to speak, Karl broke into a smile. He had spit the steak with such force it had flown across the table and hit Connie O'Brien right in the face.

Bob stood up in front of a boardroom crowded with OB&T staff. Karl sat at the boardroom table seated closest to Bob as he tapped a pen against a water glass to gain the attention of the staff.

"Team, it gives me great pleasure to introduce you to Rebecca Gerson. She's joined us from A&A and will be focusing on building out our technology, biotechnology, and financial services verticals.

"As EVP of target markets, Rebecca will join the executive committee and help us cultivate the new echelon of female risk managers and VPs of finance who are beginning to show up at some of our larger and more gender-sensitive clients."

Rebecca was a poised and perfectly coiffed forty-something in a dark pin-stripe suit. She wore a simple pearl necklace and gold earrings. According to Bob's earlier memo, she lived in Toluca Lake, was president of the L.A. chapter of RIMS, and on was on the Board of Regents at her alma mater, prestigious Occidental College.

"Well, everyone," she said, "I'm thrilled to join OB and T. Bob's been pursuing me for three years, but it took losing the California Savings and Loan account to this sleepy, not-so-small agency in Pasadena to open my eyes to the notion that bigger is not necessarily better."

She was a poised, natural public speaker. Every word was measured as if she had just received an A in homiletics from some theological seminary. "Our business is changing and OB and T is determined to stay ahead of that change. I see myself as the tip of the arrow that will spearhead our push into new businesses and, hopefully, a brand that's synonymous not only with risk management excellence but also with business and social diversity."

Karl noticed the looks of adoration on the faces of many of the female account managers. It was really the first time he even considered that their agency was exclusively run by white, middle aged males who managed other Caucasian men in sales and account executive roles, while women and a few minorities worked in administrative and technical support functions.

The firm did have one black executive, Sam Thompson, one of Bob's great social experiments that had not succeeded. Sam was a heralded football and track star from UCLA that Bob had hired after watching him compete in the Olympic Trials of 1968.

After the Watts Riots, Bob was overwhelmed with what Karl saw as white suburban guilt that prompted him to hire Sam and commit to personally training him as a broker. Bob's good intentions faded, but not his resolve to keep Sam. While Thompson was a terrific person and a great family man, he was primarily a knife-and-fork guy, good for lunches, golf and rubber-chicken dinners. He was a master at telling stories and in an industry that was full of jock sniffers and fans that remembered Slammin' Sammy Thompson's miraculous TD run against Stanford in 1966, many were delighted to have a football star on their account – even if he really didn't understand risk management.

Karl was certain Connie O'Brien was behind Bob's new affirmative action push for women. Bob was making another gamble, but this one was more serious. Rebecca Gerson was obviously talented and would not have left A&A unless Bob had promised her a shot as successor to him as CEO, a job he had already promised to Karl.

Matthew slept in, waking up to a hangover and pulsing head as his mother rattled plates in the kitchen and whisked his younger brothers out the back door to ride their bikes to school.

John had left for school at five-thirty for an early-morning weight-lifting regimen with the basketball team. Peering through the painful slits that were once his eyes, Matthew glanced around the room, resenting how the privileged space given to the first-born son already had been converted into John's room. Many of Matthew's posters were still on the wall, but the space had been reengineered around a massive stereo system that stood catty-corner to the door and the queen-sized waterbed in the center. Matthew had been ignominiously set up in a camping cot, but with John now gone to school, the eldest Patton had shifted to the waterbed. The sensation of the liquid mattress felt strange but soothed his throbbing skull. The motion made him feel like he was floating in the air. He drifted off again only to jolt awake to a distant ringing phone.

"Mom!" he yelled groggily into a pillow as he pulled it over his head.

There was no reply. He covered his ears but the phone kept ringing.

"Phone!" he yelled through the open bedroom door.

"Jesus!"

Stumbling out of the bed, he fell to the floor. He recovered himself and ran up a small flight of stairs to his parent's bedroom, grabbing for the receiver. He was surprised to hear the voice of the vice-principal of Freddie's school asking for Susie.

"Hey, Mr. White. It's Matthew."

"Welcome home from school, son. I think I recall your mother telling me you're up at Cal, right? Hey, I need to speak to your mom right away. It concerns Freddie. Seems he got into a little mischief today before school and I need her to come down and meet with Freddie and me."

Dehydrated and craving a glass of water, Matthew rubbed his eyes. The night before, one beer had turned into several pitchers with a few high school buddies at Burger Continental on Lake Avenue. His brain felt like someone was entering his frontal lobe with a rototiller. A wave of nausea washed over him.

"Um, you know," he said, fighting back sickness, "she may be out shopping. I don't know. She doesn't seem to be here and I'm not really sure how to get hold of her."

There was a sudden beep on the phone and the call was cut off.

"Sir, this is the operator. We have an emergency call from Karl Patton. Will you accept?"

Matt was wide-awake now. Running his hand through his hair, he blew out some air. "I guess so," he said.

"Okay, sir." The operator sounded annoyed. "You can speak."

"Matthew, where the hell is your mother? I just got a call from someone at school that Freddie and two other kids got caught starting a fire in the equipment shed."

"I just hung up on Mr. White to take your call."

"Why the hell did you do that? Find your mom and call me when you get hold of her. I can't leave the goddamn office. If you can't find her, get your butt down there and find out what those pimps and union bureaucrats have on your brother."

Matt smiled and shook his head. "Okay Dad, got it." *Pimps and bureaucrats? They are middle school teachers!*

An hour later, Matthew, still somewhat under the weather, was pulling out of the middle school parking lot after hearing how Freddie, Tommy Myers, and Robbie Hartman had used magnesium to burn a hole through the fence of the Little League diamond.

When Matthew had first arrived at school, Freddie did not appear particularly contrite and looked almost triumphant that he'd burned a hole the size of a basketball through the visitor's dugout chain-link fence.

Matthew frowned at Freddie. "I'm sorry, Mr. White. Mom is out and Dad is at work. They asked me to come and hear what the little arsonist did that got him into trouble."

Freddie tried to defend his actions. "We figured by putting a hole in the fence, parents could pass stuff through to their kids when they were sitting. You know, like food. It gets boring during a baseball game. Al would probably sell more snack truck food during the day if kids were eating all the time."

White suppressed a smile. He tried to appear serious, but he was fond of Freddie. Ready for retirement, he enjoyed the ingenuity of these kids, even if the result wasn't all that desirable.

"Well, Matthew, your parents need to understand that this was an act of vandalism. Freddie will have to repay us to repair the fence. More importantly, it happened on school property during a school day." He raised his eyebrows at Freddie. "Might I suggest we confine our experiments to supervised, controlled burns off community property?"

Freddie nodded.

"Okay, young man! Back to third period. I am sure Mr. Fineman is wondering where his favorite math student is." Freddie jumped to his feet and bolted for the door.

"Walk! Don't run!" White barked at the boy.

Matthew looked at the ancient educator and hesitated. "That's it?"

"That's it."

Matt seemed almost disappointed. "I mean is there anything we need to do like keep him out of school for a week's suspension or ground him?"

White opened his file cabinet and stashed Freddie's folder. "Nope, case closed. Freddie brought it to my attention that because the fire occurred before eight-fifteen, technically school had not started. The bigger issue was the fire. It was so bright that one teacher said that you needed a welder's mask to look at it. The boys were wearing sunglasses. It was actually pretty inventive."

"Inventive? Nothing personal, Mr. White, but if that had been me when I was in middle school, I would've been suspended, and that's nothing compared to what would have happened at home."

White chuckled. "Things change, Matthew. I don't think we can draw and quarter every kid who makes a bad choice. Now, what your parents choose to do to him is another matter but the school's position is simple. No harm, no foul."

Matthew shook his head. "Wow. I mean, like, *wow*. Things *have* changed. That kid may one day burn down this whole town, and they will trace it back to this moment and the day the school decided not to expel him."

"Son, do you have something to say?"

"No, I just don't get this generation of adults. You make rules and then you decide who can break them. It's all so arbitrary."

"That's a strong word," said White. "I like to think of it as clinically subjective. We take each situation and apply pragmatic logic. You don't always need a hammer to kill a fly."

"You do in my house," Matt said, walking out of the office.

Matthew was already irritated and it wasn't even noon. Just a week earlier he had been surfing all day and sleeping out at night. He did not want to be home anymore. He wanted to be with his buddies surfing and hitting the Dead concert tour that was starting on the West Coast in June. In a few weeks, he would be back at Cal and in his own apartment on Telegraph. He would see his girlfriend and rejoin his tribe. He couldn't get away from this screwed-up family circus fast enough.

Earlier in the week, Ronnie had stood in the doorway of his pool house and watched as the motorcyclist rolled his Harley Davidson soundlessly down the driveway and kick-started it. The mysterious guest had spent the night, which was a first. He usually came around after dark and left within a few hours: a "Wham-bam, thank you, ma'am" type. In the morning light, he could see him more clearly with his black leather jacket, the muttonchops, and long hair. Ronnie knew him. It was the same dude. He had been sneaking around like a dog in heat for a month.

When he confronted his mother about the middle-aged interloper and why he needed the cover of darkness and back doors, a drunken Diane Thomas told her son to shut up and mind his own business. "You're lucky to be living here. I don't need to support you. I do it because I want to."

"Mom, you're a cocktail lounge ashtray, filled with the discarded butts of a hundred guys who just sit at your table for five minutes waiting for something better to come by. Why don't have a little self-respect? The old man has moved on. Fuck, he has a whole new family."

Diane was now talking to no one in particular and referring to Ronnie in third person. "Just like his father. All no good. No good. No good."

Her speech was slurred and she shook her head back and forth, looking at the floor.

Ronnie clapped his hands to get her attention. "Diane! Hey, Diane! You think I like racking in this house of pain? I know the shit I've seen. What's your excuse? At least I'm not shacking up with every babe that looks at me for more than five seconds. Someone told me that little shit Ralph Hunt is going around telling everyone he wants to nail you. The little bastard got a student deferment so he didn't have to go fight for his country. If I ever see that son of a bitch around here I am going to top him. I should have done it in high school."

Diane considered her son with intoxicated disdain. She despised what she had become, and in the thick of her own brittle disintegration, she was blaming everyone around her. She hated her husband for leaving her, although it was hard to know which came first—her unyielding neediness or his desertion of their family. The Thomas clan had become one colossal gangrenous wound.

Ronnie's dad, Buddy, had moved out in 1964 and quickly remarried, losing interest in his children while investing all his energies into his new family. A few parents had felt sorry for Ronnie. The dads who had coached Ronnie in Pop Warner football loved his fearlessness and eagerness for approval. He was a wild kid, but he was also a natural at any sport. He needed positive reinforcement and a role model.

Despite the distractions and Diane's mercurial drinking, Ronnie focused his aggression on football, and as a middle linebacker he anchored a stingy Huntington Hills defense that made it all the way to the 1966 state Southern Section CIF championship game.

The Rancheros lost the finals 10-6 to its San Gabriel Valley rival, the Alhambra Titans, when center Ralph Hunt fumbled the snap to all-CIF quarterback, Bill Hayes. Even to this day, Hunt would tell anyone who would listen that Hayes had committed the gaffe that lost the game.

While Hayes went on to star at Illinois, Hunt Jr. stayed closer to the golden apron strings of home, relying on his father's contacts and family largesse to buy him access to USC. As an all-CIF defensive star, several colleges had contacted Ronnie, but he lacked the social skills or sponsorship to dispel the reputation of his being a head case. He was encouraged to attend Pasadena City College to get his grades up and then apply to schools once he could meet their admissions criteria.

Ronnie decided to enlist in a different school: the Marine Corps, immediately following graduation in 1967. He had driven to Chicago to visit a friend, and after a wild, drunken binge in Lincoln Park, he ended up in a Marine Corps recruiting station looking for directions to a tattoo parlor. He was promptly dispatched back to California's Camp Pendleton for basic and rifleman training before applying to become a field medic. Four months later, he was in country—just in time for the Vietnamese Lunar New Year of Tet.

When he returned home to Huntington Hills in 1970, he realized that he had traded one unwinnable war for another. He had hated Vietnam but in the Corps, he had filled an empty space that had been growing like a malignancy inside him. In country, every moment seemed magnified by a factor of one thousand. A KIA toe tag waited just out view. In about as much time as it took to flick a tripwire, life could take massive jerking turns. Stone cold boredom often dissolved in a flash into hyper-speed mayhem.

Life was a poor man's battlefield; and these grunts - men who would not have measured up to Buddy Thomas' definition of financial success – were dudes who would die for you and you for them. To be a medic was to experience unconditional love for the first time – for guys like Gonzo. He missed it – which seemed really fucked up. It was impossible to describe the feeling of being part of something that was so well anchored by a rigid set of beliefs. It was like playing high school football under Coombs except in Nam if a dude dropped a pass, someone died. It was a faith that he had never known. Aside from his little sister, no one had ever relied on him so completely or counted on him in this way.

When his *real* brothers cycled back to the World, they returned to the depravity of the inner city or to a postage stamp shithole in Bum Fuck, USA. A few guys he knew lived in Lynwood, East L.A., or somewhere up north near Fresno and Modesto. They were life's manikins, people you just looked right through as they labored anonymously on life's blue-collar assembly line. They were minorities and rednecks that had traded minimum wage jobs or a jail sentence for a draft card or worse yet, had inexplicably volunteered to defend their country. Defended from what - - no one could ever answer. Now, back from war, he was greeted each night by phantoms and a persistent hypervigilence that kept him awake for days before he collapsed from exhaustion. His body still lived moment to moment although the danger now was that there was nothing to fight.

Diane was in a vodka-fueled rage. "How would you know how I feel, Ronnie? All you do now is sit around smoking dope. You're just bitter. You blame this. You blame that. You blame ... blah ... blah ... blah."

Diane wavered and looked as if she was about to fall asleep standing up. Suddenly her eyes burst open with re-focused fury. "You don't care about anything because you don't have anything. It's easy to hate what you don't have. Wait until you're my age and it's all taken away. Wait until no one wants you. It's like goddamn musical chairs. The music stops and you're the bitch left standing up, watching other people sitting down to normal lives. I'm a first wife, a piece of discarded trash, a small-town leper. I've become all the pathetic things I swore I'd never be when I was younger."

She flipped her hair and stared at him with glassy, empty turtle eyes. "You're just one big goddamn reminder of everything we've ever lost. Now get the hell out of this house before I call the cops and tell them you're an intruder."

Ronnie walked out into the cool night. His mother was just another victim in a long line of life's wounded souls. As a medic trained in triage, he could almost trace each of her thousand cuts. It just took too much emotional energy for him to try to suture them. He was no longer offended as she disabused him. If she were lying in a surgical tent, he would merely pass her and instruct the nurse to "see that she's comfortable. She's not going to make it."

Conflict always brought back the black feelings. He felt a panic attack coming on. The confrontation's adrenaline had burned through his buzz like a flamethrower. Yet, the darkness had a way of calming. He looked forward to the night. There was less expectation when the sun disappeared in the west. People retreated to their homes and life hibernated in a bunker. It was safe for a few hours.

"Doc, if you stray too far from the herd, the lions eat your ass." Another vet once said in a VA group therapy session.

"They just wait, man. Those black-hearted motherfuckers don't even seem to be trying that hard. They wait and they watch. They want you to panic and run. The more you isolate, the further you get from the protection of the herd. We're the fucking herd. The Corps, man, we are your fucking tribe. You got to talk about it, man. You can't keep moving away 'cause those big mothers will go Daktari on your ass."

Ronnie had no idea what the hell the dude was talking about but years later it was suddenly starting to make sense. He was now far from the herd and the lions were chasing him every day. From 0600 to 1800, life was an "E&E" assignment—escape and evasion of people, places and things. The only thing that mellowed him was smoking reefer. His anger and attacks of anxiety had made it impossible to hold steady work. After years of odd jobs and unemployment, Ronnie reconnected with his old automatic weapons man, Arturo Gonzales, and the two men started a house painting business. Ronnie was a hard worker and did a decent job earning money from the parents of old friends and people who saw him more for what he done for America rather than what Vietnam had done to him.

He made extra cash selling low-grade Columbian pot to local kids – most of who hung out around the east parking lot of the high school. He was saving up to buy a motorcycle so he could bug out of Huntington Hills and move to Montana where two Marine buddies had started an outdoor guide business along the Madison River. He had spent his happiest moments as a Boy Scout hiking throughout the Sierra Nevada from Mount Whitney north to the Walker River and Bridgeport. He was resourceful and had the stamina of five men. Later in Vietnam on long-range reconnaissance patrols, they had nicknamed Doc Ronnie, the "pack that walks like a man."

He'd had a few brushes with the local police – simple misdemeanors like driving while intoxicated and domestic disputes with his mother. But Chief Pinsky was a former youth sports coach and knew Ronnie. He had a soft spot for troubled veterans and directed his men to tread lightly on the young man. He had recently taken Ronnie aside and warned him that if he was caught dealing drugs, Pinsky could not prevent the severe consequences that were certain to follow.

Ronnie suspected it had been Hunt who tipped police to his casual drug dealing. The two men had hated one another since middle school. In high school, Hunt drove his father's Mercedes and wore expensive clothes. He craved attention and popular guys like Ronnie Thomas enjoyed putting R2 in his place. But, everything had changed in less than a decade. While one boy had been fighting for his life in Asia, the other was having the time of his life attending college and making frequent appearances with his parents at community fundraisers and social events. It was Hunt's town now and R2 savored the delightful irony of Ronnie's disintegration.

Hunt was the manifestation of all that was wrong with Huntington Hills and for that reason, Ronnie wanted out. Every day started the same way—a shock of panic, sweat, and anxiety tasting like cordite filled air following an artillery barrage. But Ronnie had his plan. He would paint a few more houses and then land one final score. Instead of selling quarter ounce bags of seed-riddled dinky dow to acne-prone teenagers, Ronnie would swing for the fences.

He would rob Hunt's Markets.

CHAPTER 6

Santa Claus has the right idea; visit people only once a year.

~Victor Borge

Christmas morning arrived with a thud like a cornice of snow tumbling off the eaves of a roof. In the past, the boys would be faithfully gathered at the top of the stairs, forbidden to descend until Karl had first confirmed that St. Nick had indeed found his way into their home. The patriarch would busy himself reviewing the masterful elf's latest work while making coffee, starting the fire, and trying to shake the cobwebs that always accompanied a two a.m. Christmas Eve of wrapping, assembling, and sorting gifts.

The boys were now older and cynical to the magic of the holidays, especially Matthew who had acerbically declared Christmas as "Capitalism's Birthday." Sadly, only Max was now at the top of the stairs.

"Come on, you guys. Get up. It's like eight o'clock!" Freddie pleaded with John and Matthew.

"Get out of here, you little faggot," Matthew moaned.

John washed across his waterbed and reached blindly for something to heave at his brother, settling on a Surfer magazine that struck the door just above Freddie's head. "Come back at ten o'clock, dip shit!"

Karl was stirring and opened the master bedroom door to hear Freddie's earnest excitement. He scowled at the dog.

"That four legged leech always seems to be nearby when something is being given out for free."

The dog did not wag his tail but instead warily considered Karl with beady eyes hidden under a thicket of hair.

Freddie met his father at the head at the banister.

"Just a minute, son. I have to see if the Jolly Old Elf made it down the chimney."

Soon, Freddie could hear the pine logs crackling and sounds of surprise as Karl pretended to be astonished by the gifts that Santa had artfully laid out on the living room floor next to the boys' stockings. It warmed Karl to know that at least one of his children still held some magic in his heart.

Karl ascended the stairs, rousting John, Matthew and George out of bed like a drill instructor. "Okay, you worms. You need to be in the living room at 0830 hours."

Susie quickly swept in behind groans of protest to wish everyone Merry Christmas and to diffuse any tensions arising out of Karl's holiday fiat.

The exchanging of the presents was initially conducted with civility, with Matthew volunteering to distribute the gifts. To George, it was a disingenuous overture. It was really his older brother's way of declaring his emotional and chronological superiority. Matthew tried to appear that he had outgrown Christmas. He did not need to open presents. The vestiges of childhood must be put aside. Within minutes, however, the fragile protocol was abandoned and fighting broke out as the all-important gift distributor was accused of morphing into Mussolini, refusing to dispense presents to his siblings due to their poor attitudes.

Susie loved Christmas, but embraced it as a quaint pagan holiday, immersing herself in its wonder and ceremony but eschewing its more religious fervor. She was a new-age Californian who believed that cosmic laws superseded dogmatic religion. Karl, on the other hand, was a huge fan of dogma and the sanctity of Christmas. He hated it when people spelled the holiday "XMAS" because he felt it diminished the role of Christ. Karl's orthodox support of Christ's birthday confused his sons. One minute he was leading a prayer or reading from the Bible and the next minute he was punctuating his displeasure by yelling "Jesus-fucking-Christ."

Susie had dismissed her husband's profanity as a hangover from his past life. She had made friends with a West Los Angeles psychic named Carole Damon, who had told Susie that Karl had been a Templar knight in the Third Crusade, rising to the call of Pope Gregory VIII and his band of crusaders in the 12th century. Susie kept an open mind to new-age spirituality resulting in a library of coffee table books on the paranormal that offered her boys a range of thoughtful subjects such as reincarnation, psychic pets, vortexes, Native American mythology, Buddhism, Taoism, Hinduism and astrology. Susie's curiosity with the spiritual world seemed to spring naturally out of her Northern California roots and Irish Catholic mysticism. She followed cultural trends and often dragged Karl and the boys along for the ride.

The prior Christmas, she had given the boys Bio Mates—a complicated handheld device that allowed users to track their emotional, intellectual and physical biorhythms. According to the television commercial, scientists had recently discovered what the Chinese had known for years: natural biorhythms ebbed and flowed like sine waves within every living thing. As one's natural currents moved north towards their zenith or fell south to their nadir, they crossed over invisible meridians – latitudinal lines that if charted, could indicate one's probability for a positive or negative life event. These "crossover" days were important to understand so one might avoid mishaps that prior to biorhythms would have been dismissed as fate or dumb luck. They were, in fact, predestined celestial landmines that one's Bio Mate could help predict and avoid.

The Bio Mate was immediately taken advantage of as the rationale for avoiding chores, school, church, and other obligations. Freddie became terrified to leave the house on physical crossover days. "Mom, it says here that Lincoln, John F. Kennedy, William McKinley, and Robert F. Kennedy were all shot on physical crossover days. I should not ride my bike today. I'll need a ride to school."

Karl became annoyed with the succession of new age, self-help talismans that began to appear around the house. There was "pyramid power," a brief craze during which anthropologists and scientists claimed to have harnessed the power of the ancient structures to preserve and heal. A strange plastic pyramid appeared over the kitchen fruit bowl and another rested on the bedroom nightstand where Susie placed it on Karl's back when he complained of a backache. "So much for back rubs," Karl mumbled.

In 1975, Susie had gotten each of the boys a free session with Carol Damon who would read their auras and tell them about their past lives. Matthew was fascinated by the psychic's inventory of his past, knowing it defied Karl's traditional religious convictions and would annoy his father. It was also another arrow in his quiver and a credible bridge to connect with the earthy, beautiful girls who floated around Cal like dandelion seeds.

Occasionally, Karl objected to the mixed messages his wife sent because they undermined his notion of organized religion. "Are you kidding me, Susie? What's next? A Ouija board?"

"No, Karl, I wouldn't let the boys play with those things. It's like holding an open house for wayward spirits."

"Well, thank God you have your boundaries," he remarked with considerable sarcasm.

Susie ignored him. "I just want the boys exposed to a range of religions and spiritual perspectives so they can form their own theology for living. After all, you are a Taurus and exceptionally stubborn and closed to new ideas or change."

Karl groaned, knowing that he had lost another spiritual skirmish.

Susie loved it when her boys exhibited curiosity about new things and enjoyed giving her boys gifts rather than receiving them. Each Christmas her sons attempted to reciprocate, watching her with earnest eyes as she feigned wonder and surprise at the pathetic and sometimes insensitive offerings—boxes of See's Candy (she was dieting), two-dollar perfume (it was rumored to be French), Harlequin paperbacks (the guy on the cover did not look like Karl), a Swiss Army knife, and a hardboiled egg cup.

"You're all so creative. I just love everything," she said, winking at Karl as he proudly displayed yet another hideous bowtie Freddie had given him. She rose from the couch and gathered up the paper and clothes cast into reckless piles as the boys busied themselves with their new gifts—records, speakers, a transistor radio clock, a baseball glove, basketball shoes, Topsiders, and leather personal planner folios with the names of insurance companies—holiday swag that Karl had received at OB&T and was now re-gifting to his boys.

Freddie was the only sixth grader with a Fireman's Fund personal day planner. The most disturbing aspect was that Freddie had actually began to use it, recording play dates, work assignments, and the dates of quarterly earnings releases for companies that he and Susie were now following on the stock market.

Outside, the warm Christmas Day had melted into pastel pink and purple twilight. The boys had returned to their rooms with their gifts. Susie hesitated in the living room, listening to Mel Torme croon of ski hills, snow, and romance in far off alpine chalets. Susie recalled her last ski trip to Lake Tahoe. It had been an eternity ago, in 1956 with friends— the day she broke her arm at Squaw Valley, before Karl, before her four boys—all a hazy recollection, soft light from a distant star. The memories were like faint voices of carolers who fell off in the distance as they moved to serenade another home.

Yes, it was another Christmas. In the corner was the tired and worn 1975 Sears catalog. It had seen more action this year than a tree house *Playboy* magazine.

Susie secretly made herself a new year's resolution. This year, she might get her own colored pen.

Ronnie turned on the TV and took a swig from a Miller beer. He lit his cigarette and inhaled illuminating its tangerine tip.

KTTV Channel 11 was playing an endless loop of old Christmas movies. He eased back into the couch and looked around for the scrap of paper with his sister's new phone number. It would have been nice to see Joanie today. Diane had left him a note saying she'd be spending the holidays with friends in Palm Springs—and an envelope with a Christmas card containing $250.

He remembered his first Christmas in Vietnam as part of Johnson's seven-thousand-troop expansion. It had been suffocating and hot. The whole goddamn country was a wet wool blanket covering his head until he could barely breathe. Christmas music was piped through the camp public address system with promises of snow, candles in the windows, and frosted windowpanes.

A lot of the guys were homesick at the holidays. Ronnie liked being in country and away from the dysfunction and pretense of Christmas. He did not have to try to appear happy when his family was a fucking shit show. He could sit in his hooch with his buddies, get stoned, and then eat a turkey dinner. He might even go into Tran Lei and get laid. It was just another day.

In Vietnam, Doc Ronnie, the baddest motherfucker in the Valley arose from the ashes of Ronnie Thomas, the spun-out teenager. The mixed-up high school kid was dead, wasted in a firefight of bitter words, and sliced to pieces by his parent's selfishness. He was now Phaedrus, the dude from the book, *Zen and the Art of Motorcycle Maintenance*—a shadow looking back across his own past life.

Ronnie could have lost it when he topped those five dinks in Phu Bai. He was a medic and had been trained to save lives, not waste them. He was scared shitless when the NVA attacked his position, but they had held firm. He had picked them off one by one with a PVS-2 as they ran across an open square between two gutted government buildings. The last guy's head had sort of disintegrated while his body kept running. He remembered laughing out loud. It was funny and surreal, like watching a chicken run with a severed head. Just remembering caused the dark mood to grow in his chest, the precursor to the panic that always followed.

He lit a joint and muttered, "You can bug out now, Marine. Drive on!"

As he refocused on the movie, Ward Bond was chasing Jimmy Stewart through the swirling snow of Bedford Falls. The phone rang shattering the silence.

It was Joanie. Her voice was tender and reminded him of fresh air and Friday nights. His little sister had always loved him and looked to him to protect her from the jagged edges of their scabrous lives. But now he couldn't speak.

"Bucky? You there?"

He was crying now, and he couldn't stop the tears from pouring out on to his face and moustache. "Yeah, baby girl. It's me. Merry Christmas."

Junior Riggs finished filling up the red Mercedes and walked to the window. His was the only gasoline station open for miles on Christmas Day. Two years earlier, Junior realized he could sell twice as much gas on holidays and still be home in Monrovia in time for dinner with his parents. Working in Huntington Hills had its dispensations. He could charge a premium for an oil change and basic automotive repairs because most of these white men were too proud to confess they had no idea what was actually happening underneath the hood of their cars.

"Could be the distributor cap or the head gasket," Junior would say, waiting for an informed rise out of the silver-haired men who appeared to have not worked at hard labor a day in their lives.

The men would look nervous. "So how much does something like that cost to fix?"

Junior would shut the hood and shake his head. "Tough to tell until I get inside of her and see what's makin' her tummy ache. I'll give you a two-hundred-dollar estimate and then call you if I find anything else. These foreign girls are part-tic-u-lar. They are, like most women, fun to drive but expensive to keep happy."

Men in town would normally defer to Junior the way a patient might empower a doctor. Huntington Hills was a good gig for Junior and he thanked his stars that his father had the good sense to buy the franchise from Mobil in 1965. He worked hard not to waste the gift he had been given by his Pops.

"Junior, Merry Christmas, my man!" Ralph Hunt II rolled his window down and greeted the angular gas station owner with a familiar grin. Tall and rangy, Junior Riggs sported an afro trimmed tight to a high forehead and striking olive-green eyes. He had the flush nose of a prizefighter, lean cheeks and a thin face that exaggerated the size of his mouth. Junior was all eyes and teeth. The boys used to say that when Junior smiled his grin would eat his entire face.

"Mr. Hunt. What brings you to our fine establishment on this holiday? Merry Christmas!"

"Just spent the morning playing golf and need to top off Red before going to Mom and Dad's for dinner. Call me 'R2.' Mr. Hunt is my Dad."

"Okay, Mr. Hunt," Junior said as he opened the hood to check the oil.

Hunt reeked of alcohol. Junior knew Ralph Hunt Senior and was sad to hear about his illness. The elder Hunt was one of the few business owners who had argued back in 1965 that a black-owned enterprise would be important to a town like Huntington Hills. Junior's father, Raymond "Pops" Riggs, and Mr. Hunt had been good friends for a decade and it was a Riggs family rule that Hunt Senior would never pay for gasoline at Riggs Mobil.

This Ralph Hunt was another thing entirely. Junior had seen spoiled kids before and young Ralph Hunt was as putrid as sour milk. Hunt had gone to college and probably mingled with a few black athletes in his time. Some dude might have even shown him the dap one night and given him the impression that he was an honorary brother. Dudes like Hunt were as depraved as the narrow-minded peckerwoods that had worked so hard to keep civil rights from happening. At least with a bigot a brother always knew where he stood. With a rear-echelon liberal, you got a little further into his circle before he got uncomfortable and created a reason to keep you out of his club.

Nothing had really changed since civil rights except maybe now there was a lot more white guilt and awareness. Most whites acted afraid of blacks in this town and spoke in slow, obsequious tones, not wanting to offend them. After Watts in '68, it was clear they were afraid that there was going to be an insurrection. He laughed as Hunt talked through the hood of the car about loving South Central Los Angeles as if it was his second home. Junior rolled his eyes. He lived east in Monrovia.

"All good, Mr. Hunt." He slammed the hood shut.

"R2, please, and Merry Christmas. Keep the change." Hunt handed him a $10 bill for $5.50 worth of gasoline.

"Thank you, Mr. Hunt. Please pay my respects to your parents and tell your daddy to quit staying up nights dancing to *Soul Train*."

Hunt laughed a little too hard at Junior's bad joke. He rolled up his window and sped on to Huntington Hills Drive, running a red light.

"Merry Christmas, du mi ami," Junior said in Vietnamese as he stuffed the sawbuck into his shirt pocket.

He chuckled. The cops would probably never pull Hunt over, and if they did, they'd probably just tell him to take the back streets home. A white man had to be plenty fucked up to get a ticket in this town.

Junior had been pulled over more times than he could care to remember, mostly by rookie cops who took one look at his beat-up Chevy and the color of his skin and then asked him where he had been, and where he was going. After making him wait fifteen minutes while they checked his plates, license, registration and car for vehicular violations, they'd send him on his way, having saved Huntington Hills from possible infiltration by the criminal element. In five years, he had yet to find a commute that would avoid seeing a police car.

Junior glanced at his watch. Ten till four. He looked toward the alleyway. She was there again, like clockwork, the old woman he called The Crab Lady. She peered into the alley through a crack in her back fence. She appeared every morning and late afternoon, waiting until the trash from the market had been emptied into the large bins, and then scuttled across the alley with her broom to peer into the bins for food and discarded goods. If anyone opened the loading dock door, she would busy herself sweeping around the bins and barking thick, accented admonishments that the market needed to keep the alley clean. Junior figured she was alcoholic, insane, or both. Even Huntington Hills had its share of hidden poverty and mental illness.

Junior felt lucky. He had his mind and a place to go. It was time to close up and go to Pops' for Christmas dinner. The feeble sun moved behind a cloud and he shivered. It would be nice to be home in his own neighborhood with his family for the holidays.

CHAPTER 7

May all your troubles last as long as your New Year's resolutions.

~Joey Adams

The week between Christmas and New Year's arrived like the eye of a hurricane, offering a momentary respite during which Susie might reconstruct her predictable November routine and gather up the debris of December celebration.

The dead calm worried Karl. Like a seasoned meteorologist, he knew the back half of the holiday still packed high emotional winds and potential for damaged feelings where Susie was concerned.

Susie's matriarchal rule was traumatized each year when five men were suddenly home and idle. It was an extreme time that exaggerated the normal warts and imperfections of daily life. The soiled laundry and dirty dishes grew geometrically. The low-pressure system of lazy teenagers on vacation collided with the restless winds of an idle husband creating a tempest that only increased Susie's personal pressure cooker.

Her avalanche of anger always started with a snowflake of self-pity. Susie would start talking to herself as she picked up clothes that had been dropped haphazardly, as if the owners had all caught fire. She began to exhibit all the signs of a person ill with the poisoning from soiled routines and polluted thoughtlessness.

Karl always was bewildered when Susie wasn't herself. Only he held the tenured role of moody shape shifter and mercurial overlord. Susie's role was to be a placid lake of restraint and a predictable oasis that offered protection to all from the rise and fall of the testosterone barometer. When she was in a foul mood, the entire equilibrium of the family unit was destabilized. Every male went to bed at night praying her irritation would not result in one of her infamous resolutions.

On the eve of America's bicentennial year, patriarch and matriarch switched places. The boys were stacked like cordwood on the den couch watching an endless string of college football bowl games, while Karl prepared a presentation for the following week.

Karl had been holed up in his office for quite a while, brooding and irritated over Rebecca Gerson and her threat to his planned ascension to CEO at OB&T. The boys had spent the morning attacking the Christmas leftovers; they had left a mess in the kitchen and neglected to put the turkey back into refrigerator. The turkey platter had been set too close to the edge of the kitchen counter, and Max had gotten up just high enough to pull the white porcelain serving dish to the ground. Susie's favorite platter was now in pieces as the dog greedily ate as much white meat as he could before being banished to the backyard.

"Out! Bad dog!" Susie screamed as she surveyed the mess.

She had been upstairs, wakened from her brief nap by the sound of breaking china. Every Patton male was within ten feet of the kitchen, yet no one had moved an inch to investigate.

"Shit!" she screamed. The boys opened the door and peered into the kitchen. It was rare when Susie used the "s" word. Even Karl knew that this meant trouble. Despite everyone's best efforts to avoid Susie's holiday tripwires, the dog had blown it, and she was now a volcano of fury. This year's pronouncement was communicated like a centurion announcing an edict from Caesar.

"All of you. In the kitchen. Immediately! *Now!*" she screamed as she picked up the broken dish. "You have ignored my repeated attempts to get you boys to put your food away, put your dishes in the dishwasher, hang up your towels, put away your laundry, and refrain from eating all the leftovers. In response, we will now do the following:

"One: The linen closet will be locked with a padlock Monday through Friday and you will not be issued a new towel until Saturday.

"Two: You are now responsible for your own laundry. I suggest you wash and fold it over the weekend.

"Three: You will now make your own lunches, and if you forget to make your lunch, you will go hungry."

The boys glanced at Karl. He had taken them aside earlier in the week and threatened them with reprisals if anyone proved to be the catalyst for another New Year's breakdown, but he had not planned on the dog. Susie's first official pronouncement always detonated like a grenade. Hell had no fury like Susie when she had had enough. His only consolation was the knowledge that her resolutions had the life expectancy of a housefly. The Patton men were pitiful recidivists, and the day one of them heard, "Here, let me do that!" was the moment that sanity was restored.

The days leading up to New Year's Eve in the San Gabriel Valley were ushered in with great expectation and grand ceremony. Pasadena was once again hosting the annual Festival of Roses pageant and parade. The nationally televised cavalcade that coursed along Colorado Boulevard at the foot of Mount Wilson did more to ensure the conveyor belt of western American immigration than the 1849 Gold Rush. Against azure skies and under palm trees rustling in a light breeze, people camped out all week along the parade route, celebrating the winter solstice as it would never be experienced at home – wearing tee shirts, shorts and flip-flops.

Between Christmas and the New Year, massive Winnebago motor homes would overrun Southern California like an invasion force armada regurgitating anemic, marshmallow-shaped Big Ten fans who had journeyed 1500 miles to watch their football team compete in the "granddaddy of them all" New Year's Day college bowl football game at the Rose Bowl. The neoclassical stadium built in the 1920s was a monument to symmetry and simplicity and could accommodate more than one hundred thousand diehard fans.

George was depressed. Just one year ago, his USC Trojans had beaten the Ohio State Buckeyes in an 18-17 thriller. George had been at the game with Karl, clutching ancient binoculars, watching the plays and occasionally drifting over to Coach Woody Hayes, who screamed at and cajoled his team to stop USC's final drive and two-point conversion.

This year, the UCLA Bruins were representing the Pacific Ten in the Rose Bowl, once again against Ohio State. Earlier in the season, behind the running of Wendell Tyler, UCLA had upset the Trojans to lead the Bruins to the Pac Ten crown and a rare trip to the Rose Bowl.

One mile away from the Patton homestead, tucked into stands of eucalyptus and sycamores, stood the Pasadena Grand Hotel, the grand dame of early Los Angeles art deco hotels. It was ornate, with glass-enclosed dining rooms and spacious grounds that included Oriental gardens, koi ponds, and an enormous Olympic outdoor pool and court-yard. Its façade was concealed by thick ivy that climbed and curled around gabled windows.

Each year, the hotel played host to the reigning Big Ten champion football squad. Their mission was simple: a win over the Pac Ten cham-pions on New Year's Day, sunburns, and the phone number of any Rose Pageant Princess. Once the Ohio State Buckeyes arrived in Los Angeles, they would be bused to the Pasadena Grand. Over the years, Matthew, John, George, Freddie, and a generation of bold, star-struck kids staked out the four corners of the hotel, willing to risk detainment, or even worse, an encounter with Coach Hayes, as they attempted to intercept the players for autographs.

The Bruins were huge underdogs in this year's Rose Bowl. The humongous Ohio corn-fed mutants had soundly beaten UCLA 41-20 earlier in the season. Even though the OSU Buckeyes were the enemy, the Patton boys were desperate to get an autograph from anyone remotely famous, even bulging behemoths with protruding eyebrows and necks that rose like mountains from their rippling shoulders.

Up close, any collegiate football player was intimidating. Yet the most terrifying of them all was Coach Hayes. Woody reminded George of every older man that ever chased a kid off his lawn. He was all business, with dark engineer's glasses; wild, tangled salt and pepper eyebrows; and a chin that screamed, "Fight to the death."

Hayes was rumored to hate everyone in California—USC; UCLA; referees; and the tanned, thin-wristed Los Angelinos who showed up for their team's games only if their record was over .500 and the sun was shining. The only thing Hayes seemed to hate more than his opponents in the Rose Bowl was the University of Michigan. To make it to the Rose Bowl in the 1970s, all Big Ten roads led through Columbus and Ann Arbor. Hayes was rumored to hate Michigan so much than he once told his team when they were running low on gasoline that he would rather push the bus all the way to Ohio than spend one dollar on petrol in the state of Michigan.

The theme for the 1976 Pasadena Rose Parade was "America, Let's Celebrate." The Grand Marshal was some woman George had never heard of named Kate Smith, who was famous simply for singing "God Bless America."

It was a Patton family tradition to drive up to Orange Grove Boulevard on New Year's Eve and "look at the idiots" who chose to camp outside along the parade route to ensure the best viewing location for the Rose Parade. Each float was carefully constructed out of real flowers, and every year seemed to usher in a new standard of creativity that reassured any spectator that America was indeed moving forward.

Matthew parked the car and the boys barreled out of the vehicle. Matthew laid down Karl's ground rules. "Okay, I have squirrel boy." At the appellation, Freddie made a face and sighed.

"You two meet us back here in exactly two hours or you'll be walking home at midnight. It's ten now. Don't be late. I *will* leave without you."

George was excited and nervous. It was the first year Karl had not chaperoned the boys, and it was certain to be a substantial adventure. In previous years, their father would yell at them to stay together while he shined a high-beam flashlight in the face of every holidaymaker, eliciting profanity and threats. Karl usually swore back at the invisible voices and became so tightly wound trying to shepherd his four boys through a tent city of a thousand campers that he would always cut the trip short and bribe the boys with warm donuts from nearby Winchell's.

John took out his flashlight and switched it on. George groaned. "What's with the Karl Patton flashlight? The point is to be invisible until we find a group of girls around some campfire. I don't need to see any of these lame floats. Kelly and her sister are camping somewhere out here with a bunch of other girls. We find them and I go to work getting her back, thus crossing off my only real New Year's resolution."

John was disappointed. He actually wanted to see the floats and had been reading about one that was constructed completely out of tulips from Michigan. Each entry was the size of a small house, using thousands of colored flowers to decorate a thirty-foot bear or a ten-foot-high television set, or any other number of strange and wonderful notions that symbolized America's Bicentennial.

"Dude, we look at a few floats along Orange Grove first and then we find the girls. Do you know where they're camping?"

Hesitating, George said, "I think they said they're near Los Robles or San Gabriel Boulevard."

"Georgie, those streets are miles from each other. In between, there are a zillion people with hibachis, tents, and lawn chairs."

"Well, I know she's wearing a light blue ski jacket."

"Okay, that reduces it to five thousand. Do you ever think about anything past the next five minutes?"

George shrugged. "Look, I have two hours, and I want to find her. If you're not going to help me, fine. I'll see you back here at midnight."

Already resigned to the fact that he would be looking into the faces of drunken people rather than the design of floats, John switched on his flashlight and followed it along the ground like a movie theatre usher.

"Okay, bonehead, I'll lead the way."

Matthew and Freddie stopped in front of a large crowd of people admiring the float that would carry the Rose Queen and her Princesses.

"A few girls from Huntington Hills become Princesses or even Queen every couple of years," Matthew said. "It's a big deal. The Big Ten football players come into town and immediately start trying to scam on our girls at all the different dinners and media events that they have to attend."

"What's scamming?" Freddie asked.

Matthew thought for a few seconds. "Um, it's sorta like trying to make out with a girl. You decide who you want to scam on and then you try to make her laugh, maybe take her out a few times to the movies, buy her dinner, and then maybe she will like you. Then she might become your girlfriend."

"Sounds expensive."

Matthew made a cynical face. "You and Karl. All you think about is money."

Freddie was still intrigued. "I mean movies, dinner, and whatever. That's like twenty dollars, right? Why not just pay her ten bucks a week to be your girlfriend?"

Matthew laughed out loud. "Buddy, I think there laws against that sort of stuff."

John was getting annoyed with George who was now walking ahead and yelling "Kelly Reed!" every hundred yards. His appeals were met with derision and catcalls from the dark.

"Kelly's in here with me."

"Sorry, dude. She's busy."

"Go to bed, white boy. It's past your bedtime."

It was ten after eleven, and they weren't even halfway down the parade route. The streets looked like one of those futuristic dystopias, a post-Armageddon landscape where mankind had been reduced to living rough on the streets. They were suburban wanderers, lost in a sea of human flotsam and jetsam. John just wanted to go to bed.

"George, is that you?"

George shined the light into a knot of silhouettes gathered in lawn chairs just off Colorado Boulevard. "I thought I recognized your voice. It's me. Tracy."

"Hey, Tracy. You know John. We are just looking for Kelly. She said she was up here tonight."

The blonde girl stood up from her chair. She was slender and beautiful like a magazine model, but also six feet two and towered over most boys. She introduced them to her dad and uncle from Indiana. The men stood up at once. It was as if two skyscrapers were being raised in front of him. Neither man was less than six feet five.

"Pleased to meet you boys," Tracy's dad said. "I think I know your father. He played basketball at Santa Clara the same time that I played at Stanford. He was a hell of a guard. We used to play pick-up games over in Arcadia before all you kids started showed up. Tell him Phil Harris says hello."

"Yes, sir. Nice to meet you."

"Kelly's just down the block the way you guys came," Tracy said. "They're on the other side of the street near the movie theater. I think she's with her sister, Tammy, Kerry and Tim Irwin and a bunch of his friends. I went by earlier and they were all hanging out."

"Thanks," George said as he frowned. *Shit, Tim Irwin.*

Irwin reveled in cruel, brutish humor and prowled the hallways of Huntington High with a posse of loadie underachievers terrorizing the weak, marginalized and vulnerable. He was a bull with thin blond hair that fell diagonally across his square forehead. He looked remarkably unintelligent with inkblot eyes set too close together and a tiny mean mouth that betrayed his lack of understanding of anything other than physical confrontation. Tim had been a starting football player but had been kicked off the team after getting caught with drugs. He was bad news and had his sights set on Kelly Reed ever since her freshman year. Irwin made access to Kelly hard and dangerous – which made George want her all the more. She was Tim's prisoner and George was determined to become her liberator.

John looked at his watch again and then spoke to Tracy. "I think I've seen you practicing with the varsity girls. How's that going? I see you guys thumped Duarte. Very nice."

Tracy smiled through the darkness. "I see you guys practicing a lot. You've got a decent shot. This is my Uncle Tommy. He played with the Irish and just graduated from Notre Dame."

John rolled his head back in pain. "Aw, you guys broke our eighty-eight-game winning streak at UCLA. Mr. Harris, did you play in that game?"

A deep voice bellowed up at him from the dark. "It's Tommy and I was riding the pine but I had a big ass grin on my face as we took down Wooden, Walton, and Wilkes. It's hard to believe but my man Adrian Dantley still has another year of eligibility. He's gonna be all-world this year."

George was getting impatient and watching across the street. "Sorry to break up the peach basket admiration society, but I want to see about a girl."

John was quick to respond. "Look, Romeo. I'll hang here and you run across the street and see Juliet. I'll come and get you in like, fifteen? I have to hear about this game."

George grabbed the flashlight and headed off into a restless night.

"Take your time finding me, Johnny boy!"

Kelly moved uneasily in her chair as Tim Irwin sat down and put his arm around her. He had been drinking and she debated whether to tell him to leave or just tolerate him for the sake of security on the dark, crowded New Year's Eve. She was irritated that he had arrived uninvited. The evening was supposed to be just girls hanging out. She had half-hoped that George would show, but he had been so fickle around her at school she didn't know what to think. One minute, he would shower her with attention and then seem to lose his confidence and act sullen. Things were supposed to be easy, and George was making her work too hard.

Tim leaned over to whisper to her and she could smell the liquor on his breath. She stood up and stretched her arms.

"I'm going to the bathroom," she announced as she stepped over a tangle of feet, blankets and coolers. Rounding the corner, she ran head-long into George.

"Kelly!"

"George!" she smiled. "What a small world."

"I was just … well, my brothers and I were cruising around up here and we ran into Tracy. She said you were around here somewhere. I figured you might need some help making a fire or a bodyguard or a warm body."

George realized he was sounding more stupid by the second. He suddenly held his hand up to his mouth holding an invisible microphone. "Or, I can offer you a lifetime supply of Rice O' Roni, the San Francisco Treat, and a new fur coat from Dicker & Dicker of Beverly Hills."

Pretending to shiver, she snuggled closer to George. The smell of burning wood mixing with her perfume sent a surge of adrenaline across his chest. He struggled to look her in the eye without smiling from the anticipation.

"Hmmm. I like the idea of door number one. Although girls do love their mink coats..." She dropped her hands to her waist and leaned over her hips, suddenly looking uncomfortable and jogging in place. "...I sort of need to do something right now."

George raised his eyebrows. "Oh, right. I'll wait here."

Kelly disappeared around the corner, and George leaned against the side of a brick building, heaving a deep sigh of relief. As he pushed his arms against the building, three shadows approached him.

A familiar voice growled, "So what are you doing here, fuck head?"

He whipped his head around to three hulking shapes: Tim Irwin and two large boys George didn't recognize.

"Meet my cousins from Barstow. They come up every year for the parade. This is George Patton. He follows Kelly around like he's a bitch in heat. He's a freshman and he's real smartass. A bad combination. Aren't you, George?"

"Smart? Yes. An ass? Well, I can be as stubborn like a mule and on weekends, I am a beast of burden used by my fascist father for free labor." George looked over Irwin's left shoulder, which rose like a mountain ridgeline at a forty-five degree angle toward his neck. He was emboldened to see what looked like the outline of John Patton walking toward him along with another very tall man.

"You know, Tim? You're not afraid of anything are you?"

Irwin regarded George suspiciously but eventually answered. "Nothing I see around here scares me." He looked at George. "It mostly makes me sick."

"Well, it's clear you're not scared of looking like an dick. I mean, you do it every day at school and it does not seem to bug you. I admire you for that. Most guys like you would try to transfer or something...but man, you just don't seem to care. That is so ...cool."

George hesitated. "Did you understand any of that, Tim? Or should I have used monosyllabic words like the ones they use in that Special Ed class you go to at ten every morning?"

The senior's face broke into a crooked sneer. "Okay, funny Mister Comedian man, it's going to be funny breaking your nose and jaw. Right here, right now. Just you and me, you little smart ass." Irwin moved his neck from side to side making a large cracking sound. He began started to jump and lunge aggressively toward George as if he was being introduced in a boxing match.

George smiled and looked again over Tim's shoulder for John but saw only a mass of distant silhouettes and small fires glowing in trashcans and hibachis. He suddenly felt sick realizing that he was on his own.

"Okay, okay. Look, it's not a fair fight with you and your two primate cousins. Can I have one of them on my side?"

"Who you calling a playmate, asshole?"

"What's all the noise about, boys?" John walked up followed by the gigantic Tommy Harris. George felt his knees buckle in relief.

"This has nothing to do with you, Patton. Your wise ass little brother started it." Though his voice reeked with drunken bravado, Irwin's eyes kept darting over to Harris.

John sighed and shook his head. "Tim, Tim, Tim. When we were little kids, Dave Von der Schiff beat the crap out of George. My guess is it was kind of like this situation. George most likely popped off and probably had it coming to him."

George opened his mouth to protest and John held up his hand. "He came home crying like a pussy and my old man, who is an ex-army officer, grabbed me and told me to go find Van der Schiff and kick his ass. My dad told me then that George's fight was my fight. He said we have the same last name forever. So I went out and found Von der Schiff, who is actually not a bad dude, and … I kicked his ass."

John shrugged. "Timmy, I got no choice in the matter. My dad will kick my ass, so I have to kick your ass to prevent you from kicking George's ass. It's pretty tiring—all this ass-kicking."

Tommy Harris walked over and put a hand on the shoulder of one of Tim Irwin's cousins. "Boys, I just got out of prison for hitting a guy so hard that I killed his grandma. I don't think we need any trouble here."

Irwin appeared to know he was in a bind. "Well, then, why don't you guys just get him the hell out of here!"

John smiled. "A capital idea. We are late for our ride home, and Mr. Harris is tired and wants to go sit down before he meets with his parole officer. We'll just be moving along."

Irwin nodded and the three boys created an opening for George to pass. As George stubbornly held back, John grabbed him by the arm with a vise grip that was reminiscent of his father's. "Let's go, George. *Now!*"

George stood firm. "I want to say goodbye to Kelly."

John pulled him close and leaned into George's ear, "You just did, smart ass. We're outta here."

The men walked a few yards before John turned to shake Tommy Harris' massive hand. "Thanks, Tommy. Happy New Year."

Behind them, Tim Irwin yelled. "See you later, assholes. Don't worry, George, Kelly is in good hands. She won't get cold tonight."

George stopped and began to turn.

"Just keep moving, Georgie. There's a time and a place and this ain't either," John hissed.

The boys worked their way west across a sea of blankets and campers, eventually finding Matthew and Freddie at midnight. "You're late, buttheads," Matthew yelled. "Let's go. Mom and Dad will be pissed."

A rush of fireworks, bottle rockets, and car horns honked indicated that 1976 had finally arrived. "Happy New Year!" yelled Freddie. George slammed the car door and glared.

"What the hell's wrong with him?" Matthew asked.

"He ran into Timmy Irwin and a few of his pals guarding Kelly Reed. Missed his big chance to make a love connection."

Matthew put the car back in park. "Do we need to go find that asshole and plug him up? I always thought the guy was a prick."

"Nah. We're good. Let's just go." George said.

Down Colorado Boulevard, Kelly had finally returned from waiting almost a half-hour for the portable toilet. George was nowhere to be seen. She had been hoping he might kiss her to usher in the New Year. As she walked back to the semicircle of lawn chairs, Tim sprawled in her chair, passed out.

"Anyone see George?" she asked.

"He said he had to be home before midnight. He had a curfew or something," muttered one of Irwin's cousins.

Kelly looked down the block and into a night of sparklers, skyrockets and people kissing to celebrate the bicentennial year.

"What the hell is wrong with that guy?"

Plate 2

SUBURBAN BIG GAME
hunters
use Red Ryder
BB GUNS.

Big game is prevalent in the suburban jungle. Crows, squirrels and the occasional door to door salesman are great ways to test your skill and prepare for the ultimate confrontation between you and the neighbor's rabid dog. Ask Billy Becker, the boy who stood his ground against Debbie the mad Boston Terrier of West Covina. He depended on his Red Ryder when it counted and lived to tell the story to his grandchildren.

SPRING

Spring

CHAPTER 8

The best substitute for experience is being sixteen.

~Raymond Duncan

In a rite of passage reminiscent of Malcolm McDowell's shock therapy in *A Clockwork Orange,* high school freshmen of the '70s were subjected to highly graphic movies of car crashes, mangled bodies, and twisted metal. The movies attempted to dissuade DIWs (drivers-in-waiting) from becoming DWIs (driving-while-intoxicated). Authorities felt the need to underscore that the automobile was hardly a toy. It was, in fact, according to Karl Patton, a goddamn one-ton projectile of destruction.

The New Year meant a license for George—a privilege that first required driver's education class and weekend rides with the instructor and JV basketball coach, "Party" Marty Mooney. But before a boy could even clip into a safety belt, he must endure the much-anticipated driver's education film *Red Asphalt,* a gruesome cinematic montage of vehicular death.

John and Matthew had told George about the highway safety films. As a fifteen-year-old, he had not seen many R-rated movies. Ultra-violence was an emerging form of art in the minds of directors like Sam Peckinpah and Stanley Kubrick. Graphic films were a forbidden fruit reserved for mature audiences only. To George and his buddies, the idea of seeing something in school that might fetch an "M" or even "X" rating was almost too good to be true.

The lights dimmed. The air was thick with adolescent anticipation. George sat silently, while Glenn Bull and Teddy nervously joked with paper-tiger bravado. Girls squirmed and shifted in their seats as if they were about to dissect a frog in biology. This was serious stuff. Susie had had to sign a permission slip for George to attend class that day.

The film was faithfully threaded through the projector by the AV geek, and with a flip of a switch, the film credits for *Red Asphalt* fell ominously down the screen like the broken lines of a two-lane killer country road. Within five minutes, the class was on its heels, having been among the first responders to three horrific car wrecks, including one in which a guy had been decapitated.

Someone whispered in the dark, "My brother told me *Last Prom* had a guy with a pipe all the way through his head."

Suddenly, Inez Del Riggio leapt to her feet and moaned as she tried to make it to the door. Stumbling through the flickering projector light, she vomited across the shoes of Charlie Hildebrand. Someone screamed while another voice yelled, "Hey, coach, we got a puker!" It all happened so quickly, just like the young man in the coupe who tried to try to outrun the Southern Pacific train and ended up looking like a home economics burnt chicken.

The Department of Highway Safety tried to show George and his friends what the consequences of bad choices could be for a young driver racing too fast in VW Karman-Ghia. However, most of the graduating class of 1979 was too mesmerized by the site of brains, blood, and guts to really register that those entrails could be their own if they chose to blindly pass an eighteen-wheeler on a two-lane highway in New Mexico. George decided when he did learn to drive he would avoid the Southwestern United States and train tracks altogether.

Next to facial hair or the discovery of your father's stash of girlie magazines, a driver's license was a defining moment - official recognition of a boy's ascent out of the oppressive canyon of adolescence and into the great plateau of manhood and autonomy. Freedom from parental oppression was best abetted by a motor vehicle. A car was a plane ticket to exotic places far from the supervision of adults whose principal job was to ruin your life.

By age sixteen, George was under the impression that the only difference between an Eastern bloc country and his own household was a lack of bread lines. His father had become increasingly intolerable as he stressed out at work by day and came home at night looking for a fight. Karl clashed with George on grades, bedtime, curfew, and where he was going for the evening. Matthew had returned to Cal, and John was adroit at avoiding trouble, which left Karl and George to brawl like street fighters. Susie did her best to defuse the tensions between father and son but there was no way to avoid the time they must spend together learning how to drive the family cars.

Subscribing to the Erma Bombeck School of Driver's Education, Susie refused to accompany any kid when it was time to master the art of driving the Impala and the Pinto. Susie's extrasensory perception told her that teaching any of her four sons to drive would be her undoing.

The responsibility for motor vehicle instruction fell to Karl, who dreaded the act of slipping into the passenger side of the car. Karl was not wired to be a passenger. He was master and commander and had been driving the family station wagon, as well as exclusively piloting his work car—the sleek sienna-brown Ford Granada—for years. The act of turning over car keys to a sixteen-year-old male offended him.

Susie told Karl that the boys had to practice driving on every car, including his precious other child, the Granada. The moment George entered Karl's car, the owner's tics and anxious behavior began. Disconcerted and disoriented by the lack of control, he winced and placed both hands on the dashboard as George adjusted his rearview mirror, moved the driver's seat back, and adjusted its angle. It was as if George were putting on Karl's clothes while he was still in them.

Karl immediately shouted out instructions and warnings.

"Turn on the indicator."

"Watch the curb!"

"Jesus, look out for that car!"

"Watch it! Wait, wait, wait! Okay. Now! Go! Go! Go!"

All this would unfold within the ten-yard span of driveway leading from the family two-car garage to their empty suburban street. The journey was hell for both of father and son, George needing to follow instructions to earn the privilege of continued learning, and the father grudgingly allowing his progeny to operate his favorite toy. Karl's Granada was a coddled baby that was not washed, but bathed, by whichever son owed Karl the most money, with a chamois cloth the size of a cocktail napkin and waxed faithfully for the long week's journey that lay ahead. Susie was allowed to operate his car only in the event of geopolitical emergencies such as imminent nuclear attack. Children were not allowed to touch anything. To change a radio station, adjust the air conditioning, or even pass wind in his car was a Class I felony.

On the other side of driveway were the lime-green Pinto and the Impala station wagon. The "family" cars had endured every indignity that could be visited on them by two teenage drivers and countless thankless male passengers. The vehicles' interiors resembled refugee camps, while the Granada remained as pure as the day it rolled of the assembly line in Flint. When Karl brought home his new car, Susie said, "If you need some garbage to put in your car until you accumulate a few items of your own, there is plenty in the Pinto."

Karl's driving lessons with George always ended before their scheduled time. "Pull over, pull over," Karl would shout. "You're going to get us killed."

"What?" George would yell back. "I missed that dog by three feet."

George and Karl would return home and the door would slam twice as son and father retreated to their individual caves of self-pity. Susie looked up at the noise hummed as she polished silver in a safe kitchen, content to be next of kin in the event her men did not return.

"It's Mr. O'Brien, line one."

Karl clicked the button to take Bob's call. He did not understand why the head of the agency could not walk twenty feet to see him. He did not need a secretary to call. Hell, Karl did not even want an assistant. He could do his own typing and answer his own goddamn phone. The secretarial pool was a waste of financial resources and a cesspool of petty infighting as young women relentlessly scratched, clawed, and attacked one another in an effort to rise in a female hierarchy Karl had never known existed.

"Karl, do you have a minute? Rebecca and I wanted to run something by you."

"Sure. What does Rebecca have to do with this, Bob?"

"Now, Karl. It is 1976, not 1876. We have to acknowledge the diversity that looks to us for representation inside our homogenous little suburbs and provincial little company."

Earlier in the week, Bob had climbed up to his politburo podium to espouse his collectivist diarrhea. Karl was always amused at the CEO's spasms of self-righteousness, considering Bob spared no expense for his own lifestyle.

"Since when did we become provincial, Bob? Is this comrade Connie talking or you?"

"Karl, leave her out it. This is my firm and at OB&T, I want us known as a meritocracy and an affirmative action workplace. The best man or woman regardless of age, creed, color or economic status has the same opportunity to any job, except mine, that is. "

Bob raised his eyebrows and smiled at his own joke—a disingenuous expression of mock surprise that annoyed Karl every time he witnessed it. It was a cue for his audience to laugh at his feeble attempts at humor.

Familiarity bred contempt, and Karl had endured years of Bob's peccadilloes, sudden course changes, and personality quirks. Karl had a small equity stake in the agency, but not enough to pay for four private college educations and set aside money for his own retirement. He respected Bob's marketing skill, but worried that he might one day choose to sell the agency to mollify his young wife's need to solve world hunger, and then Karl would be screwed.

He was furious as he put the phone down. This was Bob's second lecture in as many weeks, and it was clear that he was about to drop the proverbial other shoe. Karl was poorly disguising his heartburn over Rebecca's hiring, and what made him even angrier was that she was very good. She had brought in three accounts in just three months, including a major biotechnology firm that had one of the first female chief financial officers in the L.A. marketplace. ReGen Technologies had recently finished clinical trials and received approval for a chemotherapy drug that had vaulted the firm to more than five hundred million dollars in market capitalization. Karl did not have as much experience dealing with public and pre-public companies and was in awe as he watched Rebecca describe to the client how she would present the risk to underwriters in London.

"Whoever leads this year's renewal will set the price for everyone else on the slip. I have two underwriters I have cultivated for the last two years in the emerging technologies sector, and they are hungry to expand their North American presence into biotech and pharma. They also now offer unique run-off policies that consolidate risks from past liability periods into the present policy. They see some of these new industries as a nice hedge against some of the asbestos and pollution litigation arising out of U.S. construction and environmental claims."

Rebecca had looked directly at Karl when she mentioned the deteriorating construction markets. Karl immediately felt self-conscious, as if he was being held personally responsible for some of the strange and complicated claims arising from their client's portfolios.

Large claims were both a blessing and a curse for an insurance agency. Catastrophic claims hurt the insurer's loss ratio, which in turn, had an impact on broker contingent compensation— an essential but highly variable part of an agency's operating profit. It also led to complicated negotiations when insurance companies denied claims, citing obscure contractual interpretations that would allow them to avoid paying for a large loss.

Karl was an expert at engineering and contracts, and was a ferocious negotiator when managing client claims. His position was always the same: if a policy was silent on whether coverage was excluded, it was implicit that the policy should respond.

Karl was more pragmatic than claims professionals at bigger firms, who argued for the sake of argument over every policy word and often found themselves making a case for exclusion clarity in contracts that soon enough were granted to them. Claims adjustment was an art and Karl was an artist. It helped on occasion to be a little bit of a prick. The stakes were often high and if a broker could not get a client's claim resolved, the broker usually got fired, perhaps along with the risk manager or CFO that hired them. If you successfully covered a client's exposure and got them payment for an unanticipated loss, you often cemented a relationship for life—or at least until the next claim.

Karl was guarded as Bob asked him into his office, where Rebecca was waiting drinking water from a large cup.

She's kind of attractive for a lesbian, Karl thought as he observed the womanly figure underneath her gray suit. Yet she was so overtly stiff she looked like the descendent of a long line of German prison guards. Karl could detect something burning in this woman. He remembered seeing it in his own grandmother—a look of angry resolve that suggested nothing would deter her from improving her circumstances.

Karl recalled giving his grandmother his report card as a sixth grader when he got home from school. He had good marks: several A's, one B and one C.

"Not good enough," Omah would bark in her uncompromising German accent.

Each quarter Karl would bring his report card home and share it with his grandmother. Each time, the response was always the same: "You can do better."

In his eleventh year of school, Karl received perfect marks. He rushed home past his own parents to the ancient matriarch of his family as she sat with her eyes closed, recovering from a day of cleaning rich people's houses. He stood glowing as Omah read the grades and soaked in his best-in-class scores.

"Not good enough!" she chastised, as she handed back the report card to Karl and closed her eyes again.

Crestfallen and unable to penetrate the steel exterior of her unrealistic expectations, Karl turned to go back to his room. As he glanced at his perfect transcript, he noticed something that had not initially registered. His grandmother had handed it back to him right side up. She had been looking at the report card upside-down.

As shocked as if he'd been leaped into frozen Lake Michigan, Karl realized that his grandmother could not read.

Rebecca wanted to be known and respected as the best risk consultant in the insurance business. She was determined to become the first female CEO in an industry crowded with overpaid and underwhelming white males.

Though she had been dating Will Crane for seven years, he had stopped asking her to marry him, content to play second fiddle to her career and her ambition. Crane had inherited his father's wholesale industrial supply business and had effectively outsourced all management to a brilliant COO and a Harvard-educated thirty-something who worked like a dog for Will and fifteen percent equity.

In the rare instance Will could convince Rebecca to take time away from her work, he spoiled her—New Year's in Antigua, an August villa in Umbria, and a ski chalet with friends in Lech. Rebecca usually worked during vacations, often deflating Will's best-laid plans and on occasion, requiring that trips be cut short for emergencies that Will would not have thought twice about delegating to others on his management team.

Will knew he could not compete with her career, but proximity meant there was always a chance to turn her toward matrimony. He loved her and having never married or been interested in having children, he was convinced that Rebecca was his soul mate.

Rebecca cared for Will, but never allowed herself to explore the deeper waters of their relationship, preferring to stay close to shore where she could remain on her feet and in control.

Will was the perfect companion in her business—an articulate, well-traveled, bon vivant CEO of a hundred-million-dollar business, skilled at the art of making other people feel important. He was educated at Santa Barbara's Cate School and Stanford. He spoke French and passable Italian and Spanish. The fact that he was seven years her junior didn't bother anyone but Rebecca.

In her heart, Rebecca believed she wouldn't be able to keep him in this holding pattern forever. Men his age eventually knelt at the altar of younger women. She felt her tummy and tightened her abdominal muscles. The modest paunch would simply not vanish under her daily assault of sit-ups, salads, and samurai-like discipline around sweets.

Her mother used to tell her to take care of herself and to avoid the sun. A woman's skin, ankles, and hands gave away precious information about the physical package. "Keep them guessing, dear," her mother would cackle as she shared her understanding of men, despite her two broken marriages. "Mystery, Rebecca. That's what men all want—inscrutability and illusion. Never let them know what you are really thinking."

Rebecca had taken a risk resigning from a blue-chip firm to chase a CEO role. The ABC houses—big name-brand brokers—moved as slowly as battleships, but they never sank. The joke was no risk manager ever got fired for hiring Alexander & Alexander, but they could be fired for taking a chance on a small boutique brokerage like OB&T if something went wrong.

Yet working for a large, privately held brokerage firm where she made money for a small group of partners who were free to sell their firm at any time, while all she got a pat on the ass, was not her idea of an equitable arrangement. It was the equivalent of being married but having all of the assets in her husband's name.

OB&T was her best chance to become CEO and to realize her dream of security and stature. No one was going to stand in her way this time. The guys at A&A had done a pretty good job of screwing her out of a deserved promotion, but not here. Not now. No one, not Bob O'Brien; Will, her perpetual fiancé-in-waiting; or even that caveman Karl Patton was going to obviate her mission.

She could see Karl was going to be a problem. He didn't bother to disguise the fact he felt Bob had screwed him with her hiring. On one hand, she respected Karl's transparency, obvious skill, and his unwillingness to give up on becoming CEO. Alternatively, she saw his emotion as weakness and his chauvinism as terminal. This guy did not play poker or politics well. He would eventually blow himself up and then the field would be clear. She'd lay odds it would take him about a month.

Rebecca leaned on the edge of Bob O'Brien's desk and crossed her legs at her ankles. A swimmer in high school and college, she was sturdily built, with broad shoulders, a long torso, and the kind of natural beauty and carriage that often comes from athletics. Her blond hair had faded to chestnut over the years, and she was beginning to see strands of gray that cropped up like weeds in an otherwise perfect garden.

She could have used her good looks and attractive figure more to her advantage, but chose instead to work hard to disguise physical features that might distract people from her true talent. She was all business all the time.

She spoke methodically and without emotion as Karl watched her body language. "Karl, this is still a male-dominated business, but it is changing. I can get us in doors, but there are just some things that I can't do. I play golf and am a twelve handicap. I shoot skeet and ride horses, but there are some places I can't go or don't want to go."

Karl frowned. "Like what? Strip joints and male member only lunch clubs?"

Bob O'Brien stepped in. "Karl, our agency had prided itself as always being five steps ahead because we're private and nimble enough to change. What did Darwin say? It's not the strongest of the species that survives but the one that adapts best to change. The times they are a-changin' and OB&T will be way ahead of everyone if we can expand our verticals and demonstrate a level of social and professional diversity that will reflect the future of our business."

"So what now, Bob? I'm supposed to go from account management and sales to be the titty bar and cocktail guy? No offense, but the last time I checked, I was working my butt off to help build this place so we could afford someone like Rebecca to help us expand our footprint. I am up to my ass spending time in those less-glamorous industries like construction, hospitality, and aerospace. Between West L.A. Jews, Italian tough guys, price-conscious Irishmen, and micro-managing risk managers who think a good meeting involves separating fly feces from pepper, I don't have the capacity or the inclination to carry someone else's bag."

Bob had been expecting this reaction from Karl and assumed a patronizing tone. "Karl, we recognize this. That is why we are announcing today that Rebecca will be co-leading sales and account management with you." He handed Karl a laminated org chart with Bob at the top and two boxes below, one each for Rebecca and Karl. This had been in the works for at least a week.

"*We* recognize this? Is that the royal 'we,' Bob, or did someone just reorganize the company and forgot to copy me on the memo?"

"Karl, give it some thought. I think you and Rebecca will be unstoppable, and the only way for this firm to stay competitive is to subordinate the things that our competitors cannot—their own egos and traditional views on business. The world is changing and we need to change with it."

"Yeah, it's going to hell." Karl fumed. "The GOP and the economy are in tatters. Interest rates are climbing. The fucking Arabs have us by the balls. Civil rights activists are trying to integrate a historically segregated America and in the process label everyone either a victim or a perpetrator of discrimination.

"Oh, and by the way, Bob, you may have been too busy at your local DNC fundraisers and not read my recent memos about the fact that one of our largest clients is about to be crucified by the Senate for bribing state officials in West Germany. I think it was about ten million they paid to a few bureaucrats to secure a contract to buy F-109 Starfighters.

"A shareholder lawsuit will certainly give rise to claims that will likely be denied by the Lex underwriters," Karl went on, his voice rising. "We could end up with the biggest fucking errors and omissions claim of our agency's life. But, hey, if you decide that today is the day that you try to make good for two thousand fucking years of misogyny and racial discrimination, that's just great. And remember the old saying, 'Before you replace something, be sure you are substituting something of equal or greater value.' It's a zero sum game, Bob. When you redistribute wealth, you give someone something for nothing. It also means someone who did nothing wrong except work hard gets fucked."

Karl's hesitated and then turned slowly to face Rebecca. "Nothing personal."

Rebecca smiled and then half-smiled, "Oh, none taken."

Karl got up and walked down to his office. So this was it. Twenty plus years invested in his agency and he was about to get forced aside by some bullshit affirmative action quota.

Diane returned from Palm Springs with a deep tan and a case of the major guilt for leaving Ronnie behind during the holidays. She looked in the mirror and was pleased. She had lost five pounds and still had a figure that could turn any man's head. She wore low-cut, form-fitting dresses to advertise her tan, freckled 38 DD chest, and smooth hips. She swam and exercised each day, punishing her entire body. She was fighting a rearguard battle with time, attempting to deny anyone the ability to gauge her true age.

Her hair was naturally light brown, but she had elected to go with a color called "La Plage Noir," striving for an Ali McGraw *Get Away* look. She had beautiful, sad emerald eyes that rose like green planets above a sharp nose that turned ever so slightly up at its tip. She had few laugh lines and rarely mustered more than a half-martyred smile that never seemed to make it up to her eyes. Her perpetual tan made her look exotic and athletic, while her new raven hair promoted a contrarian argument that it was brunettes who were more fun, and at the same time, these dark beauties could take care of business.

She could not have invited her son to Ginny Buckingham's place for Christmas at Mountain Shadows. She had worked hard to get Melissa Storms to include her in Ginny's first wives club, where divorcees traveled, consoled one another, drank Campari and sodas, and tanned in preparation for parties where they would patrol like sharks for unattached wealthy men.

The San Gabriel Valley was still full of shortsighted men who, having tragically indulged their need for an affair or ditched their high school sweetheart for a second marriage trophy wife, were now licking their wounds from divorce and looking for a poised, mature companion. The goal was to find someone kind and not too handsome who still maintained some net worth and needed help managing it before everything was diverted to the grubby hands of past wives or spoiled trust-fund children.

Diane had tried calling Ronnie on Christmas morning but hung up after he failed to answer. When she called later, the number was busy. She really had nothing to say to her son. She loved him but could not understand the trauma he had suffered in Vietnam. When Ronnie came home, Diane initially felt a rush of maternal instinct, but she soon discovered that Ronnie could not stay sober for more than a week and would break into fits of rage at the slightest provocation. He had been living in the big house when Diane finally asked him to move into the pool cabana where he could have more privacy. The truth was that she was afraid of her son and didn't know how to communicate with him.

Ronnie was now a twenty-nine-year-old Humpty Dumpty broken into a million pieces during The Battle of Hue in 1968, and it seemed that no one could put him back together again. Their family had long since lost its adhesion. The VA diagnosis of "exhaustion" translated into a medicine chest of prescription drugs and weekly sessions with a thirty-year-old Marine Corps psychologist who had never seen a bullet fired in anger. Her son was burned out and spent like the machine gun cartridges that littered the killing fields of Laos and Cambodia. With Joanie moved out, it was just she and Ronnie. The huge empty house she had fought so hard to keep during the divorce was now a cobweb-strewn monument to her life as a jilted Mrs. Haversham.

Diane was desperate to escape the black hole that had formed out of her collapsed dreams. Over the New Year's celebrations, she had finally caught the eye of Don Randall, a handsome local architect who had recently endured an ugly divorce from his well-heeled Pasadena wife, Janine. Janine and Don's marriage had held together twenty years, just long enough to jettison their kids, who were grown and in college.

Janine had gotten the big house on Crocker Road while Don had managed to hold on to his beloved Bentley and the family cottage on Balboa Island. He kept an apartment on Orange Grove so he could be closer to his business in South Pasadena but would escape to Newport whenever traffic or his job afforded him an opening to get away.

Diane had loathed Janine Randall for years because she felt the private school princess looked down on her. From the moment she had first gotten together with Don, Diane had felt like the second Mrs. DeWinter, overshadowed by a first wife whose larger-than-life personality, counterfeit smile, and sinister presence forever stood between her and the man she was beginning to love.

Given her insecurity and penchant for melodramatic confrontation, Diane had difficulty dating and sabotaged promising new relationships by demanding overt gestures of commitment. Her fear of being used became a self fulfilling prophesy leading to a string of lovers who had cut and run at the first unsolicited "I think I am falling in love with you" or the suicidal rhetorical question, "what are you thinking?"

Susie had told her repeatedly to take things slow and give potential suitors space.

"Sweetie, play hard to get and don't jump into the sack with him on the first date. You are trying to find a partner not domesticate a wild animal. Remember what it was like in college?" Susie asked. "Nothing's changed. Men certainly have not evolved. They want what they cannot have. Play the game, but don't be a tease. Walk, don't run."

Diane could not help herself. She needed to know she was getting security in exchange for giving up her body. Still, she had resisted sleeping with Don, and things had begun to look up when he called her after New Year's asking her to a Valentine's Day party at the Los Angeles Country Club.

There was a problem, however: The Bad Habit. That was her nick-name for him. He was coming over at least twice a week now. She could always hear his motorcycle from her bedroom as it sped around West Virginia Road and then moved more quietly down Park Circle. He'd turn off the Harley and then roll it through a narrow opening between the driveway fence and tall, ruby-red hibiscus plants that buttressed the silent road. He would rap with his helmet on the back door, and she would lose all her resolve once she saw him in the window, with those pathetically martyred eyes and the "please take care of me" half-smile. She would hate herself for letting him in.

Ferociously passionate, he usually wasted no time, often removing whatever clothing she was wearing to make love to her in the kitchen or perhaps in the laundry room. He prowled her body and electrified her with his aggression. At first, she protested his animalism, wanting to be courted and coaxed into his adultery. She wanted him to tell her how his marriage was a sham and that his wife did not understand him. Or at least talk about the planets, their alignment and our astrological compatibility. Anything. *Don't just screw me.*

He would take her and then linger like a cigarette in the dark, speaking little but leaving the scent of cologne and leather in the house. He would slip into the night, always leaving her just after midnight to return to his family. She could see him, moving with stealth, losing his clothes, and slipping under the sheets as his wife stirred. The next day he would look tired and wasted, drawing sympathy for his late-night client work and energetic ambition to build his agency.

Lately, he had taken the risk of staying all night. But something had changed. He was now treating her with less deference, showing up late, and at other times, staggering to her back door drunk like some sloppy frat boy looking for a quickie. He somehow knew she was the kind of girl who would let him in. She hated that he was right, and that she had become a hopeless cliché of suburban neediness.

She wondered whether she should risk talking to someone about him. She trusted Susie, the one married woman who anchored her small group of single friends. But she worried about what Susie would say. Diane was now contaminating the last safe place to which she could retreat, her own circle of support. She was sleeping with the husband of one of her best friends, jeopardizing her new relationship, and at the same time driving away the one man in her life that she had always loved—her son.

Junior was feeling good about business. Despite the chaos of forty-four-cent gas prices and the unpredictability of interest rates that affected his loan from the bank, he was cash flow positive and able to think about making additional investments in the station or expanding his lucrative repair business.

At six feet three, Junior Riggs was quite the physical specimen. He was rail-thin to the point that Pops would joke that "the boy could shower in a shot-gun barrel". But he was strong like an ant, able to lift multiples of his weight. When he was in Vietnam, he had boxed as an amateur middleweight. But Junior had hated the army and resented its double standard: white officers telling black men to put themselves at risk for a country that would not even grant them the most basic of civil rights.

When he returned home to Monrovia, Junior was angry and confused. Pops had set him straight, putting him to work at the garage and teaching him how to turn his negative energy into money. He also taught him how to run a business.

"Now don't go blowing up my dreams. I am expecting you to run this place and let your old father settle into that nice easy chair I have at home. Resentment never paid a single one of my bills. Don't go listening to anyone who tells you that you are a failure. When you are lying on your back, you're just knocked down. It's only when you go blaming others for your problems that you become a loser."

It had been five years since he ended his tour. Junior had finally completed the transfer of ownership and had been able to buy his father out. The Mobil station's location was perfect, adjacent to the local pharmacy and Hunt's Market where women would buy groceries and then instinctively pull in to get Junior's full service—a smile, oil and tire pressure check, and a few gallons to top off their car's massive twenty-gallon tanks.

People were still gun-shy about being short on gasoline after the long lines and shortages of 1973. Americans had not had to ration since the 1940s. Junior was convinced people were consuming more gas than ever.

New smaller, compact models of cars were promising more fuel economy and better mileage than the eight- and ten-cylinder monsters that got less than fifteen miles to the gallon. Yet Californians loved their big cars and buying Junior's gas. Addiction could be a beautiful thing.

As he waited to fill up a parched BMW, Junior glanced over to the Hunt's Market parking lot. He watched with amusement as R2 Hunt carried two brown bags alongside a drowsy-looking blond woman with legs like giraffe. The overweight beefeater, now adult bag boy, had rolled up the sleeves of his shirt revealing thick, fleshy forearms. He placed the groceries in the boot of the giraffe's Jaguar and then proceeded to linger by her driver's side window continuing the conversation. From Junior's vantage point, it appeared that the blonde was in a rush and was desperate to extricate herself from the fleshy troll's small talk.

Junior remembered playing Hunt and the Huntington Hills Rancheros in high school football. The teams were well matched, but The Hills had a crazy defense with a middle linebacker named Thompson or Thomas. The boy was a crazy missile of destruction and personally caused sure-handed Mustang fullback Mel Jackson to fumble on three separate occasions with the Mustangs losing possession of two. Ralph Hunt the Second had played center. Junior remembered him because they all called him Fat Ralphie. The game had been tight, but in the end, the Mustangs lost in the quarterfinals 16-14 when that Thompson kid picked off a pass. Junior wondered what happened to all those guys.

He assumed some of his classmates went to Nam and others drifted from the neighborhood. Others joined branches the Navy or the Coast Guard to avoid combat. Some got into drugs or became gang bangers and were dead or doing hard time. A few got the hell out of Los Angeles and made something of their lives.

Junior had joined the army because Pops had served in Korea and his grandfather had been in the Navy before him. He knew the Army respected the order of rank but he had not understood that it still condoned the use of a color bar. Now, looking at R2, Junior was reminded of every comrade that died because of some incompetent O-1 pay grade white officer. Those ROTC boys were all brass balls and bravado in the rear, but when they got in the bush they were pussies—calling in backup in an easy LZ, sometimes even bringing ordnance down on their own men. But when they filed their situation reports, they might blame the forward observer for making a mistake with the coordinates. That was usually about the time that someone would suggest fragging the dangerous, lying sack of crap.

Junior had no problem with taking out an officer if he was a hazard to his men, but there were no guarantees that next guy would not be an even bigger John Wayne. The conveyor belt of useless, white enlisted officers moved as fast as the VC who flowed in and out of Cambodia along the Ho Chi Minh trail.

The flaxen giraffe pulled away in her Jag before R2 could remove his arms from the roof. He spun around but recovered enough to fake a wave. Holding his arm, he waddled back towards the market. The automatic doors opened up, and John walked past R2, escorting a pregnant woman and her small daughter, and pushing a massive cart full of groceries while holding a sack of potatoes on one shoulder. R2 ignored them.

John delivered the groceries and looked up, waving to the woman as she exited on to Huntington Hills Drive. He turned and caught Junior's eye and flipped his head in acknowledgment. Junior saluted back toward John and smiled.

Junior liked that Patton kid. The boy had approached him months before looking for a job. Things had been too tight for Junior to afford help, but he had been impressed by the boy's handshake and his ability to look Junior in the eye.

Junior had seen the kid's father come through the station over the years. He assumed Mr. Patton was ex-military—the same sort of master sergeant, like Pops. Parenting was all about setting the right example. Pops was fond of saying that "a boy won't do what his daddy says, but he sure will copy what his daddy does."

Junior watched as John pushed the basket back in the door of the market and then slowed the gas down to top off the BMW.

"That'll be $6.80, sir."

As he went to make change for a ten-dollar bill, Junior noticed a car windshield catch the afternoon sun. A brick red Cadillac Deville was parked in the alleyway behind Hunt's market, and its driver appeared to be either watching the back loading dock door or the parking lot as the customers went in and out of the store. It was getting later in the day and it seemed odd that anyone would be making a delivery this late. Perhaps the driver was waiting to pick up one of the girls who worked in the deli.

Junior returned to the Beamer in the station and made change for his twenty. "Thank you. Come again!" he said enthusiastically.

He turned again and saw that the Deville was no longer parked in the alley. He tried to recall the man behind the wheel. He had seen that guy somewhere before.

CHAPTER 9

You couldn't get hold of the things you'd done and turn them right again. Such a power might be given to the gods, but it was not given to women and men, and that was probably a good thing. Had it been otherwise, people would probably die of old age still trying to rewrite their teens.

~Stephen King

John walked toward the storage room where the box boys dangled on top of empty pallets until they heard the customer service bell indicating the need for someone to bag groceries at the front checkout counter. He dodged past the dairy case and darted left into the back room before anyone could give him another task. Tucked in between burlap sacks of potatoes and empty produce flats, he found Rick Helm and Bob McKesson— high school seniors and two of the store's ranking bagmen.

Helm was smoking a clove cigarette with the loading dock door slightly ajar to dissipate the odor. John knew they would catch hell from Andy, the store manager, if the loading dock door was left unlocked. It was supposed to be open only on Thursday load days when new groceries were delivered and the boys stocked the shelves.

The box boys liked keeping the door cracked to play a sadistic game of cat and mouse with the insane lady who lived across the alley, trying to swing the door open and catch her as she rummaged through the trash. John thought it was cruel but did not feel it was his place to admonish the two older boys. On occasion, R2 would join them; they had once startled the old lady to a point that she had fallen down. Hunt thought it was the funniest thing ever, but John had seen hatred in the old woman's eyes.

Redheaded Ricky Helm was in a lather over an upcoming Rush concert in Hollywood. "J.P., Starwood on the eighteenth. I got two tickets and Shauna Harder to go with me. We are going to 'SC first to visit her brother at a frat party and then going to Hollywood to hear Lee and Neil play *By-Tor and the Snow Dog*!" Helm broke into an air guitar riff and retracted his freckled face into a massive wincing wrinkle while he bit his lower lip.

He decided to play an entire set of Rush and then stopped abruptly in the middle of a *Fly by Night* solo. "There's just one problem. One gigantic, larger-than-life dilemma. There's nothing to take to accentuate the experience. The Greek is tapped out and Plums says that he can't get anything from his brother until next Saturday. The town's so dry the trees are whistlin' at the dogs. What's the use of going to a concert if you can't get a little mental – although we do have a case of Carlsberg Elephants and fifth row, center seats."

John suddenly remembered the baggie of houseflies George had given him in December. He had promised George he would try to find someone stupid enough to buy them as long as George split the proceeds with him.

John knew he could probably sell the flies for sixty bucks, give George his half of the wholesale price, and make a clean forty-dollar profit. Now, he just needed to remember where he had hidden the baggie. He had been upset that night and could not recall which of his several favorite hiding places he had used to keep the flies far away from the prying eyes of his psychic mother. He wondered why he even tried to keep them. He could have just as easily found more insects in the spider webs that framed their garage windows.

"Ricky, my man, you're in luck. I've got a line on some Afro-dizzies from the darkest region of the Congo."

"Afro-what?"

"These are Spanish Fly afro-dizzies - aphrodisiacs designed to make any dude irresistible to women—even someone as ugly as you. They're illegal in Europe, the US, and Botswana. The dude who sold them to us was overseas with the Central Intelligence Agency."

John was starting to screw his eyebrows up at his own fanciful descriptions, but he knew his audience. These guys would smoke their own nose hairs if they thought it would get them high. He had learned his merchandising lessons the hard way, from television cologne commercials that promised sex, fame, and fortune. If you used Hai Karate, you would literally have to fight off thirty-year-old women using martial arts moves. Drench on Old Spice and have your way with any mature woman at the dock bar. While he could have had his pick of any girl in high school, John had developed a fascination with older women. After sneaking into the local Rialto theatre to see *Summer of '42* at the ripe age of twelve, he was haunted by the star-crossed love of Gary Grimes for Jennifer O'Neill.

John tried to adopt the ways of mature men, lathering on popular colognes and pheromone-laced fragrances, often soaking his body to a point where he was highly flammable. Yet, his closest encounter to date had been with an aging female German shepherd named Lobo that tried to hump him for several blocks while he pedaled his bike home from a basketball practice. His failed liaison with Kitty had been another severe blow to his efforts to become a member of the *Summer of '42* club.

Helm jumped down out of his comfortable perch. "Dude, how much?"

John played coy. "I'm not sure. I may not be able to get the guy to sell them. After all, it's bone dry and prom night is coming up. My guess is a lot of guys are going to want them for that."

"Seventy-five!"

John kept a straight face. "Eighty," he said.

Helm threw his head back, raised his arms in mock frustration and turned his back.

"Okay, okay. Because you're a buddy, seventy-five bucks. But you have to give me one sixer from your case of Elephants."

The boys clasped hands.

McKesson looked befuddled and tilted his head at John. "Dude, what's an African Desiack?"

Helm looked disgusted. "Bobby, if you have to ask, you don't belong."

The bell rang three times. The boys tied on their aprons and rushed up different aisles to assist the checkout girls with boxing groceries.

A few seconds had passed when the dairy case opened up and R2 came out wiping his mouth and grinning. *So, ol' Karl Patton's got himself a drug dealer in the family.*

Hunt looked like a bloated piglet that had just finished feeding. His beady eyes and ruddy face were flushed with alcohol, nitrous oxide, and the delusion that this year's Huntington Hills Bicentennial celebration would mark his ascent into city and state politics.

Rebecca was having a rough week. Her mother had been hospitalized for pneumonia, and one of her largest clients had made an announcement of a major merger. She was not grafting into OB&T nearly as well as she had envisioned and was realizing that Bob O'Brien was not the kind of boss who would resolve the problem by telling Karl to either get with the program or look for a new job.

"Rebecca, Karl has been here more than twenty years and this is a major setback for him. Having to share authority when he thought he would be taking over the agency in the next five years is tough on him."

"Bob, I am sympathetic, but you didn't bring me in here to *share* authority. You brought me in to *take* it. I'm here because you understood a relic like Karl could not navigate a brave, new diversified world. The big houses are catching on to regional brokers like OB&T. We need a five-year plan, and you need a successor that will make this agency *her* highest priority. If you are going to maximize your earn-out, you need someone who is twenty-four seven, not a neo-con with four kids who believes that women should be kept barefoot and pregnant."

"Whoa, Rebecca!" Bob said, holding up his hand. "Karl may be many things and not be the most politically correct apple to fall from the tree, but that guy helped build this place. If you want to lead the agency, you will need to win over the assets—our people. You can't expect me just to blow up anyone who becomes an obstacle to your progress to the top. I do that and I start losing clients. Nope, you have to win him over. Ask him out to lunch or take him and his wife to dinner."

Rebecca scoffed. "Oh, I can just see the demure Mrs. Patton now. She probably does not make eye contact, trails behind him like an Asian comfort girl and does not speak a word unless he gives her permission."

Bob was now laughing, with a surprised expression that for some reason annoyed Rebecca. "My dear, you could not be more wrong."

Susie submerged herself in furious housework when she was upset, and right now the house was sparkling because she was enraged. Earlier in the day, she had been to Huntington Hills Middle School to meet with Freddie's counselor, Sandy Hammond.

March had been "career month" for the entire Huntington Hills district. The school administrators were determined to better illuminate for students the intricate machinery of the working world in hopes of aligning nascent avocations with future vocations.

In homeroom, Freddie and his classmates were asked to fill out a questionnaire designed to ascertain their strengths, weaknesses, passions, and aversions. The teachers and counselors were told by the new student counseling office to take the vocation assessment process very seriously. Freddie, still smarting from a week's grounding for his chain link fence experiment, was trying to cooperate with his teacher, Miss Barbara, as she handed out instructions.

The first sheet listed more than one hundred activities and came with the one simple instruction: Pick the top five activities from the following occupations that you most enjoy.

The next page offered a series of public and private sector examples. The actual testing questions attempted to frame the emotional and physical requirements characteristic of an occupation's first-quartile performers.

1. Mark the word that best describes you:
      a) follower
      b) leader
      c) fixer
      d) watcher

2. You are happiest when you are:
    a) working indoors standing up
    b) working indoors sitting down
    c) working outdoors standing up
    d) working outdoors sitting down.

Freddie had looked for another answer: E. None of the above. He did not like manual labor but liked managing other people and making money doing it. He would rather be the team manager than a player on the bench. Freddie had lots of questions. Did the job involve physical activity where one's size could be an impediment? Was there lots of sweating? Did the job pay at least four dollars an hour? Could he perform the task while watching TV? Could he subcontract the work to dumber people and pay them less money? Would someone need to inspect his work before he could go home for the night?

He raised his hand.

"I don't know, Frederick," whispered the perpetually annoyed Miss Barbara. "Just try to find one sequence of characteristics that describes you."

"What if none of them describe me?' he chirped.

Miss Barbara hissed at him. "Don't get smart, mister. Principal White made a point that you are already on thin ice after last month's firebomb. You have fifteen more minutes. "

The test results were collected, tabulated, and cross-referenced with each child's most recent grades. Together the data were somehow triangulated to provide a rich social X-ray into every student's potential as a contributing member of society. Once students were labeled and categorized, each child was scheduled to meet with a "counselor" to discuss the findings.

Susie had read the memorandum sent to their home from the school district. She was highly skeptical of educational gimmicks that periodically worked their way through her children's schools. In the thick of guiding four sons from elementary through high school, she already had experienced every charlatan and new-age educational reformer. She had seen them all—the academics, the socialists and the twenty-six-year-old Ivy-League PhDs—cycling through the school district as consultants, teachers, principals and superintendents. She distrusted any tests that attempted to pigeonhole children early in their development, before they could even begin to explore their potential.

Freddie's counselor tripled as a social studies, art, and drama teacher. Susie knew Sandy Hammond as a nice but unimaginative educator who was clearly not the sharpest pencil in the drawer. Personally, Freddie was bemused that Mr. Hammond was chosen as his ombudsman to the business world. In their only career conversation to date, his young teacher asked Freddie only what Karl did for a living. Hammond seemed perpetually fascinated with other people's careers and often quizzed kids on what their fathers did. Freddie tried to outline the concept of insurance brokerage as his father had explained it to him. However, in this case, the student could not instruct the teacher.

On the day of his career day debrief, Freddie received a packet that explained the testing methodology. He was excited. Perhaps the results would confirm his belief that he was going to become an international financier or an entertainment czar. Summoned to Hammond's office, he found his teacher, feet on his desk, nursing a mug of coffee with the word "Dad" stenciled on its side.

"Well, Patton, let's see what we have here." He opened an official-looking folder that included graphs, charts, and complicated percentages. He looked at the report as if it were written in ancient Greek. Freddie held his breath.

"So, it says here … let's see … that you should consider a career as a fish and game warden."

Freddie waited for more. "You know Mr. Hammond, my dad does insurance. Does it say anything about that? I'm also pretty good with money, and I like stocks. Although, come to think of it, I did check in the survey that I liked fires and sleeping outside in a tent. I just finished reading *My Side of The Mountain* over the summer."

"Well, there you go, son." Hammond seemed satisfied but quickly became flummoxed when Freddie did not immediately accept his fate to regulate traffic in some national park. Hammond handed Freddie a hand-drawn, cartoonish-looking brown brochure with a game warden that looked like the ranger from Yogi Bear. It read: *Fish and Game Warden: A Life of Adventure.*

Everyone had been talking all day about careers. Betsy Vanstrom was going to be in international fashion. The straight-A math savant, Peter

Platz, was going to be a banker. And Freddie? He was going to arrest people for illegal fires and not carrying a fishing license.

Initially, Freddie did not say anything at dinner, but he was worried. He had been programmed by Karl to believe that any vocation involving a shovel, heavy machinery, or a shirt with his name stenciled on it was a vine that would bear limited fruit. Success did not come from sitting in a fire tower glancing across an ocean of evergreens looking for a puff of smoke.

He did not tell his mother, but, as usual, she found out. She had uncovered the crumpled Fish and Game Warden brochure in his blue jeans pocket and gently confronted her youngest son. As he spilled his guts about being a park ranger, Susie seethed.

It was at this moment that she declared war on the school district and its vocational counseling program. To protect her boys and their friends, she would have to kill this educational profiling program before it became a flawed self-fulfilling prophesy wedging kids into limiting boxes based on the results of some dubious questionnaire. She would enlist the help of other mothers and lead a coup at the next PTA meeting. This would not be hard, as she was already somewhat of an organizer among other women in town and known for her candor and pragmatism in dealing with boys.

As Susie wrestled with her emotions, she smirked at the offspring of her New Year's laundry edict: pink, gray, and white shirts with dark stains from John's laundry hamper. The kids' clothes had still not recovered. The idea of wearing colored underwear had upset George to the point where he refused to wear his pink hangers, choosing instead to go "kamikaze" until they had been bleached back to white. Susie figured that she still needed a few more wash cycles before the pinks returned to whites.

Now, as she emptied John's pockets, mindlessly checking for dollar bills or loose change, she stared out the back window and observed as two house painters finished the back-half of the Motter's house—a similarly styled Mediterranean with seashell white paint, brown trim, and a red-tile roof. She had been watching the workers for a week and liked the way the house was shaping up. She had been meaning to give Diane a call to see if she could get Ronnie to come over and do some touch-up work around the windows and patio doors. It was, after all, America's birthday and a perfect excuse to doll up the house. Although money was tight, she could argue that it was the patriotic thing to do.

Karl would object to having someone else paint the house and would make a case that he and the boys could complete the job. Susie knew that this was a recipe for disaster and that, if pushed, Karl would consent to hiring a war veteran. He knew Ronnie had been through a lot at home and in Asia. Susie had also been meaning to call Diane anyway to find out if she had made inroads into Don Randall's heart.

She loved the intrigue and melodrama that sparked weekly among her fearless and unfiltered friends. The sorority of complicated souls would meet and speak in code at out-of-the-way restaurants, one another's homes and across four seasons of sidelines. They would laugh and talk under their breath as they kept an eye on the each other's children and their older siblings who were competing in the sporting events. The companionship was oxygen for the single and divorced mothers who were overwhelmed by life's indiscriminate blows but refused to declare defeat. They wanted their kids to know that despite their travails, divorced mothers cared enough to be present.

Their stories were often steamier than a drug store novel, and Susie was a trusted confidante. The English had it right. Gossip and sugar were the great sweeteners of tea. Susie would listen, as she always did, rendering little judgment but offering her friends sound life advice if they seemed to be asking for it.

As she considered the good fortune of her own life, Susie spotted the canvas bag at the bottom of John's dirty clothes hamper. God only knew how long his grungy basketball clothes had been concealed in this dark incubator of filth. Her hand gingerly probed the corners of the bag for socks or worse, an unwashed jockstrap, when she brushed against a plastic bag. Alarm bells went off as she removed the package, only to find a baggie filled with houseflies.

Instead of discarding it, she slipped it into her pocket. The bag was sealed tight and it looked identical to the small baggie of marijuana she had found in Matthew's pants a few years back. Maternal intuition flickered and signaled a yellow cautionary flag. Something was not right. It would be worth a brief conversation with her son.

CHAPTER 10

We are all born ignorant, but one must work hard to remain stupid.

~Benjamin Franklin

Matthew was overjoyed. He had just procured a precious Grateful Dead ticket from three friends who planned on attending the Dead's show in June at the Paramount Theatre in Portland. School would be out and Susie had agreed that barring any objections from his father, Matthew could spend June and July working in Northern California, living with his relatives at the O'Reilly family compound at Forest Knolls, in Marin County.

It was a cool, breezy East Bay morning as Matthew walked out across Telegraph Avenue and into People's Park, the site of the anti-war protests of 1969. This sacred place was ground zero for Bloody Thursday, when then-Governor Ronald Reagan unleashed his Alameda police storm troopers and their shotguns on defenseless activists. The blood of student James Rector would forever remain a stain on Reagan's hands like Macbeth's crimson spot. This hallowed ground was a place his father would never understand. Karl loved Ronald Reagan, who was gratefully losing to incumbent President Ford in the Republican primaries for president. God forbid that Reagan, the fascist murderer and cronies like Edwin Meese, would ever hold the reins of the U.S. government.

Matthew was not worried about the political weather vane in America. Everywhere, students and faculty were predicting a Democratic sweep in Congress and the White House. Matthew had read as much as he could about the candidates and seemed most comfortable with Morris Udall from Arizona, although the Georgia governor, Carter, had been winning most of the Democratic primaries.

Matthew's love interest, Mary Alice Hunter, now lived at Lothlorien, a vegetarian residential dorm filled with a strange ensemble of hippies and granola-eating activists. Things seemed to be cooling between them. She now asked that they meet either at his place or in some location other than where she lived. When they did stay together, it was always at Matthew's apartment. Initially, this agreement worked out rather well for everyone except for his roommate, who began to resent paying fifty percent of the monthly rent for a pillow and an old couch.

Eventually, Matthew divined that Mary Alice was moving on an even more liberal course than he. Her cooperative vegetarian living arrangement had ignited a burning desire to change the world and rapidly redistribute the wealth found in towns like Huntington Hills. It seemed that overnight Matthew had become the unwitting poster child for her new war on white-collar affluence.

Mary Alice made derogatory comments regarding his hometown and the fact that it was at the Caucasian end of the color bar. It seemed that no matter what Matthew did to try to shed his privileged past, the beatniks, activists, and anarchists could not accept him. His long hair, shell necklace, and determined activism were perceived as merely a rich-boy rebel veneer. He felt the constant need to apologize for his privileges and for everything that had gotten him into Cal in the first place: his grades, his family and his white-bread upbringing.

Matthew was often rankled by what he felt were the hypocritical judgments of his fellow students. Many of these "radicals" came from private high schools and communities similar to Huntington Hills and were attending college thanks to the welfare of their parents and the subsidized tuition of the state. Yet somehow they had managed to distance themselves from their parents and present themselves as new generation of self-proclaimed change agents.

Matthew did envy their convictions. It seemed he had never really believed in anything. Suburban life never required him to make hard choices. Over time, he chose a predictable theology of opposition—to Karl and his points of view. It was ironic that Karl was so essential to Matthew's sense of identity. The man he wanted to pull away from had become his raison d'être. Holmes had Moriarty. Superman had Lex Luthor. Matthew had Karl.

It was 1976, a perfect year to declare one's freedom from the tyranny of capitalism and political fat cats like Reagan and Ford. It was also a time for him to form his own opinions and forge his own way. Matthew realized if he was going to win the respect of individuals like his anti-establishment girlfriend, he would need to commit some grand act of rebellion so all might see that he, too, was a changed man.

Karl was in a deep funk. He needed to do something extraordinary to alter the course of Bob O'Brien's latest affirmative action push. While he grudgingly accepted that Rebecca had the skills and market knowledge requisite to leading the firm, he felt he possessed identical abilities. Bob was turning OB&T's succession planning into a heated competition, and Karl was now the dark horse. He sat in his office staring out across a marine layer gray morning, the haze of the spring sun slowly warming the day.

The phone rang and he picked it up. Outside his office, he could see his assistant frowning. It was her job to answer the phones.

"Karl, my favorite subcommittee chair. It's R2, pal."

"Ralph, how are you? What can I do for you?" Karl tried to conceal the suspicion in his voice.

"Well, I think it's time we get together and hit the links. Perhaps we can kill a few birdies with one ball. I'm interested in your proposals on how Hunt's risk management programs can be improved and also want to narrow down the list of Grand Marshal candidates. Say, I saw your son earlier this week at the store. I forgot what a handsome kid he is. Jesus, he must have to beat 'em off with a stick."

Karl considered declining the offer but realized it would only postpone the inevitable. Meeting Hunt on his own ground may not be a good idea. He recalled the Army and how his gunny would always scream,

"Gentleman, we must bring the fight to the enemy. However, never let him determine the place and time of battle."

"Uh, sure, Ralph. I think I can move some things around. How about Saturday or Sunday?"

"R2, please. If we are going to be doing business together, you must call me R2. All my friends call me R2. And we should be friends. Dad talks about you all the time like you are some kind of goddamn saint!"

Karl swallowed hard. He wondered if word had leaked out regarding his committee's recent ideas for the parade. He kicked himself for getting involved in something as stupid as a Fourth of July celebration.

The Grand Marshal suggestion had really been Russ's idea. Although Karl was grateful. Given all that had transpired at work and the bribery claim at Lamley Aerospace, Karl had been a bit distracted. Hunt would go ape-shit when he found out.

"Okay, Ralph … R2," Karl winced.

"Good, good …good." The prosperous voice on the other end of the phone seemed very relieved.

"Let's go off at LACC, Friday at twelve-thirty. We can meet an hour earlier in the clubhouse, have lunch, and then tee off. I'll loop in a couple of my fraternity brothers. Good guys, scratch handicappers, and funnier than hell. You can tell that beautiful wife of yours I will have you home by six p.m."

"Great," said Karl, trying to sound enthusiastic. He hung up, only to have his line light up again. He reached for the phone as his assistant scowled disapprovingly at him. He returned her grimace with a saccharine smile, but she won the day.

"OB&T, Karl's Patton's office. Oh, hello Mrs. Patton. Yes, just one moment. I will patch you through. Mrs. Patton on line one," she said.

She smiled triumphantly as Karl he rolled his eyes, cradled the phone to his shoulder, and kicked the door closed. He kicked it a bit too hard and gritted his teeth as the slam shook the large plate glass window and his Levolor blinds. His assistant looked offended, while several other assistants poked heads above their cubicles.

Before he could say anything, Susie launched a cannonade of frustration beginning with the school's assessment of Freddie.

"And now it's John."

"What the hell is wrong?"

"I just found something strange stashed in his closet hamper."

"Well, what is it?"

"Well, I think it's just a bag of house flies, but they're in one of those drug baggies, and it was hidden in his laundry. I don't know what he's up to but I don't like it. After his scare last year, I thought he would have joined the President's anti-drug taskforce by now."

"They're all retarded, every fucking kid under the age of twenty-five," Karl said. Anger was Karl's first response to anything that confounded him, and the challenges of dealing with his children ranked as one of his great uncontrolled sources of anxiety. At least at work you could fire people for acts of stupidity, although these days, you first had to put them on one of those socialist, do-gooder, Human Resources performance improvement plans. Then you fired them.

Children were different. They were like union members. You couldn't terminate them and every goddamn thing was a negotiation.

"Well, I guess Mr. Shit-for-Brains will have a lot of time to think about his stupidity. I say we ground him through Memorial Day. Take away the car and dismantle that goddamn stereo for good measure. I want that little son of a bitch riding to and from school every day on his ten-speed as his friends drive by and honk at him."

"Well, that's very helpful, but we don't even know if he's done anything wrong. It's just not like John to have something like this—whatever *this* is." Susie fell silent.

Karl had learned over the years to indulge her pregnant pauses and not fill them with suggestions. She was like a medium going into a trance and channeling some hidden source of intelligence. He did not believe in any of her paranormal mumbo-jumbo, but he had to smile at her uncanny ability to ferret out the truth. She was Miss Marple, Hercule Poirot and Nancy Drew all rolled into Elizabeth Taylor.

"So?" Karl finally said.

"I think I know what I need to do. Love you. Bye!"

Karl ran his fingers through his closely trimmed hair. He was under siege from all sides. Whatever happened to that age-old axiom about work and family having an inverse relationship? If life was shitty at work, things were supposed to be great at home. Yet as of March 31, he was adrift in an ocean of bullshit in a boat captained by turncoat Bob, a lesbian first mate, and crewed by his mutinous teens—the budding socialist, the cipher, the smartass and the pyromaniac savant.

He thought of Susie and grudgingly smiled. Susie cleared away the smoke so he could see things for what they were. She made life softer, sweeter, and easier to understand. She was his lighthouse whose beacon appeared like clockwork, keeping him away from the sharper shoals of life's impulsive decisions. *What if Smitty and I had not decided to visit San Francisco back in 1949?* He thought. *What if I had decided to go to Northwestern instead of Santa Clara?* He shuddered at the idea of those cold Chicago winters and the possibility of having married some dull, doughy Midwestern girl whose idea of a vacation was a trip to a corn-field.

Kitty sat in her car in the parking lot of Cornwell, Blakeslee and Romer and sobbed. At Susie's suggestion, Kitty had consulted an attorney to better understand her options in the event she and Garrett could not reconcile. He was more pensive these days, often returning home after midnight and easing into bed softly like a burglar, not wanting to be detected. He had already purloined so much from her but she could not accuse him. She could smell the infidelity on him, although he did his best to suggest his absenteeism was merely client work that was taxing his strength and stealing his time.

Kitty looked in the rear view mirror and dried her eyes, wiping away mascara that was now running down her cheeks. "My God, I know what happened to Baby Jane."

She took out her compact and went to work. Opening her purse, she removed several small cucumbers from a baggie and leaned back in her seat, laying the lime green wedges on her eyes. It was an old trick taught to her by her mother, a hickory-hard Southern woman who ran off with a traveling salesman and then spent a lifetime holding together a family of girls and a constant vigil for a husband who was never home.

Kitty LaTourette had been the object of desire and rumor for every adolescent boy in her small town of Cameron, Alabama. Less than twenty-five miles outside of Tuscaloosa, the melting pot that created the

LaTourette girls comprised generous portions of Nordic blonde mixed with a jambalaya of Southern insanity. Some families whispered that the LaTourettes had some Negro blood coursing through their veins. As far as Kitty was concerned, a little "colored" blood made her unique in a place that could not distinguish between history and tradition.

Cameron, Alabama was too exhausted under the weight of its own poverty and prejudice to progress in any direction. It was a stunted community where the only things that grew were weeds, cotton and debt. At around age of fifteen, its younger inhabitants started to disappear, choosing to leave and find work, trading their poverty for a better chance. All too often, they would return, sometimes years later, broken and resigned to an eventual funeral plot in the antebellum cemetery down by the river.

Kitty left Cameron when she was fourteen, never saying goodbye to her younger sisters, a decision she regretted for years, but a condition of her emancipation. Her mother knew she needed to let her eldest girl go, but felt the younger ones needed time to ripen on the vine of life.

She ended up in Birmingham with relatives and went to high school, flourishing in literature, mathematics and drama—an odd combination for a woman in the '50s. Kitty was given a full scholarship to the University of Alabama, where she discovered how to use her intellect, body, and emotional powers of persuasion to get anything she wanted.

She was president of Chi Omega and modeled swimsuits to finance her social life. Upon graduation, she went west to seek her fortune as an actress. Kitty did fairly well, grabbing some spots on television commercials and in print ads. She was an Arrow Soap girl and spent several weeks showing off the radiant skin that glowed with the regular use of Dorothy Gray cosmetic products.

In 1958, she met Garrett. He was the sinfully attractive art director for an advertising agency that was conducting a casting call for baby products. The client was looking for a Nordic beauty queen to coo with a happy infant promoting a new brand of silky soft diapers. Kitty did not get the job, but she did get invited to dinner by "Johnny Cash," a nickname that some of the girls had given to brooding Mister Erickson, the striking art director with the long sideburns and shoulder-length hair.

He radiated danger, but she was hardly intimidated - having tamed scores of less-than-domesticated men. Her old boyfriend at Alabama had been a dashing wide receiver with an adoring fan club of gentrified debutantes waiting to catch his eye. Kitty's indifference and keen insight into All-American Lance Pendry had demoted the man they called "Captain" to a pathetic, jealous private who relentlessly guarded Kitty's borders to chase off any potential suitors.

Garrett was her first exposure to loss of control. He was a wild force of nature that blew into her life – a self-centered tornado of consumption – cutting a huge swath across her existence and leaving wreckage in his wake. He made her feel like she was eight years old again, running across damp Alabama clay as the afternoon sky turned a sickening chrome green. The wind howled as she extended her arms in the heaving downdraft that whipped rusted dust devils of dirt into her eyes. Her mother would scream for her to come to the storm cellar but she would wait, mesmerized by the dark clouds rolling towards her. She dreamed of being lifted into the sky and disappearing from Alabama. *Just take me away with you, anywhere.*

She had thought she had tamed her man. Their lives before Seth and Candace were bliss—an egocentric joyride of travel, entertainment, industry galas and high-society friends. When Seth was born, they had tried to maintain their lifestyle, but Kitty could not reconcile children with the hangovers and his deep indigo moods.

She became determined to tame their lifestyle and Garrett. When Candy followed, they moved from the Westside to the San Gabriel suburbs. Kitty hoped a small town might stimulate Garrett's stunted paternal instincts. Huntington Hills would offer her children a chance for a better education and a stable life that moved at the predictable rhythm of a small town. Yet, Kitty's dreams of cadence, calm and consistency were just additional strands of the domestic barbed wire incarcerating her husband.

From his first day, when he got pulled over in his Porsche by a Huntington Hills cop, Garrett despised the community. He had spent his life lampooning and stereotyping suburban life, and now he was expected to throw off his leather jacket and boots and be fitted with a sweat suit and tennis shoes. Kitty once suggested he help out with Seth's Little League team. A coach's whistle might as well have been a bit in his mouth. It was not going to happen, and after a while, Kitty understood that when he was a part of their lives, he was merely passing through.

Now, like her own mother, she was forced to raise her kids virtually alone. Garrett was physically present, but never really home. He looked like a sailor perpetually scanning the horizon for the sight of a masthead and the next ship that might take him back to his one great love.

Garrett's surliness and Kitty's intelligent candor made it hard for them to graft into the community, and Kitty often found herself on the outside looking in on a circle of women who had no use for Southern liberals and new-age hippies. Her chance encounter with Susie at a Little League game had led to a five-year friendship that was her mooring in a turbulent sea of petty gossip and double-standard suburban hypocrisy.

Kitty lifted the cucumbers from her eyes and peered into the mirror. No signs of trauma. She placed the bag back into her purse and turned off the ignition key. It was only a short walk to The Chronicle. She would be early, but she was in no hurry, preferring to sit in the shade with the windows open, and listen to the radio. She did not feel like making small talk with anyone while waiting for her friends to assemble. They would descend on the quiet restaurant like cackling witches: Ginny Buckingham, Diane Thomas and Melissa Storms—the troika of raucously naughty first wives.

Susie had been the original catalyst for the lunch but had to bow out at the last minute because of an incident at home. Susie was never specific about the felonies and misdemeanors that sometimes redirected her energies, and Kitty respected Susie's instinct to keep her family life private.

Kitty was looking forward to this lunch and had decided to confide in her girlfriends about her failing marriage and Garrett. Yet she felt a twinge of remorse. She was violating the basic tenets of her mother's rules of silent Southern martyrdom: "Your business is your business," and "Nothing goes outside this house except shoes and a dirty dog."

As Kitty had gotten older, she saw the flaws in her mother's enabling, silent suffering. A person was generally only as sick as their secrets and if life did not afford you at least one soul mate capable of sharing your doubts and concerns, you should join a church. People needed to talk about their feelings with another human being. In this case, Kitty had three best friends with whom she could confide.

She switched on the radio and found a lonesome George Jones country western song on KLAC. The music made her ache for another time.

She watched Diane pull up beside her in her ruby red Deville. Unaware of her audience, Diane prepared herself in her car, applying a small line of lipstick to her tight-lipped mouth. She had been acting strange around Kitty lately—almost too nice, speaking in the way people talk when they know something uncomfortable about you. Kitty looked through her window and saw Melissa Storms walking through the parking lot. The petite blond broke into a sweet but affected cheerleader grin and eagerly waved back in that hyper-effusive manner that was her trademark.

It was going to be a great lunch today. It would mark the end of wallowing in self-pity and the beginning of a new life. She could depend on her friends to give her the right advice. She would call Susie later and share all the gossip. It had not been since university that Kitty felt that someone actually had her back. It was time to get on with living, with or without Garrett.

Rebecca picked up the phone and put it down. She swigged a huge mouthful of cold coffee and winced as if it were three fingers of old bathtub gin. In the last week, she had started drinking coffee again, a bad sign that some old habits from the A&A days were returning. She had hoped that the job change and move from downtown to Pasadena would give her more time to take care of herself. The reverse commute to Toluca Lake was helping, but she was not accustomed to working with a firm with so few layers of management and support staff. She was initially put off that she had to share an assistant with Karl.

She finally picked up the phone. "Carol, can you get me Mr. Patton on the phone?"

There was a long, awkward moment. Carol sounded stumped as she said, "But if I call Mr. Patton, how do I tell him you're on the line if I answer his phone?"

"Jesus," Rebecca hissed, stood up, and made her way down the hall to Karl's office. Knocking, she didn't wait for his response. "Karl, am I interrupting?"

Karl motioned her to a chair and then crossed both hands on his desk, looking ready for a fight.

"My ingénue boyfriend, Will, and I are having dinner at our favorite restaurant next weekend. We'd love it if you and your wife could join us. I think you will really enjoy Will. He's a rather old soul for thirty-eight and I am *dying* to meet your wife. From what Bob says she is some kind of oracle on men and boys."

Boyfriend? "Um, sure," Karl said, flustered by this unexpected olive branch. "I'll need to check with the boss, but that sounds fine."

"Let's say six p.m. at La Espadrille."

Karl was still not thinking straight. "O.K. Six p.m. at La S'bian."

"Excuse me?"

"Check. La Espadrille. We know it well. Love it. Love the food there." He pretended to be marking it in his Day-Timer while his ears turned bright red.

"Oh, and I will wait a few minutes to tell Carol that we are having dinner together. It may be too much for her if we tell her to put it in our diaries at the same time."

Karl did not laugh, but then realized she had made a joke. "Oh, yeah. Ha!"

Rebecca bolted upright and shook Karl's hand with a firm grip.

"Great, see you next Saturday."

She smiled. Oh yes, she had him.

John arrived home early from school to get ready for work. He was upstairs putting on a button down, tie, and dark blue jeans when he remembered that he needed to take the baggie of dead houseflies to the market to give them to Rick Helm. He felt guilty perpetuating fraud on another person. However, it made him smile to think that all these idiots who thought it was so cool to get stoned would actually be eating houseflies. Personally, John did not get the fascination with alcohol and drugs. It only led to bad consequences and loss of control—double millstones that could hold back any kid trying to break away.

He went into his closet and noticed his dirty clothes hamper was not in the corner. He was not overly concerned. He sometimes found it downstairs in the laundry room, and Susie never checked it that carefully.

He jogged downstairs and glanced at the clock. It was ten to three. He was working the three to seven shift. It was also load day, which he dreaded. He hoped the morning guys had unloaded most of the groceries and that they were sitting in the aisles in boxes, ready to be opened, priced and stacked. He walked into the kitchen expecting to see Susie, but she wasn't there. He heard the dryer shut behind him and turned to see his mother standing in the laundry room door.

"Looking for this?" she said, holding the baggie in her hand.

George had decided to skip freshman baseball this year so he could focus on his grades. He was still playing his last year of Babe Ruth baseball and did not want the punishments that always accompanied poor marks. Susie had warned him that things changed in high school and that "grades start to count." He did not like the sound of a permanent academic scorecard and was secretly terrified at the thought of geometry, algebra and pre-calculus. There must have been a recessive gene in the Patton family because everyone excelled at mathematics except George. He loved to write and excelled in English. He could write limericks, poetry, short stories, plays, and detailed book reports.

His freshman teacher, Miss Shorenstein, sparked his love for English that spread quickly like a grassfire. Miss S. was one of Susie's favorite high school teachers and after seeing how John and Matthew had flourished under her tutelage, Susie simply refused to accept tired or inferior teachers for her boys. When George brought home his class schedule and Susie saw Jim Purga as his algebra teacher, Susie was on the phone the next day with the high school registrar, Ms. Seligman, moving George's classes around to ensure he got Tim Kanner as his mathematics teacher.

Kanner was an ex-Vietnam medic and some claimed, a certifiable nut job, but he was also one hell of an educator and Susie loved his unconventional style. She understood that George was a right-brain kid who needed concepts, stimulus, and high-energy instruction. Purga's rote style and brimstone rigidity would drive George right into a C — a grade that was good for only two things: graduation from high school and a chance to attend Pasadena City College to try to build a college worthy transcript.

George raced home to finish his homework so he could go over to Teddy's house that night. Teddy had somehow procured the latest edition of *Oui* magazine that had naked pictures of Ursula Andress. The German actress was one of George's favorite Bond women and a fixture in his pantheon of fantasy wives. The day before, Teddy had been whispering to him about the magazine when he had heard the phone click.

"Oh, crap. Someone was listening. Dude, if it is my mom, I am so screwed. I gotta get rid of this porno magazine now."

George was quick to react, "Teddy, if you throw that mag away before I have a chance to see Ursula Andress naked, I will freakin' kill you before your mom does. I will be over tomorrow afternoon."

George walked in the back door and heard it slap against the doorjamb as he threw his heavy Schwinn book bag on the ground. Max trotted up to him and wagged his raggedy tail. Leaning over to pet the dog, George surveyed the empty kitchen. Normally, dinner would be cooking and the room would be alive with talk. He hesitated and strained to hear people talking in the other room.

"Whose is it, John?"

"I can't tell you, Mom. Just believe me, it's not mine."

"Well, what is it?"

"I told you. They're just stupid house flies."

"Then why have them in a drug baggie?"

Silence.

"You *can't* tell me whose they are or you *won't?* Do you really want your father involved? He is due home in one hour, and he's in a bad mood today."

John whipped his head up from between his knees. "You told him?"

"I most certainly did. I found something suspicious in this house and we do not allow sketchy activities. So, give me a name. Whose is it? Is it Robbie?"

"Why do you always think its Robbie?" John said angrily.

"Seth, then."

John laughed sardonically. "No. He hasn't spoken to me since that night at his house."

"What night?" Susie said, suddenly feeling as if she'd uncovered an unsolved crime.

"Nothing. We just haven't talked much since December. We sort of had a fight."

"About what?" Susie was boring in as only she could. She was the expert interrogator and this egg was about to crack.

"It's a long story. Mr. Erickson and Mrs. Erickson are having, well, problems, I guess, and I just was trying to make her feel better. Seth came in and thought that I was, like, hitting on his mom. Which I wasn't, I swear! But he got pissed and I left and it's all screwed up."

John did not want to cry, although his eyes welled with tears. Susie realized that she was interrogating the wrong man for the wrong crime.

At that point, George could not stand eavesdropping any longer and peeked around the corner. "Hey, what's going on?"

Susie's face morphed in a flash from empathy to epiphany. As she rubbed her second-oldest son's shoulder, she held up the baggie.

"George Patton, is there anything you would like to tell me about these before your father comes home?"

CHAPTER 11

PFC Raymond "Junior" Briggs had been dropped into a red-hot landing zone in Pleiku Province in the fall of 1968. He was part of Company D, First Battalion, and Seventh Squadron Air Cavalry, which had been sent to rescue an AH-1 G Cobra pilot shot down while supporting ground operations. The location was particularly tenuous because the clearing only afforded two birds to land at a time. They were facing a force of at least four companies while they could only land two squads with each sortie. Once the landing zone closed off, the guys on the ground were on their own.

Junior was the second man to hit the ground out of the helicopter and found himself pushing through dense undergrowth as he established the rescue team's blocking perimeter to the LZ's southwest. There was tremendous automatic fire coming from the area directly opposite his position. He could see that enemy mortars were now probing, slowly bracketing his position.

Sgt. D.K. Norman, Company D's redneck gunny, moved up toward Junior's location and motioned silently that there was enemy movement farther to his left. Sgt. Norman did not look or sound intelligent. He approached a firefight the way he approached everything—with angry, pig-headed determination and a face frozen in a perpetual sneer.

"Riggs, the LZ's gotten too hot. 3rd platoon is still airborne. You get your skinny ass another fifty meters over by that clearing. I want you to hold that position until Charlie is crawling up your butt looking for peanuts." He grabbed their new radioman and shoved him toward Junior.

"Gilliam, get your sorry green ass over to Briggs and call in whatever coordinates he tells you for aerial assault support."

Junior swore under his breath. "Bend over, my brother. Here it comes again."

The last thing he needed was to be saddled with a kid who had been in country less than a week. He glanced at the terrified operator and moved over to grasp his arm. "Gilliam, keep your head down and stick with me."

As Sgt. Norman hustled off in a low crouch, Junior surveyed his fields of fire. The grass was so high he couldn't see anything except the furious blue and red tracer rounds that were buzzing less than a foot above his head. "Okay, Cherry. You radio in exactly what I say, and I'll try get out of this in one piece. We got movement and heavy fire on the other side of this zone. I expect Charlie will try to overrun us sometime in the next half hour."

Almost immediately, their position was in trouble. It was hard to see anything through the pop smoke of grenades that had been set off to mark the location of the landing zone. The automatic weapons fire intensified. He had set up his blocking location fifty meters short of a clearing that would have afforded him an excellent field of fire.

"Gilliam, you stay chilly and keep that PRC close and open. Hold on to that weapon and make sure it is locked and loaded. You're the FAC on this perimeter. Whatever you call in will get blown to pieces, including us if you fuck up."

The radioman did not move and stared into the overgrown tufts of grass. Junior crawled forward and came to the edge of the LZ where he could now see the other side of a twenty-meter clearing.

Within seconds, a concealed bunker opened up on Junior's location with withering fire. He could see a dozen of the enemy moving south in an effort to flank his blocking position. "Jesus Christ!" Junior screamed as he rolled over on his back. "Cherry, call in AS for this location. Have them fire for effect on this exact spot. We're going to wait and then pull our asses back ten meters."

Gilliam frantically yelled into the horn and Junior hoped that he had gotten the coordinates correct. He was more terrified of getting wasted by his own assault support than a fixed bunker.

Slipping backwards, he grabbed Gilliam. Moments later, gunships riddled the area with thousands of rounds, churning the earth and filling the air with shredded grass. The entire sky had been torn open. When the helicopters leveled off, the radio crackled, "That should do it, Alpha. You let us know if you need another light up."

To Junior's relief, Ruiz, Alomar, and Jackson finally arrived to lay down suppressing fire. Junior directed the men as they reinforced his position. "Alamo, cover that depression to the left. The gooks are moving down there trying to cross the eastern side of the clearing. We should expect them any second."

Gilliam was now blubbering and talking to himself. Junior gripped his shoulder and looked directly into his face. "Listen, brother, there's a reason all us black and brown men are over here in this shithole trying to protect a couple of white pilots. This is where the heat is going to come from. We need you to choke down that fear and get your sorry ass on the horn with those AS ships. This is going to be a bloody fucking foxtrot where we all going to have to move together and time everything just right. You do your part and we get to go on a little I & I tomorrow. You fuck up and you'll be body bagged. Got it?"

Gilliam stopped crying and clutched his gun. Alomar screamed, "We got movement! Twenty hostiles coming from about fifteen meters."

The men opened up their weapons and the first few North Vietnamese fell. The bunker opened up in retaliation.

"Incoming!" Ruiz screamed. "They got us locked in. Two more rounds and we are fucked. We got to move."

Even though they were about to be overrun, if they abandoned their position, the left flank of the rescue LZ would collapse. But they couldn't remain where they were. Another mortar round exploded dangerously close to their right.

"Okay, Alamo, you have to lay down on that bunker. We need to cross that clearing and take their position. We can pivot left and roll up the gook squad. Smoke the clearing and follow me. Cherry is with me. Ruiz, you provide supporting fire with Alamo. Jackson, move left and set up across from Charlie. Expect covering fire in five."

The men opened up with the M60 machine gun and their M16s. Junior and his radio operator moved northwest and then darted across the clearing when a burst of automatic fire ripped Gilliam's chest, practically cutting him in half. Junior dragged him to a tuft of grass and felt his rage and adrenaline explode.

Junior emerged behind the bunker and threw three grenades inside. A large explosion hurled him several meters away as ammunition exploded through the air like skyrockets. He fell into a small depression that skirted the back of the bunker and scrambled east toward the area that he had told Alomar to expect the NVA counter assault. He could see two squads of men. The North Vietnamese silently crouched to the ground, unaware of Junior's flanking position, as a hidden machine gun sent enfilading fire across the clearing into the American's lines. Suddenly, the NVA machine gun was silent and the enemy troops began to move forward to flank the Americans. Junior pulled the pins and unleashed white phosphorus and M26 fragmentation grenades, opening up with his M-16.

Five NVA soldiers evaporated in the blasts while two others screamed having caught fire. The remaining men scattered. Junior moved forward and fired continuously, well after they had melted back into the elephant grass.

Junior yelled to Ruiz and Alomar, "Gilliam is down. Bunker secure."

Ruiz darted across the smoke filled clearing and fell next to Junior. "Riggs, you are one insane motherfucker."

Junior looked at his watch. They had held the blocking position for over an hour. He could now hear the whump-whump of a medevac as the wounded Cobra pilot was being extracted from the area near his wreckage.

At eighteen hundred hours, the enemy counterattacked again. Ruiz had retrieved the radio from Gilliam and was listening as elements of Company D were given the command to launch a counteroffensive, pushing the enemy even farther back from the landing zone. Like a phantom, Norman appeared once again, this time with four additional men—Francisco, Portrero, Griffin, and LaPorte, all black or Hispanic.

Seems like the darker your skin, the closer they wanted to get you to the shit, Junior thought.

Junior grabbed the radio and moved forward as the point of an arrow that would fan out through the grass and wheel forward. Taking point was the riskiest position, but Junior would not ask any of these men to do something that would put them at more risk than he was. As he moved forward, he could hear enemy radio chatter and movement. He decided to hold his men back and once again call in assault support directly on top of his position.

"Black Ops, Black Ops. This is Delta One. I need a couple of shadows to lay down some rockets on this position." He gave his coordinates and waited. The C114 gunships rose from behind a hill like a swarm of angry wasps. Junior scrambled back, cutting his face on the sharp grass as he ran erect toward their LZ. The earth behind him opened up in flames.

As the U.S. soldiers were retreating to the UH-1H helicopters that had now landed safely, Ruiz was hit with two rounds that shattered his pelvis and nicked an artery. Unaware of the severity of his own injuries, Ruiz turned to fire on the enemy that had now rushed into the smoke of the sterilized field.

"Get the fuck going, Junior. I got this," he screamed.

"You're coming with me, brother," Junior said, as he threw Ruiz over his shoulder, carried him to the medevac, and returned to Ruiz's position to provide fire until he was certain he was last to get on the helicopter.

Back at base, Jackson and Griffin were all marveling at Junior's heroism and courage. The men would later learn, however, that it would be Master Sergeant D.K. Norman that was recommended for a citation for gallantry under fire.

It was then that Junior became bitter about this white man's war and swore he would never again stick his neck out for someone who didn't care whether he lived or died.

The transistor radio was playing the Temptations as Junior got up from behind his cash register to answer the double ping that meant a customer at the pump. Looking out the window, he saw it was the same cherry Deville that he had seen in the alleyway a week or so ago. He came over the window and glanced in. The face was familiar. It took a few seconds, but then Junior remembered.

"Say, I know you, man. You played for the goddamn Rancheros. Man, you was one hell of a middle linebacker. I expected to see your crazy ass in the NFL."

Ronnie seemed uncomfortable being recognized, like a celebrity trying to remain incognito. "Shit happens, man. Ronnie Thomas," he said, reaching for Junior's hand for a soul handshake. "Did a tour. Things got kind a fucked up ..."

"Say no more, brother. Corporal J.R. Riggs, Garry Owen, Seventh First. Most of you rich, white people just call me Junior."

Ronnie smiled and felt as if someone had turned the air conditioning on in a hot room.

"Sheee-it, son. You Air Cav boys were a bunch of teat-sucking, mama-sans. Second Marines! Keep moving! The tip of every mission's fucking bayonet." He held out his Semper Fi tattoo proudly, turning his arm out as if he was about to give blood.

Junior saw the Hue tattoo. "Damn, boy. You ran into some serious shit."

Ronnie's face darkened and he looked through the windshield. "Just got to keep moving and drive on, man."

Junior turned to the pump and was silent until the tank was topped off. "Got that right. Keep moving, man," he said to Ronnie. "Just drive the fuck on."

George had been grounded for over several weeks for his part in the Spanish Flies episode. Susie had secretly laughed but aggressively lectured her sons on the reprehensible act of intentionally doping one's date.

Matthew was coming home from college this weekend and George had overheard that Susie and Karl were going out Saturday evening for dinner. They would not be home before midnight, which left him plenty of time to host an impromptu pony kegger with several girls and a few of his buddies.

George had put Teddy in charge of getting the pony keg. Teddy was a master at procuring alcohol from any of a dozen Asian-owned liquor stores throughout the San Gabriel Valley. Like a veteran check-kiter, Teddy never frequented the same establishment.

The transactions were always the same. Teddy would dress up in his church clothes as if he was coming home from a business meeting. For whatever reason, the absence of facial hair and obvious youth seemed lost on many Korean and Chinese liquor storeowners. It could have been that they found it hard to discern a kid's proper age. Matthew's theory was that in a tough economy, most liquor stores were so focused on staying in business that they were willing to look the other way and risk selling to an underage kid.

Teddy normally approached a store several times, testing each clerk for weaknesses and blind spots. Today, he tried a new store, Lantern Liquors in nearby San Gabriel. As he placed his customary six-pack of malt liquor on the counter, an older Asian woman of indecipherable age peered at him from behind reading glasses.

"You twenty-one?" she asked, peering into Teddy's sixteen-year-old eyes.

Teddy sighed abruptly and looked offended. He reached for a wallet that held no ID. He had read that Asian cultures cared very much about face. If he looked as though she had insulted him, he might be able to pull it off.

"No, no. It okay," the ancient woman said, hurriedly putting the alcohol into the bag and bowing obsequiously. "You young. Very, very good to be young." She smiled a crooked smile as Teddy offered her an officious nod. As he indignantly marched to his car, he made a mental note, "Lantern Liquors, older woman, four p.m. No problems."

Kitty called Susie, ostensibly to debrief on her lunch with the troika, but instead found herself pouring her problems through the phone. "I know he is having an affair. I met with Cliff today and he gave me all the information I would need to begin filing for a separation and, if necessary, divorce.

"I'm afraid my Cinderella story of sorority girl meets Prince Charming and lives happily ever after in Camelot has become a Tennessee Williams tragedy," she said, giving into tears. "I get to play the wasted spouse who cannot keep her hot-blooded husband at home. And then to crown my aging tigress misery, I am offered a consolation prize of affections from an adolescent ..." Kitty abruptly stopped herself. She had not wanted to say anything about the incident with John.

"Kitty, why didn't you tell me about John?"

"Darlin', we Southerners defend the reputation of any man if his intentions are honorable. Your young lothario made my year, but I believe he understands now that he was aiming his arrow in the wrong direction."

"How's Seth?"

"That poor boy. He is a confusion of hormones, anxiety, and anger. In many ways, he is the proverbial acorn that has not fallen far from his father's oak. I'm afraid it may take him longer to forgive his father and mother than his best friend."

Susie leaned back in her chair and scratched Max's head as he stretched out next to her.

"John is a sensitive child," Susie said. "He's different from my other three. He has a remarkable ability to conform and adapt. He is a chameleon, but inside I think he is still a million little pieces trying to form his own man. These are such hard ages for boys."

"Darling, for a woman, forty-five is not exactly a walk down Bourbon Street. I find parts of my body moving and shifting every day. I look at the bulge on my tummy and say, 'Weren't you on my thigh yesterday?'"

Susie laughed out loud and saw Freddie look up from his homework. She lowered her voice and became serious. "Who do you think Garrett is seeing?"

"If I had more courage, I'd find out the identity of this home-wrecker. It could be one of the hundreds of eager young females he hires as models, account executives, or assistants. Deep down, I can't really blame the girl. He is a hammer forever looking for nails. I know my foundations were rotted long before Garrett chose to burn down our home. It's sad; because I still love him and I was brought up to dutifully suffer like all Southern women."

"Dear, as my loving prehistoric husband would say: bullshit!" Susie was surprised she had said the word out loud and then covered the phone and spoke in a hushed tone. "That creep has violated the sanctity of your family, and for that he has to pay the piper."

"Well, he will start by paying my attorney's fees because they are going to be very expensive."

Susie smiled, "Trust me. Cliff Blakeslee is the best. You will have all the financial support you need to begin a new life with the kids. You just have to take it one step at a time and not get overwhelmed when the shit starts hitting the fan." She laughed out loud again. "My god, I *am* starting to sound like Karl."

Karl swore as he felt his golf shoe skid out from underneath him. He opened his trunk, removed his ancient golf clubs and walked into the Los Angeles Country Club. It was annoying enough to have to take an afternoon off from work, but to end up on the west side of L.A. on a Friday night meant a two-hour commute back to Huntington Hills. He looked around to be certain no one had seen him almost break his leg.

He was a twenty-five-plus handicap and loathed the idea of spending five hours wandering in high weeds and trees looking for a dimpled white ball. Worse yet, he would have to endure R2 in his green grass element – the proud, fat manatee with his counterfeit modesty and his three-hundred-yard drives. Karl could only assume that the other two players were cut from the same soiled fabric as Hunt.

The course was immaculate, and the weather was a glorious seventy degrees with a slight wind coming off the ocean just five miles to the west.

"Karl! Over here." R2 waved as he rapped a ten-foot putt that curled three feet to the right before stopping on the lip of the hole and falling in. "Bingo. So, you have trouble finding the place? It is a dangerous distance from the cocoon of The Hills. I used to come down here a lot in college. The girls at UCLA were smarter. We always said 'SC to bed and UCLA to wed.'"

He punched Karl in the side and caught him flush before Karl could tighten his abdominal muscles, knocking the wind right out of him. R2 turned his flabby back, which was already showing layered lines of sweat, and picked up three balls with the end of his putter. He flicked his wrist and the putter, flipping the balls up and into his hand, one by one.

"Holy shit! Where'd you get those relics?" Hunt chuckled as he moved over to examine Karl's ancient Patty Berg undersized woods and irons. R2 leaned in and Karl could smell the alcohol.

"Did anyone tell you that you are playing with women's sticks? I mean, wow! Those clubs are vintage Babe Zaharias!"

"It's all that was left in the garage after the terrorists got through losing my clubs at Arroyo Seco and Eaton Canyon," Karl said.

"José!" R2 yelled at one of the men near the golf carts. "Get Mr. Patton my dad's clubs and bring them both over to ten. We'll go off the back nine. You'll be carrying my bag and Mr. Patton's."

"Yes, Mr. Hunt, sir." The elderly Hispanic caddie moved quickly to grab Karl's bag from his shoulder so he could store it

Karl turned and reached out his hand. "Karl," he said.

The caddie smiled and a shadow of empathy fell across his face. He grabbed Karl's hand with a confident grip. "José. Good to meet you, Mr. Karl."

Hunt yelled as he turned his back to the two men. "José, tell Bobby we're off as a twosome around one o'clock. My two other guests are going to join us later for drinks but cannot make it this afternoon."

R2 slapped Karl's shoulder again and leaned into him, nodding toward José. "Best goddamn Mexican caddie north of the Rio Grande. He can read these greens better than a Chinaman can iron shirts. Not sure he can read a book, though!" R2 laughed at his own joke, not waiting for Karl to reply.

Lunch was a bloody steak and three-cocktail affair, with R2 desperately trying to get Karl to drink another Bloody Mary. Karl waited for the questions regarding the parade and insurance, but R2 seemed to be dodging both, spending spent most of the lunch trying to further ingratiate himself with stories of a recent trip with some fraternity buddies to Cabo, a tiny fishing village in Baja, California.

After only one drink, Karl felt himself warming to his lunch companion and at the same time loathing his excess. He clearly had no moral compass and seemed to measure his life by what he had done the previous week. How could one generation veer so far afield the other? The old man was one of the smartest, classiest guys Karl had ever met.

By the time they teed off, Karl was feeling tipsy and wanted to lie down by the pool. R2 had consumed two beers and three cocktails with no effect. He talked the entire time he addressed his ball on the tee. Turning effortlessly, he hit a low line drive that rose down the right side of the fairway, gently drawing to the left, landing and rolling about 90 yards off the green in a first cut of very light rough. Off in the distance, Karl could see José making the sign of safe like an umpire.

"Position A. Jesus, it kills me when that old Mexican makes that 'safe' sign. I love that guy."

Karl put the ball on the tee and it promptly fell off. He grumbled and leaned over to balance the ball, which had a small scratch and dirt marks on its side.

"You need a few balls?" R2 chuckled.

"I lost 'em when I got married." Karl joked.

Hunt grunted a bottomless guttural chuckle as Karl took two practice swings that left deep gashes in the pristine tee box.

"It's been a while," he said as he brought the club head to the ball as if it were a baseball. The swing was not bad. However, his stance had been purposely aimed left as if he had expected to hit a looping slice. Instead, the club head came across the tee striking the ball dead left. It ricocheted off a parked golf cart and caromed into a group of caddies preparing two carts of women golfers.

"Oh, shit!" bellowed R2. "Fore!"

The caddies dove in different directions and the women glared at Karl and R2. Karl held a new ball up and nodded toward the women.

"I'll just drop out near you. We can put some distance between ourselves and the ladies."

The round was excruciating for Karl. He had lost seven balls before the turn and had a pounding headache from the sun, R2's incessant banter, and the waning effects of his liquid lunch.

On the turn at the first tee, he whiffed two consecutive drive attempts and got so angry that he picked up the ball and threw it 150 yards into the fairway.

"Best shot of the day," R2 said, as he walked by him. Ahead of them, Karl could see that José was slowly indicating that his thrown drive was indeed, "safe."

"So, we can see that golf is not your game. How are you as a broker?" R2 was suddenly serious and had seemingly transformed from a good-time Charlie to a bloodshot drunk pointing a broken bottle. "Dad says that we should move our business to your firm. I wanted to know what we could expect from you *personally.*"

Karl did not pick up on R2's implication and began to share how he would personally oversee the review of all the policies and a shift toward self-insuring more risk, which would reduce costs.

"Cut the crap, Karl. You want our business and you know what I want. We can help each other out. Dad is turning things over to me, and one of the first things I want to do is be sure the markets benefit from every relationship we maintain our distributors, media, and vendors. This is the age of the quid pro quo and any well-run business benefits from every relationship."

"The business benefits or you benefit?" Karl asked, with an edge to his voice.

R2 smiled. "It's the same thing. I *am* the business." He turned his back and putted across thirty feet of carpeted green, not even waiting for Jose to pull the pin. The ball angled to the right and then worked its way left across a difficult double break, ramming into the back of the cup just as José lifted the pin.

"Incredible, Mr. Hunt. I have never seen anyone make that putt from that distance on this green. Incredible."

R2 turned to Karl. "Your son does a good job at the store. From what I hear, John is an A student. It would be a tragedy to see him labeled a druggie and maybe ruin his chances for college. Seems like a good kid. I'm not saying I have seen it myself. But I overheard him trying to sell drugs to one of the box boys the other day. Now I myself strayed as a young man in high school and college, so I make no judgments. But not everyone is as understanding as I am. Certainly not my old-school father."

Karl watched as R2 walked to the next tee box and hit a perfect three wood onto the green of a short par four. Karl did not say a word but took the club that was handed to him by Jose. He was seething as he turned and struck the ball on the screws of the club. It lifted in the air and lingered above the green before dropping down like an egg from a nest within a foot of the cup.

R2 walked past him and slapped him hard on the back. "Nice shot. If you'd sunk that, you'd be buying drinks for the clubhouse. See what happens when you set your mind to things, Karl? You get exactly what you want."

Teddy walked into Lantern Liquors at four o'clock on Friday afternoon. The elderly woman he had met on his previous visit was there, but a teenage girl now accompanied her.

The older woman said something in Chinese to what was most likely her granddaughter and smiled. The girl looked at Teddy and offered a knowing smirk.

"My grandmother says you are her number-one customer. She also says you are much older than you look. I don't suppose you brought your ID with you today for these two pony kegs?"

Teddy was about to have a heart attack. It was too late to procure alcohol at any of his other stores, several of which had recently thrown him a curve with newly hired Caucasian clerks who would card an octogenarian.

He padded the back of his jeans and looked disappointed. "Oh, shoot. I only brought cash. Is that going to be a problem?"

The older woman watched as the two of them spoke and tried unsuccessfully to follow their conversation, nodding her head and smiling.

The girl hesitated, spoke to her grandmother in Chinese and then grinned at Teddy. "No, you're in luck. But give me the address of the party. I might want to stop by with some of my friends and test the beer. We need to make sure it isn't flat."

Teddy could not suppress an answering smile. "Sure, bring as many of your girlfriends as you like, especially if they look like you."

"You Hills boys think all Asian girls look alike, don't you?"

Teddy was now on his heels, uncertain how to respond.

The girl smiled. "I'm just messing with you. We'll be there."

Teddy handed her George's address and carried the two pony kegs out to his car. He put the tubs in the front seat and piled the ice high in the back. He would store the beer overnight on ice in the DeSantis back garden and then run them through the hole in the ivy fence to the Motter's yard, and then lower them into George's back yard in the late afternoon.

"Check to see if the beer is flat." Teddy said out loud as he laughed. "She sure wasn't flat." After a three-year drought between girlfriends, things were finally looking up for Teddy.

Matthew pulled on to Bedford Street, observing the immaculate gardens and impeccable lawns. He slowed his roommate's borrowed Toyota truck and eased parallel to the curb. He looked out across his own family's lawn where two eroded circles of broken grass and dirt marked a makeshift pitcher's mound and home plate. The sturdy St. Augustine grass was patchy and sunburned where over-the-line, wiffle ball and football games had conspired to turn Karl Patton's lawn into hardpan.

Matthew had come home for a mini-break and to talk through his plans for the summer with his parents. He had already contacted his great-uncle and had two promising leads on construction jobs in Marin and the East Bay. He had agreed with Susie that he would take some time off for their annual trip, which this year was a change of plans from their rental beach house in Balboa. This time, the family would drive up to the Bay area to see Susie's family. Matthew was concerned that his father would not ratify their midsummer plans since it involved driving more than two hours and included seeing the crazy Irish. Yet he also knew that his mother could sell his dad on anything.

He had decided on his drive home from Cal that he was not going to share his college transcripts with his parents anymore. He did not like the arbitrary judgments of his work by academics or amateurs who had studied the real world but never really worked within it. On this point, he and his father wholeheartedly agreed. However, Matthew also considered his father among the legions of pea-brained, humorless dinosaurs who made life so hard on the next generation.

When he had learned that his parents would be out Saturday evening, Matthew purposely waited until the weekend to arrive home. He would be in town several days and then back to school. His dad had invited him to a Cubs game at Dodger stadium, and that would be plenty of time together with the old man.

His father was always in a good mood when he could see his beloved Cubs play the Dodgers. Karl was a rabid Chicago fan, having grown up in the shadows of Wrigley Field and watched the Bears at Soldier Field. The Cubs were not expected to be good this year, so it might be an excruciating ride home. It was always painful driving with Karl, as the location of all L.A. sporting events required his Granada to travel through some very tough neighborhoods.

Walking through the front door, Matthew carried his dirty washing to the back porch. He could hear a hair dryer upstairs indicating preparations for an evening out.

"Anyone home?"

He heard Susie's voice from upstairs. "It's about time you got home! Dinner's in the oven. Sloppy Joes. Only take two. The others still need to eat. George is in his room and John is listening to headphones and won't hear you. We'll be back around midnight! Welcome home, honey."

Matthew could smell her perfume, always the first sign that his parents were entertaining for the evening. The scent still flooded him with memories of being a kid. The only time he smelled a French fragrance was when his mother was going out with his father. It was strange that Chanel reminded him of people leaving.

He looked around and felt his muscles relax after the long drive. It was nice to come home, even to this crappy old house. Max jumped through the dog door and raced over to brush against his knee. Matthew crouched down and roughed up the dog, who responded with weak bites and playful growls. "Hey, Maxie. How you doing, boy? Avoiding Ku Klux Karl these days?"

Matthew caught a glimpse of someone moving through the back yard. From the breakfast room window, he could see George and Teddy Galloway stumbling across the lawn carrying what looked like a small beer keg. They dropped it into the dark ivy under a crown of camellia bushes and then turned to disappear again behind the garage.

He sauntered outside and over to the back garden trash area. "What are you fuck-ups doing?" he asked.

George jumped and let go of a metal washtub full of ice, which spilled into the dirt. "Shit, you scared the crap out of me! Where did you come from? Are Mom and Dad still upstairs?" Matthew nodded at George but did not say anything. Teddy gave Matthew a big grin and moved his head forward and backward like a chicken. "We're having a little fiesta tonight with some mujeres calientes and you're invited."

Garrett had been calling Diane on and off since Tuesday. She had not answered her door when he knocked. The one time someone did answer the phone, it was her son, the psychotic baby-killing zombie who said he had no idea where she was and hung up the phone.

He had made up his mind that he was actually going to leave Kitty, but he wasn't sure he wanted to be with Diane. She was a sort of transition fling at first, but her neediness and lust for attention had infected him. He found himself wanting her and then hating both himself and her after they would meet to have sex. Garrett had been cheating on Kitty for most of their marriage, but it had never occurred to him that the day would come when he would finally leave her.

After college, he had spent a month in Rome and taken to the Italian way of life. Most Italian men viewed infidelity as a physical thing that bore no relationship to the integrity of one's marriage. It was natural that a man would want to be with other women, particularly younger women. "Capri is an island for lovers," an older Italian had shared one night in the Piazza del Popolo. "It is where a man takes his girlfriend, not his wife."

The table of men had laughed and raised their glasses, while the young art student from California soaked up every ounce of Italian culture and chauvinism. The old man went on to explain, "The mother of your children is a Madonna to be worshipped. A girlfriend is an island that must be explored. Your football team requires your loyalty. The mafia is to be respected, and your church gets your soul. Government? Well, our politicians are like weevils and must be picked out of our daily bread or ignored."

Most of Garrett's affairs had been cheap, vacant liaisons with anonymous women he met at airport bars and on commercial shoots. He had once contracted a venereal disease in Thailand and was relieved to learn that he had not passed it on to Kitty before having it treated.

There had been a few close calls, especially the secretary who had threatened to commit suicide. Dean Jackson, his partner, had done him a good turn by firing "Miss I'm-Going-To-Kill-Myself" for the egregious offense of lying about taking a sick day. She had been lying. She had been with Garrett Erickson in Santa Barbara.

In the 1960's and early 70's, Garrett had been an anti-war activist and McGovern supporter. He was devastated when Nixon maintained the Whitehouse in '72. He savored every corrupt second of the Watergate affair and felt the thrill of vengeance as he watched the façade of the Grand Old Party burn to the ground. He hated the conservatives. He had grown up a Marine brat who did not see his father for years at a time. He loathed the brutality of the armed forces and the raw and uneducated people conscripted and used in the name of duty, honor, and country. It was all bullshit.

Old men made wars, young men fought them, and their families suffered all the traditional casualties of war. The ethos of U.S. imperialism was out of control, leading the country into Vietnam and creating a generation of shattered kids. Now it was all coming out: the secrets and the lies propagated by a corrupt government selling the American people on the need to assassinate citizens of other nations in the name of democracy. Ho Chi Minh had been a goddamn ally of the United States in the Second World War, helping fight the Japs before we betrayed him and handed Indochina back to the French and their colonial rubber interests. The cheese-eaters promptly lost at Dien Bien Phu, and the bastard Johnson upped the ante and escalated the war.

Garrett's mother had faithfully accommodated each move to every godforsaken backwater base in the country. Marine Master Sergeant Lou Erickson had finally found his niche as a demolitions instructor in Camp Pendleton, near Oceanside, California, in the forties following World War II. Garrett had been fourteen years old. The move from South Carolina to California had been easy in one sense, but difficult on a high school freshman who did not play sports. He subsequently fell in with some of the wilder kids and delinquents that lived on the fringes of Norman Rockwell's white-picket world. His brushes with authority led to monumental knockdown fights with his father when he was home, followed by his mother always pleading with him to stay and complete high school in Oceanside.

He kept his word and graduated and then left. Garrett worked his way through two jobs and a series of junior college classes finding he had a flair for art and film. Transferring to the University of California at Davis, he graduated with a degree in marketing. After moving to L.A., he got a job with a small agency as an art director and quickly used his bad-boy image to attract edgier clients willing to risk brand safety for creative awards and recognition. Most clients did not realize that Clios and other creative awards benefited the agency and the art director much more than they helped push product.

Garrett could sell a cup of sand to a dying man in the desert, and he always seemed to get what he wanted. He had won over the sleek Southern model who would later become his wife, but in the transaction, he had traded his days and nights of decadence for endless afternoons of Little League and Fourth of July picnics.

This was his chance to get away. Kitty was realistic and he was sure she knew at some level that it was over. The kids would be fine. They had a chance to escape the fucked-up childhood that had backed up on him like sewage from his parents' dysfunctional living arrangement.

He really did not love anything, least of all himself. The people in his life could make him feel content or amused. But he did not feel joy, the way he felt riding a hundred miles per hour on his motorcycle or when he made some outrageous statement to a client in an effort to shock him into buying into Garrett's post-modernist view of the world. Diane was the first tremor of emotion he had felt in years. He was not sure whether he loved her or he just loved how she made him feel. For now, it didn't matter.

He was moving back to West Los Angeles to what he hoped would be a life that held more future than past. Yet, Garrett knew he was not good at being alone. Diane had become his mother and his lover. Like most fallen women, she made few demands. They could find a small place in Venice Beach and forget. He realized he needed her and assumed it would be easy to convince her that there was nothing left in Huntington Hills for either of them but heartache.

La Escadrille was tucked under evergreen awnings between two high-rise office buildings. The walls featured the faded patina of an al fresco café one might discover while touring some ancient Provençal village.

The maître d' recognized Rebecca immediately and kissed each of her cheeks as he shook Will's hand with delight.

"Bonsoir. So good to see you both. I 'ave your table set, and a magnificent white truffle foie gras saved for the four of you this evening."

"Thank you, Maurice. These are my colleagues Monsieur and Madame Patton." Rebecca said.

The maître d' darted a hand toward Karl. "My pleasure, Monsieur and Madame. Welcome to La Espadrille."

Karl leered at the French waiter. He had distain for the Gaelic culture, their geopolitical duplicity and their intellectual arrogance. General George S Patton had made the famous remark that he would rather have a German division in front of him than a French division behind him. Karl was about to make a remark about Indochina but was cut off by Susie.

"Thank you for your kindness. We understand your cuisine is delicious."

Karl smiled at Susie's impeccable timing and beauty as he glanced over to Rebecca. He had to admit she also looked striking. Losing her customary business suit, Rebecca wore a silk cocktail dress that accentuated her figure and made her look years younger. With her hair down and spilling over her shoulders, she looked less like Madame Defarge and more like Catherine Deneuve.

Susie leaned into Karl and whispered, "Lesbian? You ought to be ashamed of yourself."

The dinner was delightful and it seemed as though they had the entire restaurant to themselves. When patrons came in, they were ushered to the inside tables. From Susie's vantage point, it appeared that anyone who inquired about eating outside was told that it was reserved for a private party. Very private, since they were the only group seated in the patio area.

She's good, Susie thought, admiring Rebecca, but at the same time wary of the woman's understanding of what Karl had at stake.

Susie leaned back in her chair and moaned, "I cannot eat until next Thursday. That was the most sinful meal I have had in months."

Karl raised his glass to Rebecca, "I offer an Irish blessing from one of my wife's derelict relatives. 'May the roof over our heads never fall in and may those underneath it never fall out.'"

"Hear, hear," chimed in Will, who was clearly tipsy but having a good time discussing the economy with Karl.

Rebecca sipped the wine and watched Susie, who turned to catch Rebecca's glance. "So Rebecca," Susie said, "Tell me all about yourself and don't leave anything out. Karl has such a poor power of recall, I hardly know a thing about you."

Karl heard his wife begin to probe Rebecca's defenses as Will Crane discussed William Deming's post-war reconstruction of Japan and the rising tide of the Asian global ambitions. He looked intently at Will as he allowed himself to loosen up. Inspector Susie was now in the house.

Ladies and gentlemen, I give you sodium pentothal. She is painless and undetectable. You will wake up feeling fine but you will have spilled your guts and betrayed your deepest and darkest secrets.

He relaxed. Let the games begin.

CHAPTER 12

*Like other parties of the kind, it was first silent, then talky,
then argumentative, then disputatious, then unintelligible,
then altogether, then inarticulate, and then drunk. When
we had reached the last step of this glorious ladder, it was
difficult to get down again without stumbling.*

~George Gordon, Lord Byron

The doorbell rang and several freshman girls in tight pastel halter-tops and blue jeans crowded the doorstep.

"Hey, George," Denise Taylor and Lori Hoover cooed. "Thanks for hosting tonight. What's with the balloons and the signs?"

George glanced at the placard on the door that read *Happy 70th, George and Grandpa.*

"Yeah, we put up all kinds of balloons and crap to make the police think that all the cars in front of the house are from people coming to a family birthday celebration. The cops are much less likely to crash the bash if they think the noise is coming for somebody's party for their kid and their Grandpa."

The girls laughed and Denise pinched his cheek. "You are a crafty boy, George. I keep forgetting that!"

Blushing, George motioned toward the patio like a doorman directing royalty to the VIP section of an exclusive club.

"My evening is now complete. You girls are the first to arrive, which means you must christen the keg in the back. Teddy and Plums are setting up on the patio."

He allowed his eyes to travel down the line of appealing girls. This was the inner circle of his peer group—the "babes" as he and his hard-up friends referred to them. Sally Baines suddenly appeared and floated through the entrance on a scent of flowers, just as she had in his dreams—although tonight she was fully clothed.

"Hey Sally," George said in as nonchalant a voice as he could muster. Inside, his heart was doing handsprings and he was biting his lip hard. The blonde was a lioness of wild hair and curves.

"Hey, George," she said, offering a crumb of a perfunctory smile while glancing over his shoulder to see who else had arrived.

"Right this way." As he turned to close the door, a work boot the size of an anvil blocked the door. "Not so fast, Georgie."

Ray Hulick, Steve King and Tim Rose—three gigantic jocks—filled his doorway. "Johnny said you were having a gig tonight, and we thought we'd offer a little security."

"Oh, sure," George said, wanting to kill his brother for mentioning the kegger to some of the box boys who worked at the market. Hulick was an all-state wrestling champ, while King was a pitcher on the baseball team. The boys were all athletic wunderkind playing varsity sports as sophomores.

"Georgie, porgy, puddin' and pie," grinned Rose. "How's it hanging?" He flicked George in the crotch with his enormous frankfurter index finger and caught him flush in the fruit bowl. There was a millisecond delay before the sickening feeling rolled up into George's groin and gripped his stomach. He leaned on his knees as the upper classmen chuckled.

"Aren't you guys due back at the California Youth Authority? Try not to eat the dog's food out of his bowl, and be nice to the girls. No touching …"

The three behemoths smirked and moved single file through the door, across the dining room, and out to the patio. Guys like this scared George because their size invited confrontation and had a way of disrupting a mellow party. They seemed to find trouble the way a gun fighter might attract unwanted attention by his reputation or nickel-plated six-shooter. Certain jocks seemed to exude the challenge: "Can anyone here take me?"

Fifteen minutes later, a clutch of upper classmen and recent grads –Tim Irwin, Frank Howes, Phil Moore, Dave Winslow, and the Lewis brothers – all lumbered into the back yard from the driveway. Max barked cheerfully announcing that the older boys, most on spring break or attending Pasadena City College, had arrived. George could not believe that Irwin would have the guts to come to his house after their encounter at New Years.

"Hey, worm," Frank said disdainfully to Teddy. "Where's Matt? He said for us to stop in tonight, but I don't see him." Irwin turned and smiled at Kelly Reed, who had wandered into the back yard without George seeing her.

"Hey, girl. I bet you thought you got rid of me?"

"I told you, Tim. Just friends."

The other seniors snickered and Irwin's face turned cold. "I figured you were too young."

Kelly looked bored and grabbed a plastic cup. "Wow, what a brutal comeback. That's right. I'm just too juvenile. Damn, I forgot to bring my Raggedy Ann doll with me tonight. Curfew's nine o'clock, so I better have my half a beer now, throw up and go home. Excuse me."

George laughed out loud as he realized that Kelly had finally had the courage to confront Tim. George was eager to make up for his year-end fiascos and had spent several weeks orbiting her at school and at parties, signaling that he had matured in the last few months.

"What's so funny wise ass?" Irwin barked at George.

Moore and Winslow grabbed the irritated hulk. "Easy, Tiny Tim. We just got here and we don't want to piss off our hosts. At least not until we drink their alcohol."

George was frozen in place as the two seniors steered Irwin toward the plastic cups. Irwin never took his eyes off George.

"Allow me," Kelly said, handing him a beer cup and smiling. "That wasn't very smart."

"I don't know what that dick is doing here. However, you're clearly worth the risk. I've sort of been hoping for a second chance."

"Gee, I hadn't noticed. Well, I'm here, aren't I?" Kelly laughed and moved into a charm of girls that had gathered near the outdoor fireplace.

George turned to see three more people he did not know come through the back gate. He was starting to get worried. It was almost nine p.m. and all the wrong people were showing up. He moved quickly inside to his father's office and brushed aside the curtains, peering out into the front yard at the row of vehicles parked from his house down the street. Additional cars were inching past the house, with kids craning their necks to see if they could make out a friend's Ford or Chevy or recognize a face to justify crashing what had turned out to be the only party in town.

George heard an explosive cheer and sprinted back through the house to find a large group engaged in a drinking game. Each contender was required to down a beer and place the empty cup on his head before consuming the next beer. The winner was the first to guzzle four beers.

In his first drinking competition ever, Teddy showed remarkable stamina and stayed within striking distance of his college freshman opponent, Phil Moore. On the second beer, Teddy hit a snag and instead of swallowing the amber liquid and lifting up an empty glass, he poured half of the beer on his head and began to drink his third, which squirted out his nose. As beer spewed out Teddy's nostrils, Moore triumphantly howled, spitting beer on two girls who screamed and retreated back as the crowd. Teddy managed to finish his beer but was now clearly trying to induce a belch to create more room for the final glass.

Moore and Teddy reached for their final beers at the exact moment. The restless throng of teens broke into frantic chanting, "Drink, drink, drink!"

"No! Oh, my God, Susie, you are too funny!" Rebecca Gerson shouted and laughed as she laid her hand on Susie's arm.

Karl glanced over and saw Susie speaking in low conspiratorial tones to Rebecca, who was captivated and consuming every word Susie was confiding. Rebecca's eyes dilated at certain parts of the story and at one point, she looked shocked and glanced over at Karl exclaiming, "No, he did not! He did not say that, did he!?"

Great, Karl thought. *They are goddamn ganging up on me.* He tried to lean in and hear what the women were discussing, but Will had just asked him a question regarding insurance. He had realized an hour earlier that Rebecca did not handle Will's risk management business, part of the decision they agreed to early in their relationship to keep business and personal lives separate. Karl was not part of this neutrality pact and waded in, telling Will how he could have contingent liability exposure because he chose to do business with a single Asian distributor. If the sole supplier temporarily went out of business as a result of a loss, Will's business could suffer business interruption but have no coverage. Will took out a notebook and wrote something down.

Screw it, Karl thought. *Let the women dog pile on me. I'm going to sell some insurance.*

John had just backed the Impala out of the garage and left it at the edge of the driveway to block cars from parking on their front lawn. Glancing out to the street, he saw three girls fall out of the passenger side of a new Oldsmobile Cutlass. The driver's door opened to reveal Sam Noonan, one of George's friends. John was pretty certain the boy was still driving on a learner's permit.

A BMW was moving up the street as Noonan sat in the passenger's side of the car rummaging through the glove compartment. The BMW was moving slow but did not seem to take note of the car's interior lights and in a sudden twist of metal, carried on right through the Cutlass's door, ripping it off with one clean pop.

John ran over to see if Sam was all right. He had disappeared and John was terrified that he was wedged under the BMW. The girls screamed, as they brought their hands up to their mouths. Suddenly, Noonan leaped theatrically out of the passenger side the car, unscathed, and raised his hands. The girls screamed with joy and relief, running over to hug him.

John was still shaking his head when he saw Scotty Eldred stagger out of a new BMW whose front resembled an accordion. A brown and tan driver's side door lay mangled on the ground next to the Cutlass.

"Dude, what did you do? I ought to kick your ass!" Eldred yelled at the younger boy. Sam Noonan appeared to have not been drinking, but Eldred was clearly stoned.

John knew that Scotty's father, Herb Eldred, was a high-powered attorney at some big firm in downtown L.A. The Eldred family lived up in the Hills on Arden Rd.

"Oh, shit. That's trouble," John muttered.

Sergeant Vince Nobalski had been working for Huntington Hills Police Department for ten years. Vin had moved to the San Gabriel valley in 1967 from a shift in Central Los Angeles. There was lots of action in L.A., but it was getting too dangerous for an officer with a young family to work in that community. Huntington Hills Police Chief Norm Pinsky had decided to put state funds to work for more community based drug enforcement and had invited Vin to start a task force. Vin jumped at the opportunity. He went from murders and drug deals to cats in trees, domestic disputes, and the occasional driver who had tipped a few too martinis at the country club and needed an escort home.

The call had come in from two different neighbors on Bedford Street complaining of noise and traffic congestion from a party. Vin dispatched officers Walsh and Maddox to check out the disturbance. He assumed it was teens having a party while Mom and Dad were out. Just then, a third call came in notifying him of a traffic accident on Bedford Street.

Vin took a drag from his cigarette and exhaled across the lamp light of his desk. It was going to be an interesting night after all.

The policemen arrived and were now taking information from both Scotty and Sam. They seemed intrigued by the smell coming from Scotty's car. Officer Bobby Maddox shined a light into the Sam's eyes and then into Eldred's pupils.

"What exactly are you guys doing at the birthday party for a 70-year-old man?" Maddox asked. Both kids stared at the officer with blank faces. He pointed the light back at Eldred. "You been doing anything you shouldn't, son?"

"That's entrapment, isn't it, Officer?..." Eldred peered at the cop's nametag, "...Maddox? My father is an attorney and has advised me that I do not need to speak to the police unless an attorney is present."

Walsh overheard and sauntered over to confront the tall, dark-eyed Eldred. "Just calm down son, this isn't an episode of Perry Mason. You are correct that you do not have to answer. But understand, we *can* arrest you for suspicion of being under the influence and refusing to cooperate with an accident investigation. We need to know how this happened."

Eldred pointed at the freshman. "Well, freshman dipshit over here opened his door without checking to see if a car was coming."

John shook his head and walked up to the officers. "I watched the whole thing, officers. His BMW never slowed down. The Cutlass' door had been wide-open for a few seconds when it was hit."

Eldred mocked John. "A few seconds? Dude, really? How would you know? Do you have like a stop watch?"

Maddox moved in and tried to defuse the situation.

"Whose house is this?" Walsh asked.

"Mine," said John. "I'm John Patton, sir. We were having a party for my grandfather and we asked a few friends over, and then a lot of people we did *not* invite ..." he looked pointedly at Eldred, "... started showing up and it got kind of crazy. We could actually use your help, Officer Walsh, just getting people to go home." He pointed again at Eldred. "The first guy we would like to leave is Mr. Magoo here."

Eldred was defiant. "Your grandfather? That's funnier than shit. Fine with me. Officer, my dad is an attorney and ..."

Walsh cut him off. "We heard that, son. Let's just get the information and start moving everyone on home." Walsh walked over to interview the girls and Noonan, who was now seated on the curb with his head in his hands.

A devastated Noonan looked up at the officer. "Can you have someone call my mom?"

Teddy got a jumpstart on his beer as Moore lifted his cup to the shrill cries of encouragement from his friends. Teddy was now under the delusion he could drink faster than the older boy and win. However, trapped gas from his previous gulps had now swelled into an esophageal balloon and as he quaffed his first mouthful of Coors, he felt beer surging up his throat. There was simply no room left in his stomach.

A torrent of beer heaved up out of Teddy's mouth and across the table splashing several of the spectators who screamed and fell back. Directly across from Teddy, Moore had just raised his glass and placed it on his head when he witnessed the explosion. He leaped to one side and grabbed Stewart Campbell, a tall freshman, swinging him around as a human shield. Campbell took the tidal wave of beer and backwash head-on, while Moore remained clean and dry—and smiling crookedly.

Matthew Patton sat in a patio chair and belched. He stood up and clinked the mouth of Judd Quinn's Coors beer with his own beer bottle and laughed as foamed exploded up and out of the bottle's head.

"You dick!" Quinn laughed as he stood up to escape the volcano of beer.

"Uh oh…" Matthew remarked as he turned to see the blue lights of police cars reflecting off the sides of the Gilmores' house next door. "Oh, man. There goes the party."

Freddie was sitting at the bottom of the stairs, watching the commotion of kids coming and going from the house. He had been instructed by George to not let anyone past him. "I'll pay you ten bucks, just don't let anyone up here," George said.

George and Kelly Reed sneaked upstairs into his bedroom. Freddie could now hear Crosby, Stills, Nash, and Young music through his brother's closed door. George was eager to take care of unfinished business from New Years. A guy Freddie did not know and his girlfriend approached and he turned them away.

"Sorry, no one's allowed upstairs."

"Look. I'll give you five bucks."

As the kid pleaded, Freddie was suddenly struck with an inspiration. Ten minutes later, Todd Lewis forfeited twenty bucks to Freddie to use John's room to get together with Janie McLeod, a high school flame that was home for spring break from Washington State. Freddie let two other couples pass his roadblock, charging a ten spot for use of his room and twenty bucks for Karl and Susie's master because "it had its own attached bathroom."

"Don't touch anything in my room." He ordered as he took out his wallet.

Ray Hulick looked at the eleven-year-old as he passed him the saw-buck. "I may just have to mess up your sock drawer, you greedy little Scrooge."

"Thank you," Freddie said, thrilled with the left-handed compliment.

Matthew surreptitiously opened the front door peephole that was protected by a wrought iron grill. He could see John talking with the police and some guy he had never seen before also talking with the cops. He turned around to see Hulick and some girl he didn't recognize coming out of Freddie's room.

"Whoa, whoa, whoa! Off limits gang! Get a hotel room."

"We already paid for one. Ask Mr. Sheraton." Hulick said, pointing at Freddie.

Matthew looked disgusted. "Hey, butthead, you can't charge people to use bedrooms. Mom and Dad will be home in an hour."

"Plenty of time to clean up," smirked Freddie as he counted his cash.

Matthew shifted away from the stairs and saw that the family den door was open. Two boys he didn't know were pouring beer into a glass and letting Max drink the contents. They were sniggering and elbowing one another. Matthew opened his mouth to protest when he heard a deep voice.

"Open sesame, white boy!" An Asian man in his early twenties with a gold tooth was smiling and looking into the window grill. He had a Fu Manchu moustache that fell down from his thin lips and a spiked crop of jet-black hair.

His face disappeared and was replaced by a cute female face with large teardrop eyes. "Hey, I'm Chai and I'm looking for Teddy. My parents own Lantern, you know, the store that sold you guys the ponies. These are my brothers and some friends. I told Teddy we would come by."

A voice outside yelled. "Got to check those pony taps, man, to make sure, you know, everything is working. I see the cops are here."

Matthew opened the door and three slender, tattooed guys that looked like Triad members walked into the house followed by the teenage Chai.

Matthew guided the men through the house and deposited them on the patio steps. "He's outside on the patio. Look, I don't want to be uncool but you got to make it quick. My guess is the party's just about over. In fact, we'll pay you to take the ponies back with you when you leave. We got to clean up before the old man comes home. He can be a son of a bitch."

Matthew heard a shout inside and turned to Chai.

"Look, if you find Teddy, you can take him with the kegs."

He rushed inside just in time to see John come inside the front door and slam it behind him. Max heard the door bang and waddled into the foyer with an incomprehensible bark before falling over on to his side. He was still wagging his tail but had trouble standing. Inside the den, there were sounds of hysterical laughter.

"What's wrong with Maxie?" Freddie shouted.

"Those knuckleheads got him drunk," Matthew snapped tilting his head toward the den. "Look, we gotta get our shit together and clear everyone outta here. What the hell was that all about in front?"

John looked frantic. "That stoner Eldred caused an accident and now his freaking dad is outside, claiming the car accident was our fault and yelling that we are liable. He is like a grand jury attorney or something and he says he can sue us. Dad is going to shit a brick when he hears this. I can't understand what this guy is saying, but he wants to see Dad. Right now."

Matthew glanced at his watch. It was now ten-forty. George was nowhere to be seen.

"Freddie, where the hell is George?"

Freddie allowed a wide smile to crack and looked up toward George's bedroom. "In his room with that girl named Kelly."

There was another yell, and the crash of furniture coming from George's room.

"You asshole! Get the hell out of here!"

Matthew bolted up the stairs just in time to see Tim Irwin punch George in the face and knock him to the ground. Matthew flew at Irwin and blindsided him from the back. Ray Hulick thundered into the room to help and quickly administered a chokehold on the enraged senior. Kelly screamed at Irwin and knelt down to attend to George, who was propped up against a beanbag chair.

Someone was now furiously ringing the front doorbell. Matthew got up and began to move to the hallway.

"Ray, kick that asshole out the back door. Georgie, you okay?"

George looked up as Kelly laughed nervously putting two hands on his face and kissing his eye. "Did the monkey leave a mark?"

Matthew was down the stairs in two leaps and slid into his father's study where he could peer out the front window to see who was leaning on the bell. In the weak porch light, he could see Herb Eldred in his tartan pajama bottoms, leather slippers, and green bathrobe. He had angry salt-and-pepper eyebrows and round studious glasses. Scotty stood behind his father as Herb held up the birthday placard, twitching back and forth as he glanced toward the stumbling, laughing silhouettes that were now moving freely down the driveway.

Matthew was still unnerved from the confrontation upstairs but was forced into action. Turning to John, he barked a series of orders. "Go get George and make sure he is all right. Tell him to get his ass in gear and clear out the back yard of people. Then, go room to room with a trash can and check for any beer cans or cups.

"Freddie, go upstairs with John and check every bedroom, make any beds, and get a flashlight to check outside for beer cans. I will deal with Mr. Eldred."

John ran upstairs and went to fetch George, but Freddie didn't move. "What's your problem?" Matthew said.

Freddie rubbed his forefinger and thumb together the way a cutthroat maître d' might extort a tip from a rich customer.

"If you want to be able to use those fingers again, you will do exactly what I tell you" Mathew said. "Your compensation will be waking up alive tomorrow."

Freddie scowled at the obvious physical disadvantage between him and his oldest brother. "Someday you'll work for me," he said, "and I'll put this in your performance appraisal."

Matthew opened the door and slipped in front of Herbert Eldred before the older man could force his way into the house. "I'm Matthew Patton, sir. This is my fault. We were having a family get-together for my grandfather and my brother. My parents said we could invite some friends over. Word got out and a lot of kids that we did not invite showed up thinking it was a big party, including your son."

Eldred glared over his glasses at Matthew. "Son, do you expect me to believe that? Where the hell are your parents?"

Matthew hesitated. "Well, they're actually at the hospital. My grandfather started having some pains in his chest when he heard the car accident. Then the police showed up and I guess it was too much for him. There were too many kids trespassing that we did not invite."

Turning away, Matt pinched the bridge of his nose as if he was trying to defer tears. "He was in pretty bad shape. Dad's really upset right now. He wanted the names of all the kids who came on our property without permission."

John was listening upstairs through the window as he picked up two beer cans. *Man, he's good.*

Garrett Erickson waited on Park Circle for almost two hours before the silver Bentley pulled up. The couple sat in the car kissing for several minutes. He strained to hear the muffled conversation and the silly giggling. He felt his fists and jaw clenching. When she got out of the car, he felt a sting of rejection at the sight of her figure silhouetted against the light of the front door. He moved his hand down his neck and grimaced, feeling a flutter in his chest.

It was Diane. He didn't really care who the other guy was, but he was not prepared for the anger and sense of betrayal that engulfed him. He waited motionless as Diane lingered over her date for one final kiss and then coquettishly drew herself away, placing her hand to her mouth and saying something else that drew an immediate blown kiss. The brake lights illuminated and the English engine purred. The mystery man backed up until he was practically on top of Garrett and then sped off into the night.

Garrett followed her and watched her as she turned on lights and poured herself another drink. She was smiling. He had rarely seen her smile. She looked beautiful in the black gown and heels she'd probably worn to some vacuous country club dinner where everyone drank themselves into believing their lives were perfect.

He watched her as she slipped off her shoes and walked toward the back door. She appeared to be thinking about going down to the pool house to see her derelict son, but as she peered into the darkness, she seemed to think better of it. Turning back to the kitchen windows, she stood admiring her own reflection, placing her hand on her waist like a runway model and smiling as if she were posing for a society page.

He had to have her now. He did not even care if she even wanted him in return. It seemed appropriate that his last act of insubordination in this fucked-up, pretentious, two-faced asylum of a town would be to force himself on one of their own. He would have his way and leave her in the dirt of his disgust.

He tapped on the back door and saw her smile invert. He grinned and bowed in a theatrical way. She opened the door only partially and spoke to him harshly. "Garrett, it's over. I can't have you coming in and out of my life like a stray tom cat. You have to work things out with Kitty. She's my friend, for God's sake, and I've met someone else. Go away."

He put a finger to his lips as if to hush her and pushed his way in. She responded with a look that combined contempt and fear. Taking off his jacket, he spun back toward her, and in a split second, struck her in face with the back of his hand, knocking her down with such force that the windows shook. She fell hard and for a moment, dazed, she remembered that the last time the windows had rattled with such force was when Los Angeles was hit by the '71 Sylmar quake.

Matthew shook hands with Herb Eldred and watched as he grabbed his son's arm and forcibly pushed him into the passenger seat of his sedan. "Jesus Christ, Scott. You could get our ass sued for showing up uninvited at some family party and causing an old man to have a heart attack."

"Dad, you don't believe that crap do you?"

The street was now awash with red and white taillights as kids scurried away from the party like cockroaches. Matthew yelled behind the Eldreds as they melted into the night.

"Thanks, Mr. Eldred. Dad will be in touch."

Herb waved a dismissive hand in the air without turning. Matthew continued to the street and shook Officer Walsh's hand. "Officer, thanks for helping us clean up things. I guess Gramps' party was the only game in town tonight."

Walsh gave Matthew a wry smile. "You tell your grandfather that it's best to keep his invitation list confined to people over sixty years old."

Matthew glanced at his watch. It was eleven twenty-six p.m. when the police left the premises.

Karl handed the valet his ticket and waited for his car. Rebecca came up and gave Susie a big hug.

Turning to Karl, she held out her hand and gave him a firm handshake. "You, sir, are a lucky man. I have never met anyone quite like your partner. She knows more about men than any chauvinist I've ever met." She glanced at Susie and laughed. "And I would be honored to meet your uncles and parents sometime in San Francisco. They sound like my kind of people."

Will gave Susie a peck on each cheek and shook Karl's hand. "Karl, call me on Monday. I am serious. I like those ideas, and I think we are ready for a change. I just need to reengage with my CFO, who may be using the same insurance agent that my great-grandfather used."

Turning back, Rebecca laid her check against Karl's. "A genuinely fabulous night," she said. Gesturing for him to move closer, she whispered. "I am sure you're relieved to know I am not a lesbian—or, perhaps, disappointed. Personally, I am comforted to know that *you* are not a member of the National Socialists."

Karl went crimson and then looked from Rebecca to Susie. Rebecca eased into the front seat of Will's convertible, covered her hair with her hand, and laughed as the couple sped into the night.

As Susie and Karl wound home along the Pasadena freeway, he wouldn't stop talking. "I mean, how the hell did she know I thought she was a lesbian unless you told her? I mean she uses words like 'partner' instead of 'boyfriend' and shit like that—all those bullshit lesbian phrases."

"Honey, those are the semantics of modern times and you have not been keeping up. And as for *'figuring you out'*? My love, you are as subtle as a belch in church. That woman is brilliant and she could see your dinosaur tail dragging behind you and your tiny little T-Rex arms from the first time you met. She gets it. Rebecca deserves to be CEO of OB&T."

The car drifted and hit several lane markers in succession. Karl turned to Susie, his face illuminated by the dashboard dials of his Granada. "What? Are you shitting me? Whose fucking side are you on? I don't care if she is a goddamn hermaphrodite. That job is supposed to be mine."

"Whatever happened to let the best man win?"

"Man! Did you hear what I said? I said, 'Man!'"

"Sweetheart, that woman is actually too good for OB&T. I think she could run the biggest firm in your industry. She is selling herself short to get ahead because women have to be twice as good to get half the credit."

"Where is all this Helen Reddy shit coming from?"

"Karl, I came here tonight to help you. I think this woman is more qualified than many of the men in your business. We could argue about you. But she deserves a shot and you should be smart enough to recognize when you can learn from someone. She can't succeed without you. If you were smart, you could have your cake and eat it too."

Susie sounded tired and stopped talking. She yawned and looked out into the dark.

"Woman, I do not know what you are talking about."

There was a protracted silence and then Susie finally spoke. "That really is the problem, Karl, isn't it? Until *you* clearly *get* what I am saying, you are *not* going to get the top job. If fifty percent of your employees are females, you cannot effectively represent the company as their leader until you understand what makes everyone tick. Diversity is not about promoting under-qualified people. It is about having leadership that represents the majority of the people and promoting a culture that responds to what motivates them.

"If you can prove to your people that you have the intuition to do that, you can succeed. Until then, you just think you know what's best for them. That's kind of obnoxious and presumptuous. It's like you're the king and they're the servants. That's not a democracy."

"Business *is* a dictatorship," Karl answered. "Maybe it's a benign one, but nevertheless, one guy has to call the shots."

"Or one gal."

"Whatever. Jesus! What the hell did she say to you?"

Susie sighed and said nothing. She leaned her head on the car window and fell asleep. Karl just wanted to go to bed. He looked at the clock. It was almost midnight.

CHAPTER 13

He who lies for you will lie against you.

~**Bosnian Proverb**

Karl changed lanes and switched on the turn indicator to exit the freeway. Susie took a sudden deep breath and opened her eyes. As she adjusted to the streetlights and stretched her arms, she flipped down the eyeshade and opened the illuminated mirror.

"Karl, I actually think Rebecca is the least of our worries. I think we have a bigger problem with that ass Ralph Hunt."

"Yeah, I haven't had time to get my head around what to do yet. I almost punched the prick at his golf club last week. I was thinking I might call Cliff Blakeslee to see if we can legally do something. R2 still does not know that we recruited Jack Swigert for parade. Having an Apollo 13 astronaut leading our parade on the two-hundredth birthday of the nation will be quite a feather in the town's cap.

"The little horse's ass will go berserk, but this is one thing he cannot unwind. But the guy is vindictive and he'll try to get back at me by ruining John's reputation. The asshole does not have anything on Johnny—just a conversation between stupid kids about aphrodisiacs. Yet, I wouldn't put it past him to suggest your son was dealing other things. We'd have to sue his fat ass to get him to shut his mouth. My guess is that it could get ugly."

"Oh, now he is my son?" Susie reached over and began to course her fingers through her husband's short hair. Karl relaxed and confided what he already had known for some time.

"Let's face it. No matter what happens with Hunt, we both know that I am not getting that promotion, and no CEO job means no bump in pay or equity. We are probably stuck with that broken tile roof for another five years." He looked in the rear view mirror and turned on to Monterey Road. "And I am glad you like Rebecca because she is going to be my *new boss*." He could not help sounding sarcastic.

Susie laughed at his display of self-pity. "Poor Karl. You've had a female boss for years. You just don't acknowledge it. And besides, I wouldn't be too sure that it doesn't mean good things for you. I also don't care about a new roof or replacing that horrible green shag carpet. I just don't want Hunt to hurt our son's reputation."

She sounded emphatic and energized. "Hunt has no evidence. It's all strictly circumstantial. I think the bigger issue is if John gets fired from his job or Ralph tells Coach Mooney about John supposedly selling drugs, it could cause him some pain. Marty doesn't suffer fools or have patience for kids who screw around."

"Well," said Karl, "John should not have taken the stuff from George. Where the hell did George say he got them anyway? I wouldn't be surprised that the next time you take the boys to Doc Gildersleeve, he puts that little light in their ears and says, 'Mrs. Patton, do you know that both your sons have shit for brains?' Karl made a sound of disgust. "Can we at least contact the parents of the kid that sold it to him?"

"Oh, I have a good idea who sold them to George. My guess is the guy was teaching him a lesson by taking advantage of him. You don't need to worry about that piece of it."

"Is it someone we know?" he asked

"You don't really want to know, do you? Then you are burdened with all that information and you feel the need to act, but you don't have the time so you just get mad and you start yelling. It's a lot of wasted energy. And no, the dealer's name does not rhyme with Merickson."

"Well, Mrs. Mind Reader, what am I thinking right now?"

"You're wondering how you could have ever convinced someone as brilliant as me to marry you. You are thinking about what a good time you will have next week with Matthew when you take him to the Dodger game."

"The little pinko would probably prefer to see the Reds instead of the Dodgers."

Susie ignored him. "You are thinking about how proud you are of your sons. No, I take it back. What you're really wondering is what Rebecca Gerson told me, and what I told her?"

"Bingo!"

"You'll have to wait until we get home and then use your Gestapo techniques to get it out of me."

"Zat can be arranged. Vee have vays of making you talk," he said.

Turning on to Bedford Street, Karl could see some cars down the block and wondered whether those grab-assing Doney kids were having a party.

The lights were on in every room of the Patton house. Susie winced, disappointed that Matthew had not enforced Freddie's curfew of eleven p.m. The house would be demolished, with dishes left in the sink. It would be another hour before she got to bed as she swept, cleaned up empty glasses, washed dirty plates, and returned open containers of food to the fridge.

Karl frowned. The Impala was blocking the driveway. He parked on the street.

"Who the hell parked that here? We'll get a ticket for blocking the sidewalk after midnight."

As they walked toward the house, Susie saw Freddie open the curtains in Karl's den and then turn to someone, presumably to alert them that parents were home. Her eyes squinted and her mouth turned to one side in cynical suspicion. Something was clearly not right.

Diane held up her hand as Garrett slapped her again. "Who the hell was that, you whore!" He struggled to remove his belt.

Diane did not yell or even cry out. In a strange way, she felt like she deserved this. She had so offended the laws of morality that this beating seemed a logical reckoning for taking a friend's husband as her lover.

Garrett was now acting the enraged cuckold. He picked her up by her hair and she shrieked in pain. "You were supposed to come with *me*," he shouted as he lashed her side with his belt buckle. "This was supposed to be *our* night. Who the *fuck* do you think I am? I'm not the guy you say no to. I'm the guy women *leave* their husbands for." Each time he underscored a word, he throttled her with the belt buckle and his forearm.

He picked her up again by the hair and kneed her in the nose, knocking her backwards. She struck her head on the wood floor, saw a flash of white—and that was all.

When Diane opened her eyes moments later, she saw two men wrestling in the pale light of the kitchen. The other man was smaller than Garrett but he was lightning fast and drove Garrett into a cabinet with his shoulder. Shirtless, he didn't make a sound when Garrett slumped to the ground and coughed, gasping for air. He brought his right hand up above his shoulder and then down at an angle like a sledgehammer, striking Garrett's chin and knocking him unconscious.

The Good Samaritan was over to her in a flash, gently lifting her head. She tried to say something and then Garrett moaned. The mysterious superhero turned away from her and returned to kick Garrett's limp body before dragging him out onto the back porch.

"Hi, Mom. Hi, Dad. How was dinner?" Freddie was way too awake and too chipper. Susie was immediately on the prowl for additional clues as to what had transpired in their absence.

Matthew walked into the kitchen and opened the refrigerator to get some milk. "Oh, hey, how was your dinner?"

"Since when do you ask about my dinners?" Karl asked.

"Dad, I *am* in college now. I want to understand what my parents do." Matt said, seemingly offended.

"Uh-huh," said Susie, lost in her examination. She scanned the kitchen. It looked clean. Too clean. No dishes. The dishwasher was loaded and running. No dirt on the floors. She walked past the den, where George and John were watching television. John was seated like a parishioner in church, not draped over the arms and pillows as he would normally be on a late Saturday night. George lay on the ground, seemingly fixated on the television.

"Hi," John said.

"Hi, Mom. How was dinner?" George asked.

The foyer looked clean and there was no evidence of any disturbance. She walked into the living room and through the dining room yelling back to the boys. "So what did you fellahs do tonight, if I may ask?"

John walked into the kitchen and had obviously been listening. "We just sort of hung out, watched some boob tube, you know."

"Really? Sort of hung out? What was on?"

"*SWAT*," George said from the other room, as John blurted, "*Saturday Night Live*. I mean both shows were on, and we listened to some music in my room."

"You and your brother listening to music in your room? Together?" Susie sounded like a district attorney.

"Yeah. Is there a law against that?"

"No. No law against that particular thing." Susie said the words slowly as she circled John and Matthew, homing in close enough to smell their clothes.

Freddie was getting fidgety and John looked sheepish. Matthew stared at his parents without blinking.

"So, so wide awake. All of you. Something has got you all a bit wound up. George, come in here for a minute!"

Susie heard him groan. "I'm too tired, what is it?"

"George, *now*!"

There was a slow moan and shuffling. Susie gasped as she and Karl took in the purple bruise and swelling that had closed George's left eye. "Jesus Christ, George. What the hell happened?" Karl asked.

"Oh, this? We were playing basketball, and John hit me with an elbow on a rebound."

"Since when do you guys start playing one on one?"

George looked offended, "Hey, what's with all the questions? We used to play out there for hours. He came down on my face with the rebound. It looks worse than it feels."

Susie was now staring at Matthew, who was rummaging in the refrigerator for the milk.

"Such incredible displays of fraternal affection and teamwork tonight. You boys must be so tired. Okay, up to bed, all of you… except *you*." She grabbed Freddie's arm and held him back. Behind Karl's back George, John, and Matthew stopped, frowning at Freddie and making threatening gestures. Matthew mouthed the words, "*We will kill you.*" Susie whipped her head around to see all the boys raising their arms as if they were stretching and yawning.

"Yup, big day tomorrow. Got to go to church," said George.

As the boys slowly walked upstairs, John turned to George and elbowed him in the ribs hard.

"Got to go to church? What the hell was that all about?"

Diane woke up in her own bed and could see only her son's back as he crouched over the telephone. "Yeah, forty-seven Park Circle. Thanks. And hey man, don't use the sirens. I got it under control and we don't need a big scene."

"What the hell happened, Ronnie?" Her son turned to her, and she saw the purple welt over his right eye.

"Jesus!" she whispered and tried to get up. A shot of lightning struck her right side and she moaned.

"Hey, I think you got a broken rib, Mom. You need to relax. I called an ambulance. We're going to get you checked out. Called the cops, too. They're on their way to pick up that worthless piece of shit. He's on the back porch. I tied his ass up. It was all I could do to not cut his nuts off."

"Oh, Ronnie." Diane said, sobbing. She tasted sour chrome from the blood oozing into her mouth.

"That motherfucker did a number on you."

The police pulled up and pounded on the front door. Diane could hear yelling downstairs as the initial response team of cops mistakenly shouted at Ronnie to "keep your hands where we can see them, dirt bag!"

Diane hoisted herself to the end of the bed and felt a wave of nausea as she grabbed the bed stand. For a moment, she almost lost consciousness but managed to move to the door and grab the railing of the upstairs banister. The police now filled the doorway and Ronnie's hands were handcuffed behind his back.

"Hey, you assholes! That is my son. The guy that beat me up is on the back porch."

Vin Nobalski shouted to his men to release Ronnie.

Diane sat on the top step of the stairs as her son and an EMT charged up the stairs to attend to her.

"Careful," Ronnie said. "She may have internal bleeding."

"What are you, a doctor?" the EMT asked sarcastically.

Diane exploded at the young ambulance technician. "He's a field paramedic, a foot soldier, and a goddamn Vietnam war hero, which is more than I can say for you."

Susie glared at Freddie. "You have one chance to tell me the truth and then everyone is going to get punished. Empty your pockets!"

Freddie looked at her with surprise. "What?"

"I said, empty your pockets!"

He did as he was told and laid fifty-five dollars on the table along with a paper clip and a phone number.

"Where'd you get this?"

"I earned it."

"Doing what?"

Silence.

Just then Max weaved into the kitchen and hesitated. He fell over on his side and vomited on the tile floor.

"What the fuck?" said Karl.

"Did you guys have anyone over tonight?"

Freddie looked as if he was going to break, but he remembered the three threatening looks he got from his brothers.

"It depends what you mean by *over.*"

"Listen, you little son of a bitch. You got two seconds…"

"Karl!" Susie interrupted. "Please go check the trash and see if there are any suspicious items in there. And please don't yell at your youngest son."

Karl grumbled and went outside. Susie got up and checked the dog, who managed to wag his tail. As she cleaned up the dog's vomit, she continued Freddie's interrogation. "Okay, whatever they offered to pay you, I will double it."

Freddie could not get the confession out fast enough. "…then the car door got torn off and George made out with this girl in his bed and this Moore guy beat Teddy in a boat race and Teddy puked and they gave me like fifty bucks …"

Outside, Karl opened the trash bin and found plastic bags crammed with beer cups. He jumped back at the sound of a slight moan rising out of his pink camellia bushes. Leaning down into the shaded vegetation, he came face to face with Teddy Galloway, who was slowly emerging from an ivy cocoon covered with leaves and pale crimson petals that stuck to the side of his ashen face.

"Oh, hey, Mr. Patton," he said as if arising from a nap. "Is it okay if I spend the night? Where's George?"

"He's in deep poop, Teddy. And so are you."

Plate 3

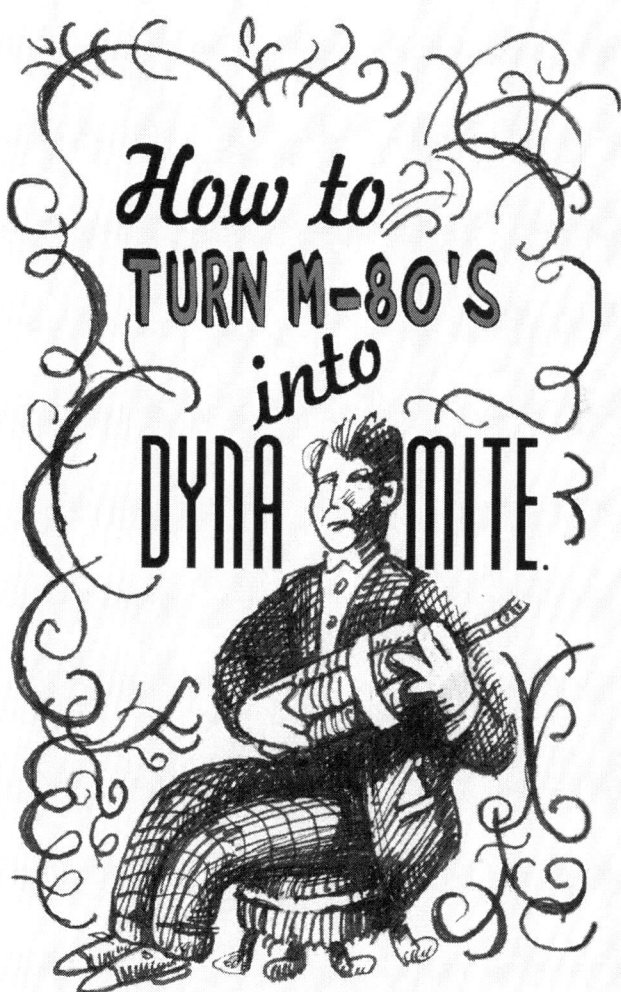

First of all, never do this without the supervision of a liscenced pyrotechnical professional. Next, tie six M-80's together with duct tape. Braid the fuses around each other. They should be at least 9 inches long. Get the pyro guy to light the fuses. Run like hell.

SUMMER

Summer

CHAPTER 14

*"A hero is no braver than an ordinary man, but he is brave
five minutes longer."*

~Ralph Waldo Emerson

Junior Riggs sat in his car outside his parent's house listening to "I'll Be
Good To You" by the Brothers Johnson. He was tired but feeling very
good. Summer was coming and gas prices would once again rise. Pops'
heart was acting up again and he needed to check in on the old man
to be sure he was following the doctor's orders to relax. As he walked
inside, his father tackled him and lifted him up in the air.

"Lord in heaven, son. We just got this telegram. It was addressed to
you, but it looked so official and all. Well, damn it, we just opened it up."
He was holding the letter, reading parts and then thrusting it into the air.

"Says here they completed an investigation 'surrounding the actions
of members of Company D, Seventh Air Cavalry in Pleiku Province on
November 22, 1968.' They are 'awarding the Bronze Star to Corporal
Raymond Riggs, USMC, Private First Class Hernando Ruiz, and Private
First Class Demarco Jackson for demonstrating extraordinary courage
in the face of an overwhelming force and for putting themselves at risk
for wounded comrades until all personnel had been evacuated from the
combat zone.' My God, boy, I am so proud of you. You never said a damn
thing to us 'cept you was glad to be home. Mother, we have us a bona fide
war hero."

Junior was speechless. He allowed himself to be hoisted once again by his father, kissed by his mother, punched by his brothers, pecked by his two sisters, and slapped on the back by their next-door neighbor, Darnell Walton, who had come over to investigate the commotion at the Riggs house.

Within an hour Junior would be at back work in Huntington Hills, but word would move faster than a fire could eat tinder dry brush, telling all of Monrovia that it had a genuine hero living among them.

R2 was in a rage. Inadvertently tipped by an overzealous city hall official that the community had selected an astronaut to marshal its parade, the younger Hunt was furious at being outmaneuvered by Karl and was hell-bent to rain down revenge on the Patton family.

As he rounded the corner of the produce aisle to determine which box boys were working, he ran into Andy Haskell, his gregarious young store manager, and John Patton.

Before Hunt could open his mouth, John grasped his hand. "Mr. Hunt, it's been an honor working with you, sir. I've learned a lot and appreciate the chances you gave me. I have some other commitments this summer and won't be able to work steady. Today's my last day."

Hunt was dumbfounded. He managed to grunt, "You're, uh, welcome," as John and Andy continued through the store saying goodbye to the bakery, meat, and produce department personnel.

The phone rang and as Karl reached for it, Carole raced to her desk and skidded across it, knocking over a cup of coffee, screaming into the handset, "Mr. Patton's office!"

"Jesus Christ," Karl said as he gently returned the phone to its cradle and watched Carole pick herself up.

"Mr. Hunt? Yes, sir, one moment. He is in his office."

Carole turned toward Karl, whose annoyed countenance had changed to concern. He mouthed the question, "Older or younger?"

Carole looked triumphant. "Older, and he is on line two."

Picking up the line, Karl tried to sound matter of fact as Hunt said, "I'm not sure how you managed getting that astronaut from Apollo 13, but I am proud of the job you did on the parade working group. I understand there were a few politics you had to navigate but all's well that ends well."

Karl breathed a silent little sigh. "Ralph, it was a pleasure and I am glad it worked out. Russ and Dom deserve all the credit."

"Son, don't be so modest. Things generally do not happen until someone kicks some rear ends."

Karl hesitated and Hunt filled the silence. "Look. I know we were talking about our business insurance here at the market. I'm not sure if he shared it with you, but young Ralph has a college roommate that he just feels more comfortable working with. I'm certain he's not as qualified as you or your firm, but if the young man is ever going to run this place, he has to make some decisions for himself—and live with the consequences."

Karl smiled and leaned back in his chair. "Ralph, I am a father and I know exactly what you mean. We have to let our boys figure it out and if we try to manage every decision, they won't make it in the real world. Personally, I'd rather have you as my friend. Sometimes it's important to keep business and pleasure at arm's length. How you feeling, by the way?"

"Oh, my damn doctor is a like some Civil War sawbones. He keeps warning me that he may have to take my leg below the knee. Diabetes is a bitch, son. But I've proved a lot of people wrong before. Don't bet against me. You know, Karl, you are a rich man with that great family of yours. You and Susie ought to be proud. I don't think you have to worry about those boys or their future. And if any of your kids needs a job next school year, have them give me a call. And thanks."

"Yes sir. I leave the worrying to Susie and I just whack whoever she tells me to hit. But I'll tell the boys that. I feel a lot better knowing I can still ask you for the occasional advice or a favor."

"Happy to help" Hunt said. "Oh, and I understand your father was in the hospital in April. I just ran into Herb Eldred, who told me you were really caught off guard at your dad's 70th. Kippy and I send him our best."

"Sir? I, I …" Karl stammered as he tried to make sense of what Hunt was saying.

"No need to relive it, son. I hope he's feeling better. Love to meet him some time. He must be a hell of a guy. I'll see you in a few weeks at the parade."

Ronnie pulled up in a station wagon and began to lay out his equipment. He grabbed and balanced a heavy aluminum extension ladder from the roof of the car and swung it over to the front lawn. He carefully laid down a large drop cloth where he inventoried his tape, plastic sheets, paint, brushes, rollers, goggles, masks, and disposable milk cartons.

Gonzales followed in his van and helped carry the ladder to the front of the house. It was a three-day job, with touch-up work around the windows, doors, grill and eaves. There was also some additional work for Ronnie inside of the house. He could gross more than four hundred dollars before the job was over, getting him one step closer to Montana.

His mother had informed him of her decision to sell the house. She said she could not depend on anyone to rescue her from her circumstances and wanted to have enough money to make it on her own. It had been the first time in years that he had seen her pull herself together, and he was glad she was making some decisions on her own. She had been in a deep funk since the incident with Garrett, and she hadn't heard from Don Randall, the white knight in the Bentley who she had hoped would rescue her from her circumstances. She was quite certain that Don's ex-wife, Janine aka The Dragon Lady, had already alerted him that he was dating a sullied woman.

Although the police had been discreet, Ronnie was sure that everyone knew about the incident. Garrett's arrest, Ronnie's intervention in saving his mother, and their family reconciliation had been a major step toward healing what was left of the Thomas family, but it had not changed Ronnie's resolve to move on. To move, though, he needed money. He would finish painting the Patton's, hit Hunt's Market, and then hang around for a few days to allay any suspicions before disappearing to Idaho, where some friends had a place near Sand Point.

He knocked on the front door and waited. A familiar voice shouted at a barking dog. The door opened and Susie smiled. Barefooted, she was wearing a floral sundress and looking more like Elizabeth Taylor than ever. Her beauty had always made Ronnie short of breath. Today, however, he managed a smile.

"Ronald Thomas, right on time. My, how you have grown up! I was hoping you would get here early so I could surprise my husband by starting the painting. With the Fourth coming and the kids out of school, life is a little crazy."

"No problem, Mrs. Patton and thanks for giving us this gig."

He could tell by the way she was speaking to him that she knew everything – Garrett, Diane, his dad and even the drugs. Strangely, though, he felt no judgment coming from her, and he understood why his mother considered Mrs. Patton such a good friend.

"This is Arturo Gonzales, my partner and longtime friend."

"Mucho gusto, Arturo," Susie said with a half-mast grin. "I'm sorry, but I have to put my ten years of Catholic-school Spanish to some use."

"De nada, Senora Patton." Arturo grinned. "Donde aprende su espanol?"

Susie concentrated and then looked relieved. "Oh, en mi escuela in San Francisco. La mayoria de las personas en el mundo hablan lenguas aparte del ingles. Es importante conocer coco minimo dos lenguas. Pero necessito practicar."

"*Claro!*" Arturo nodded his head. He turned to Ronnie. "*Muy bien.* She speaks much better than your pidgin Spanglish."

"Okay, okay. So we now all know I was not listening in Senora Amante's Spanish Three class."

Susie shook her head. "Ronald, none of my boys could learn from that woman. I tried to get Dr. Brown to fire that vindictive hag. She hated George."

Turning to the young Latino, she gave him a devilish grin. "Arturo, como se dice *witch* en espanol?"

"*Bruja?*" Arturo blushed.

Susie laughed. "Yes. That's the word I was looking for." She continued berating the school district. "But, alas, the district had no backbone."

Arturo beamed as if he had given the right answer in class. Ronnie grinned, too. Susie was cool. Yep, this would be a good last gig.

Kitty carefully finished packing her wedding china in a storage box and then sat down and cried quietly. Since the incident with Garrett, the town criers had been busy broadcasting the lurid details of Garrett's extracurricular activities. Diane was apparently only one of several women in the area who had succumbed to her husband's dark charm. Kitty was humiliated and angry at the schadenfreude that swirled around her. She was amazed at the crocodile tears and faux concern expressed by those who seemed to be wallowing in her misfortune. She felt as if she were performing a community service by helping them forget about their own unfulfilled lives.

A few people had stepped up, filling the emotional breach that had been torn in her life. Susie, of course, had been a jewel, inviting Seth over to reconcile with John, as well as giving him a place to hide and a respite from the life that now haunted him. Seth loved his father and was understandably confused over his affairs, his arrest, and the scandal. Thank God that school was just about out.

Diane had gone to Kitty's house before Garrett's arraignment to make her amends. She had offered to drop charges against him if it would help ease the pain she had caused. Susie had encouraged Kitty to meet with Diane, but left it up to Kitty to decide whether forgiving her would heal the bitter antipathy she felt surrounding Diane's betrayal.

"Kitty, resentment is pure arsenic. We have to forgive others to heal ourselves. We share invisible emotional meridians and odd connections that tie us all together. It's ironic, but by forgiving those who wrong us, we heal. By helping those who hurt us, we recover. To keep sane, we must let go of the rational instinct for revenge and restitution. 'Leave vengeance to God and Karl' is what we say in our house."

The first wives' club had mobilized and lifted Kitty out of her trough of misery. Ginny Buckingham and Melissa Storms had established a rock-solid defensive perimeter of dinners, activities, emotional support, and advice. It had been Susie's suggestion to have Cliff Blakeslee be present when Diane shared the details with Kitty and her apology. Cliff carefully recorded all of Diane's admissions to use in the divorce proceedings.

Kitty had listened to Diane without looking at her. When she finally lifted her eyes to Diane and saw her pain, demoralization, and crushed self-esteem, Kitty understood what Susie had been trying to say. It would have been more convenient to vilify Diane as the wretched home wrecker and send her away with a scorched Southern upbraiding from which she might never recover. Kitty could almost see Diane in a cheap motel room as her lifeless hand knocked an empty bottle of tranquilizers to the floor. Yet, in her moment of bitter triumph, she would have nothing. She knew she had to heal her herself, and if she put vengeance ahead of her own recovery and her children, she might never find herself again.

Kitty stood up and wrapped her slender arms around Diane, absorbing ragged, convulsive sobs. She repeated the same three words over and over, "You are forgiven. You are forgiven."

Days later, Kitty felt herself becoming whole again and as word spread of her magnanimous gesture toward the friend that had slept with her husband, she became a symbol of the potency of absolution.

George sped home from school. He was almost over his post-party incarceration and eager to map out his summer plans. There were only two weeks until vacation and his trip to San Francisco to visit his mother's crazy Irish relatives. He was excited about the upcoming road trip and even more enthusiastic about returning home for the town's Fourth of July celebration. His father and mother would be very involved with the parade, which would give him the perfect opportunity to meet his friends for a little Independence Day battle.

He could hear John's stereo playing. He opened his door, listening to Al Green croon "Full of Fire." It was weird how sometimes you turned on the radio and it was playing the exact lyrics you were thinking. He opened his drawer and lifted his tee shirts to reveal an arsenal of fireworks. He had amassed M80s, M40s, smoke bombs, fireworks, and bottle rockets. The war was planned for noon on the Fourth at Bruce

Hegarty's house. Four boys, four forts and ordnance worthy of an artillery barrage at Stalingrad.

He opened his drawer to reveal the gun. McKesson's old man had a boat moored in Balboa and possessed every conceivable marine product known to man. George remembered Mac talking about his Dad's emergency flare gun. For an IOU of twenty five bucks, he had "rented" the gun and procured two flares. Those other guys would never know what hit them.

George heard a noise and quickly covered the fireworks, closing his door. He froze, listening again for the unusual sound. He could hear the roof tiles outside his bedroom window shifting as if someone was trying to break into the second story of the house. He crept over to the curtains and threw them open, coming face to face with Arturo Gonzales who had placed a metal putty knife in his teeth. George grabbed his ears and screamed, "I didn't tell anybody, I swear to God!" On the other side of the window, Arturo Gonzales was shocked to see the kid from Ronnie's pool house.

In the front of the house, Ronnie heard Arturo yell *"Madre de dios!"* as he tumbled away from George's window rolling off the tile roof and falling six feet down to the back yard ivy.

John had ridden his bike to Hunt's. He was still grounded from using the car for his part in the Patton Pony Keg Party. Chaining his Schwinn to a streetlight, he glanced over at the Mobil station where Junior Riggs was wildly gesticulating to a customer. The elderly man was laughing and slapping Junior on the back. John got a good vibe from the young gas station owner and regretted that he had never had a chance to work with him.

As he entered the market and felt the blast of the air conditioning, John saw R2 chatting up an attractive brunette woman near the lettuce while Armando, the Produce manager impatiently waited to get on with his work. Every few seconds, Hunt would spray the lettuce and fruit with the coiled misting hose while Armando cringed.

Andy Haskell looked up from the bakery, where he was helping a customer. He held up a finger to John and picked up the phone to call

Donna in Accounting. He pointed upstairs and indicated for John to wait in the back of the store while his final check was being prepared.

John decided to poke his head in the storage room to see if any of his buddies were on break. The loading dock door was ajar. He opened it, expecting to see Helm outside smoking a clove. The crab lady was in the alleyway. Having been discovered, she looked flustered and began to sweep a small piece of plastic that had fallen outside the trash bin.

"You need to keep zis alley clean. Otherwise I vill call zee police!" She yelled in a thick accent toward John as she waddled toward the white back yard gate.

"Yes, ma'am. Sorry," John said sympathetically.

As John turned to reenter the store, R2 blocked his way. "Get the hell out of the trash, you old bitch," he yelled, "or *I* will call the police."

The old woman stopped and glared back at him. R2 turned back into the store and stared at John. "Just tell your old man that he may think this is over, but it is not. I will be running this place and will run a lot more before too long. This is a small town, son. Reputations are easy to lose and harder to recover. The old guard is changing, and we are all going to have to get used to a new world order. Tell your old man the king is dead. Long live the king."

John stared at the bearded man and composed himself. R2 was a human fire hydrant - squat and wide, with thickset arms and legs. John wondered if he could take him as he smiled and extended his hand.

"Mr. Hunt, hey thanks for the opportunity to work here. I learned a lot."

John glanced past R2 to see Donna Giddings, Ralph Hunt Senior's sister and the finance manager for the Market for more than thirty-five years, who was holding out his final paycheck. "Here you go, young man. Good luck with your junior year and we hope we see you back at the store."

"I don't think John will be coming back, Aunt Donna," R2 volunteered. "He sounds like he's quickly outgrowing our little town. "

John took the check and turned to R2. "Well, Mr. Hunt. It's true that I want to leave California, but my mom says that if you want to make God laugh, tell him your plans. I don't know what's going to happen."

Donna Giddings laughed out loud as John exited the store. "What an impressive young man. I wish I had been that mature at his age. Now, when you were sixteen," she said to Hunt, "we couldn't even trust you to close a door." She glanced over at the loading dock door and moved to shut and latch it. "We obviously still can't."

The following week, the *Pasadena Star Herald* published a front-page article about Junior Riggs and his Bronze Star. The headline, *Monrovia Man Wins Bronze Star for Heroism—Seven Years After Battle*, caught the attention of the media and generated a landslide of calls from opportunistic local leaders and politicians who wanted to meet and take a photo with the hometown hero on the eve of Bicentennial celebration.

The *Los Angeles Tribune* picked up on the story and contacted Riggs at his station. Junior spent over a half-hour talking to the reporter. "Look, man, I appreciate all the attention but there was five other guys that should have also got recognized," he said. "We was just doin' our jobs. I am glad someone set the record straight. You could say by not speaking up, one individual allowed himself to take credit for something that everyone did. There's lots of guys who did their duty and no one recognized them for what they did. Shit, people was spitting on us when we was coming home. Baby killer? Most of us never heard of Mai Lai before Life published them pictures. A lot of men of color fought for Vietnam's freedom when they were being denied civil rights at home. That's just wrong, man…

"…Yeah, my parents are awfully proud. But it's hard for some of us to see Laos and Cambodia now falling to Mister Charles. It makes a lot of people wonder whether it was worth it. All I know is we didn't have no choices. We did what we were told to do – an' always by white officers in the rear. I don't need a medal to prove I did a good job. If I'd been white, it would have been different. Maybe, I don't get shot at as much and I still get my Bronze Star…"

The following day, the San Gabriel section of *the LA Tribune* ran an article headlined, "*Veteran Says Medal Is Tainted By Racism.*"

Pops was furious with his son. "Boy, did you not listen to what I was sayin' about letting your actions and not your words do your talking? All these people are proud of you for what you did and you go pissing on your own medal?"

Junior couldn't believe what he was reading. The journalist had taken many quotes out of context and encouraged Junior's candid recounting of racial inequities and the hypocrisy of America's democratic double standards. Although he had successfully reentered into society with his own business, he now felt like he was being dropped into another hot LZ. He was still being asked to fight a war he could not win.

The ghosts of fifty-five thousand killed in battle were writhing in their graves as the dominos of Southeast Asia fell to communism. Vietnam had been the first visible tumor on the body of American hegemony. The country was fallible and this failed war was not to be reverently celebrated but instead buried and forgotten. Junior's Bronze Star had presented a tiny southwest corner of America the rare chance to thank one man for giving his best for his country; but in less than twenty-four hours, *The Tribune* article had purloined a community's opportunity to suture its war wounds and had extended the racial fissures that continued to engulf a generation.

CHAPTER 15

"Like those in the valley behind us, most people stand in sight of the spiritual mountains all their lives and never enter them, being content to listen to others who have been there and thus avoid the hardships.

~ **Robert M. Pirsig**

Matthew sat cross-legged in a tepee that had been hastily erected in a public park in Portland, Oregon. The makeshift encampment had sprung up over the last week as Deadheads gathered like Mecca pilgrims in local parks and campgrounds. Small groups migrated back and forth from the line that was already forming for admission later that Friday night to the Paramount Theatre. Matthew had driven all day from Marin with three Cal friends to see friends at Portland State and watch the Dead close out their West Coast concert tour.

He had been living with his relatives in Marin who found him a job as a gofer with Swinton Construction. Matthew discovered that the early mornings and long days of hard labor were challenging. The majority of the workers were not college educated and enjoyed teasing the kid they referred to as "Cal." Matthew had heard ad nauseam from Karl about any job involving manual labor and how those who worked in these jobs did so because they had to, not because they wanted to. Matthew resented Karl's generalizations and judgments of blue-collar workers.

Matthew was proud to be a manual laborer. They were the backbone of a country about to elect a pro-Union Democrat as president. In just five months, the party of FDR, Truman and Kennedy would kick the warped Republicans out of the White House and the nation would be on a path toward building stronger unions and dismantling the corrupt, unregulated free market that favored so few and hurt so many.

Two earthy ponytailed hippies now kneeled across from Matthew and his buddy, Billy Montague. A young man with a rust-red dread-locked beard seemed eager to make a sale to the two neophyte mind travelers. "So, man, just try one of these before the concert. You'll enjoy everything more. It's like inserting an equalizer in your head—more bass, more treble and no interference."

Matthew was having second thoughts about trying a hash brownie but he wanted to do something that he knew his father would never do. He wanted to be his own man and create further distance between himself and the man who often warned him that he 'had brought him into the world and he could take him out of it.'

He looked at Billy for help but found only neutrality. "Hey, man, I'm pre-med and driving. I strictly observe others if they choose to alter their states of consciousness."

Matthew pointed to the smallest, most benign-looking brownie and said, "I guess I'll take that one."

Rebecca had been installed as the new president of O'Brien &Taft. Although Karl had grown fond of her, he wondered whether he could really work for her as her number two. She had made it clear to Karl that she was eager to have him run loss control, claims, and account management, and was open to increasing his equity stake in the firm. Still, he felt like an election-night loser in a bitterly tough race. It had been difficult to discuss any concession when there was still even the smallest chance that Bob might flip-flop on his plans.

His funk deepened when he received the call from Russ Quintana. "Buddy, I heard from Swigert's people. He has a family commitment in

Colorado and cannot attend the parade. Karl, he is so, so sorry. He tried to call Jim Lovell and the other guy, Haise, but both of them have prior commitments. He may be able to get Gene Kranz, the flight director, but I'm not sure just how many people know about Apollo 13 anymore and whether a NASA theme sort of gets us away from our vision."

"Jesus! I couldn't get laid in a whore house with a hundred-dollar bill."

"Look, Karl, let me work on this, but my guess is we have to do some damage control with the town planning group and go with plan B."

There was a long pause. "Plan B?"

"Yeah, I assume we have a back-up. The more famous the guy, the more likely stuff like this can happen. So who is our fallback?"

"We don't have one. I guess it's R2."

"Karl, are you shitting me?"

"Houston, we have a problem."

Karl hated summer. He felt a three-month school vacation for children was an anachronism. It was the last manifestation of an age of buggy whips and agrarian living, when laborers of all ages were needed to plant, tend, and harvest the community's food. The notion of hard labor in the fields had been lost in the industrial age, along with a work ethic that had suffered a sickening setback with the birth of the Baby Boomers.

Kids had the audacity to view chores as an imposition of hard labor rather than a privilege to contribute to family and society. Summer was a time when industrious young men and women should be harnessed like plow horses and sent to labor anywhere, earning the redeeming calluses gained only through the use of a shovel, plow, or milking stool.

Karl considered the extended summer break collectivist pollution drift from Europe. Like much of Gallic culture, it was the outmoded invention of a lethargic liberal government. Time off from hard labor could easily turn any man into a cheese-eating milquetoast with a doctorate in surrender.

Susie agreed that ninety days with no structure could exacerbate the already terminal condition known as adolescence. Idle hands were the devil's workshop. Boys needed to be busy.

On Memorial Day, Karl gathered John, George, and Freddie in his office. "Boys, your Mom and I are underwriting your college education, and we can't keep paying allowances. From now on, weekly chores will be done because you live here. If you want to earn money, you will need to get a job. As far as I'm concerned, allowance is a relic of the past. It's like welfare. People began to view it as an entitlement and …."

"Karl," Susie interrupted. "The boys don't need a political science lesson."

"Well, anyway, we are not a goddamn money tree for you to shake for the rest of your lives."

The primary source of any income for a kid was yard work. Somehow, cleaning someone else's yard for money seemed less onerous than cutting one's own lawn. The main tool of the trade was the ancient lawn mower—a rusted manual cutting cylinder with a rotating blade. The simple mechanical design was unimproved since it was invented sometime before Christ most likely by a Greek teen who could no longer stomach cutting the family wheat with a scythe, but was told he could not attend the Poison Oracles concert at the local amphitheater until the field was clean.

A lawn mower was harder to push than a shopping cart with a broken wheel. To operate the cast-iron monstrosity, a 125-pound kid would have to back up several paces to build enough momentum to cut through any lawn higher than a half-inch. As the blade ripped through the various varieties of suburban grass—Bermuda, St. Augustine, fescue, and Kentucky blue—the whirling blades filled the air with green shrapnel and debris. By the end of a lawn-cutting session, a kid resembled a bizarre grasslands creature covered in flecks of emerald, sweat, and the insects du jour. It seemed the grass fell everywhere except into the ancient canvas grass catcher that hung precariously behind the machine on two hooks adjacent to the back wheels.

After cutting and raking up the grass, kids were expected to edge the lawn with a device that looked like the unholy union of a jousting stick and a pizza cutter. The metal blade knifed along the sidewalk and garden beds as one carefully trimmed the rectangle of property to geometric perfection. An uneven or overgrown yard was tantamount to poor hygiene. It suggested to neighbors that things were not well. A homeowner who could not control his lawn was most likely unable to hold the rest of his life together.

Leaves were cleaned up and accumulated with a medieval device called a rake. It was a cumbersome implement made from fragile metal strips that made a distinct scratching sound as they were dragged across garden beds and backyards. If raking were not tedious enough, it was always followed by a final indignity involving the deposit of the debris into the trash.

A boy might try to launch leaves into a neighbor's bushes or ivy, but in the tight quarters of suburban Los Angeles, gardeners were expected to place leaves in trashcans and then stomp down on the debris to make room for more clippings. Invariably, the trashcan would tip, vaulting its rider and a day's work of clippings onto the cement, where the budding landscaper would lie for moments, bleeding and angry. Eventually, however, one became expert in jamming eighty cubic feet of leaves into a twenty-gallon trash can. It made Karl quiver with pride to see his sons bouncing up and down in the cans, tamping down debris like serfs in the fields. There would be times, out of sheer elation, that he would come out and jump in the trashcan with them.

Freddie loathed manual labor. He quickly figured out that everyone needed his or her windows washed, especially in the permanent sunshine of Southern California summers. With the help of Susie, he formed a window washing business and subcontracted with several friends to help him cover local condos and ranch-style homes. It was a no sweat, high-margin, low capital-expenditure business requiring only one arm, a minimum wage assistant for bigger jobs, squeegees, ammonia, rags, and an FM radio—and there was little competition. Freddie and a friend could complete a sixty window, three-thousand-square foot ranch home in about three days, bringing in over more than one hundred and fifty dollars. He quickly figured out that apartment complexes often had identical floor plans, a fixed number of same-sized windows and air conditioners. With Susie as his chauffeur, he went door to door in upscale condo complexes, offering to clean windows for forty dollars a unit - usually completing his work in less than two hours.

The local YMCA also helped out the community by creating a job bank where locals could call and offer one-time yard work, plant-watering, pet-sitting, and house-cleaning jobs. Kids were a default labor force and they were desperate for money. Neighbors felt an obligation to keep neighborhood kids employed and out in the open where they might find less trouble, more supervision and greater self-esteem. This meant buying bad lemonade, subscribing to an illiterate national publication sold by kids called Grit magazine, buying packets of Burpee seeds that one would never take time to germinate, stocking up on Girl Scout cookies, purchasing inedible fruit cakes at a holiday bake sale or accepting earnest offers to rake leaves that did not exist. Parents understood that everyone needed to work.

Matthew looked up and saw wide green eyes and a monstrous Cheshire cat grin on the shape-shifting face of a security officer who was checking the bags and backpacks of the hundreds of people waiting to be allowed into the concert hall. Matthew suddenly froze and started to inch backwards.

"Dr. Billy"

"Whoa, Secretariat. Easy boy. What's up?" Billy said with amused sympathy.

"Everyone's face is sort of melting and underneath the wax are wide-eyed grinning cats like the ones in Alice in Wonderland."

Montague chuckled quietly and placed both hands on Matthew's shoulders, holding him firmly and pointing him in the direction of the man checking bags. Billy leaned in and spoke into Matt's ears.

"I'm afraid I have some bad news for you, Matthew. It appears that your brownie was not made with hashish, but actually contained some kind of hallucinogenic. I don't think its peyote or else you'd be throwing up right now. My guess is lysergic acid. If I'm right, the chemical is now reprogramming your HT2 receptors to produce massive amounts of serotonin. Your cerebral cortex is kicking into overdrive. This will affect your emotions and cognitive abilities. Your locus ceruleus is incorrectly translating the external stimulus you are receiving through your ears, eyes, and other senses and distorting the information.

"In other words, you are going to see some bizarre crap for the next several hours. The good news is nothing is real. It's like seeing ghosts."

Matthew stared at Billy with panicked incomprehension and then spoke in the soft voice of a child. "I don't like ghosts."

"Matthew, this has happened before. It's gonna be fine. Once we get inside, I can get you somewhere where you can mellow out. These guards are smooth dudes just fulfilling a basic role of security to ensure that we will all be safe while we are inside the concert.

"Just look ahead and hand them your ticket. You have no illegal paraphernalia on you. You are an emissary of peace. The theatre is a melodious place - like a beehive full of honey. We are drones gathering at its center. Jerry Garcia is the King Bee, and tonight he will share his musical nectar with us. This is a time to create our own mythology."

"King Bee? Nectar? Mythology?" Steve Ashmore laughed from further back in line.

Billy pivoted and hissed. "Cool it, dude. Someone slipped our man something potent and he may be in for a major bummer."

Matthew cast a dull stare at Ashmore and then rotated robotically to study the plaid pattern of the shirt of the boy standing in front of him.

"Oh, crap. That dude just grew a horn."

Billy was as cool as a mountain morning. "Matthew, it is only your brain creating hieroglyphics. He has no horn. He's normal. Think of this concert as a four-hour ride at Disneyland. It's all here for your entertainment."

Matthew seemed to understand.

"Like the new Space Mountain ride. I've got lots of E tickets and I can go on the ride over and over."

"Except the ride lasts like ten hours and everyone has horns!" said Ashmore, raising his eyebrows.

Montague shot his friend another dirty look.

"Just wait until we get inside. It will be very mellow. Lots of fun, happy people."

Matthew appeared to be relieved. "Cool. Yes. Just as long as there are no dragonflies. I hate dragonflies."

Behind Bill Montague, Steve Ashmore turned to his girlfriend, Libby Robinson, and made a mischievous face. "I didn't know he hated dragonflies."

Libby gave her boyfriend a scolding look and then smiled kissing him on the nose. She swiveled her glance toward Matthew. "Baby, don't be mean. Matthew's in for a bad trip. Does Billy know what was in that brownie?"

Ashmore surveyed all the longhaired partiers assembled in the uneven serpentine line that weaved out of the theatre and up SW Broadway. "Doctor Billy thinks our friend from Southern California ingested a brownie with LSD in it. Matthew is officially on his way to finding his spirit animal—or meeting Satan for a light supper." He laughed and Libby punched him.

"Don't. This happened to me once and it scared the crap out of me. That's why I only drink a beer now and then."

Ashmore mocked her with an overly sympathetic face. "Yes, we know what a lightweight you are. But we still love you."

Steve put his arm around her as they inched closer to the entrance. "Look, he is with Dr. Billy. He'll be safe. Billy is a calm influence. It's like a supervised lab experiment for Billy when shit like this happens."

Libby frowned. "So were those CIA tests when people they doped freaked out and jumped out of windows. I hope he doesn't get too bummed out. It could get really weird for all of us."

"You always were a sucker for lost puppies and stray animals." Steve pursed his lower lip and shrugged.

"Baby, this is not cool. I don't think Matthew is the kind of guy that can handle something this intense. Maybe we should take him to a doctor or something. The last thing we need is to for him to get wigged out and try to run eight hundred miles back to Marin."

Libby's eyes followed Matthew. He had now concentrated his stare on a moth that was flying in and out of the light from the streetlamp. He reached out his hand and snatched at it in the air.

Susie was organizing the family for the seven-hour trip up to the Forest Knolls. Northern California was home for Susie, and while Los Angeles was where she raised her family and did the laundry, Marin

County was where she had learned to understand men, life, and the notion of family.

Susie considered the family road trip an essential part of reconnecting her boys to their heritage. In the days before emission standards, mandatory seat belts, and minivans, the family station wagon—a V-8, 360-horsepower gas guzzler—served as a modern-day Conestoga wagon on steroids. Over two decades, the Patton Impala and others like it transported more families to more domestic destinations than any commercial airline.

The trips never turned out as planned, which excited Susie and annoyed Karl, who liked certainty and predictability. Susie knew that being stuck in the close quarters of a station wagon with nothing to do across hours of endless interstate was more than most kids could handle. Invariably, she would try to get the boys to play games or sing. As they grew older, however, it was harder to distract them.

Vacations could still be thankless for mothers as roadside motels often lacked basic amenities. Laundry must still be washed, dried and folded but now was managed among strangers and other vacationing families in Laundromats. Breakfast and lunch preparation was managed with plastic cutlery on narrow Holiday Inn formica counters.

Road trips meant hassle but also escape from the tedium of daily routines. The family that drove together and ate every meal together, stayed together. During the school year, Susie might preside over as many as three dinners—her own while preparing food, one while sitting with the boys at six o'clock supper, and another at eight pm when Karl came home from work.

For Susie, happiness was the journey itself. For Karl, there was no joy in the means. He could not rejoice until his passenger vessel had eased into the parking slip of their planned destination. With the first dawn of any car holiday, a mixture of dread and foreboding was sparked with the ignition of the family station wagon. Like the crew aboard the Pequod, the boys knew that with each mile they would be further indentured to the whims of their very own Captain Ahab, who would not rest until he could safely guide his ship to their distant motel. The expedition would span 600 miles, a coastal mountain range, two rest stops and one empty gallon bottle of Mott's apple juice, which Captain Karl decreed would be used as a urinal, avoiding what he considered unacceptable delays.

The process of relieving one's self was humiliating, as it involved crawling into the back of the wagon and trying to hit a target the size of a baseball while being heckled by raucous spectators.

The luggage was secured to the automobile's roof rack with a gray canvas cover and rough hemp rope. The cargo was tied with angry knots that would have confounded Houdini. The back of the car was a jigsaw puzzle of cardboard boxes filled with groceries, clothes, and odd supplies. A sleeping bag cushioned the ground between the containers, offering Freddie the only remaining place to lie down. Over the course of any road trip, Freddie would be found unnaturally curled in breech birth position between an ice chest and cartons of food.

Anxiety was palpable. It was dawn and each son was now old enough to know what to expect. George felt ill and out of sorts. Privately, he was confronting his Four Horseman of Travel—the possessed driver, the eventual need to pee, the endless purgatory of Interstate 5, and the most fearsome specter of all—carsickness. Freddie was a walking self fulfilling prophesy - so terrified of getting sick that he once threw up before the car got out of the driveway. Karl did not help - pumping the brakes harder than an organist during Handel's *Messiah*. The car's motion was similar to the sensation of being on a trawler in a force ten gale.

"Dad, can I please put down the window?"

"Go to sleep, George. I've got the *air conditioning* on."

He directed his comment toward Susie. Secretly, he would have loved to open the windows to the 100-degree heat, but Susie hated June in Central California. Karl did not like what air conditioning did to his mileage. He resisted turning it on and always attempted to trick everyone by first putting using the recycled economy air, which felt and smelled like Max's warm breath, before finally yielding to the family's protests about the car's heat.

John was first to barf. He had put up a good fight with his queasiness, lasting until the car was winding up a deserted stretch of California interstate near Ventura known as the Camarillo Pass. He tried to roll down the window, but he had been reading, which elevated his nausea to such a level that the simple motion of turning the window handle sparked an eruption of scrambled eggs that hit the top of the windows and sprayed back toward the middle seat. George hollered as if an alien had burst out of John's chest.

Karl swerved, pulling over to the shoulder of the road, a skidding plume of flying pebbles and dust. In the rear of the car, Freddie had covered himself with a towel as he tried to urinate into the Motts jar. As Karl hit the brakes, the "tinkle jar" slipped free from Freddie's hand spilling one hundred and fifty miles of urine onto the family sleeping bags. It was only eleven am and the Impala already smelled like men's room at Dodger Stadium.

It now appeared as if Karl was going to spontaneously combust.

"Goddamn it. How old are you kids? Sixteen? When are you going to quit puking and peeing all over the goddamn car?"

John groaned as he hung his head out the window. "Dad, you have to stop pumping the brakes."

"It's my fucking car and if I want to pump the brakes, I will pump the hell out of them until everyone pukes!"

"That's a nice thought, Karl." Susie said, taking out a moist washcloth and paper towels and calmly administering Dramamine and housekeeping service.

Susie had convinced Karl to detour for a day and a night through San Luis Obispo to break up the long drive and to visit the famous Madonna Inn. Known as the Pink Palace, the garish motel was a three-diamond "must-see" in the AAA Road Guide. Its rooms were individually themed and included a suite with its own windmill and a cave. The men's restroom was a kitsch grotto where boys could pee into a crescent-shaped abyss that was perpetually perfumed by a waterfall of scented toilet water. Yet the notion of any detour that added time to the car journey made Karl and the boys cranky.

Susie's only antidote to carsickness and bad attitudes was double doses of Dramamine. By the time they hit Ventura, she had gently doped the older boys into a temporary truce and restless stupor. Meanwhile, Susie kept Freddie distracted by asking him to identify as many license plates from different states as possible.

Lunch was at a roadside park outside of Buellton, California, the home of Anderson Pea Soup. Rations included PBJs that bled through white Wonder Bread to form soggy, clotted tarts. Grapes and Cheetos followed, chased by warm Shasta Lemon Lime soda. Food tasted better on the road.

John always felt more alive when he was outside the city limits of Huntington Hills. He was wary of his propensity to nausea and his anxious, irritated driver, but these were minor inconveniences in exchange for the chance to venture to new places beyond the San Gabriel Mountains. He was energized by the sense of adventure that always came with new people, places, and ideas. He needed to feel that he was moving—in any direction.

Around three p.m., the family pulled into the check-in area of the Madonna Inn. George was in awe of the giant rock formations that climbed up from golden, summer-baked hills. A split-rail fence outlined the property, and several wide corrals held llamas, buffalo, and an assortment of farm animals.

"Hey, it's a Push-Me-Pull-You." Freddie yelled pointing at the llama. The boys all shifted to the left side of the car to peer at the odd menagerie. Susie got out of the car and reached down to touch her toes and then slowly rose up, rubbing the base of her back.

"Need any help?" Karl catcalled leaning over to the passenger side and winking.

She kept walking to the entrance but turned her head toward the station wagon.

"We got a single room with four roll-aways, Romeo."

He was starting to relax. He gazed at his sons who were transfixed on two woolen buffalo. It was a double dose of Mutual of Omaha's *Wild Kingdom* - his animals watching their animals.

Matthew had been trying to speak to the twirling girl for an hour. He had taken his shirt off and in the process of struggling to remove it, had spun around and managed to lose Bill Montague. Awash in a suffocating sea of tangled hair and body odor, he threaded his way through a mosh pit of standing-room-only dancers near the stage. It was impossible to tell the men from the women.

He was now certain his head was morphing into a massive yellow gourd. He was surprised to see that people were not fleeing at the sight of his watermelon-sized skull. Earlier, he had wondered where he could find a pen or pocketknife to puncture a small hole at the base of his skull so the fluid building in his head might have a place to drain.

Dr. Billy had talked him out of his need for a shunt and explained that his head was fine, but Matthew had become annoyed with his friend's patronizing tone. He vaguely remembered shoving Billy into two women and knocking the three of them down, laughing hysterically and running down the dark aisle of the theatre. He was now circling a spinning dancer and was attempting to strike up a conversation.

"Hi, My name ... Matthew...

"What's your...?

"Live...?

"How do you...?"

Perhaps she was a German and did not speak English. It was exhausting watching this human dreidel. He checked his watch. It was nine o'clock. As the lithe dancer raised her arms, Matthew grimaced at a healthy crop of underarm hair. She seemed to be transforming before his eyes into a gyrating Hindu deity. The music began to heave, rising and falling in waves. Individual notes fell dripping from a thousand guitar strands of catgut. Suddenly, metallic-tasting pedal steel twisted the air while the Dead's drummers Bill Kreutzmann and Mickey Hart thumped their bass drums and rattled Zildjian cymbals. The music crested like a shimmering wave and then fell to the floor, crashing into pools of quicksilver. He looked at his watch again. It was five after nine.

Matthew sat down and felt his own heartbeat. *Thu-thump, thu-thump, thu-thump...* He looked at his watch. *Nine-ten.* Someone brushed against him.

"Sorry, man." A wolf-boy apologized to him telepathically and melted into a sea of pulsing lights. The lupine lad seemed friendly enough and something compelled Matthew to follow him. He suddenly stopped, panicked that he would not find his way back to his spot – the standing room only place at the edge of the left pavilion seats. If he got lost, he might never make it home. As a wave of guilt crashed over him, he contemplated writing a letter to his parents apologizing for turning his brain into Smucker's Jelly and for leaving his towels on the floor. His father was not such a bad guy for an escaped war criminal. Nazis had families. Two women with prehensile tails walked by eating what looked like hot dogs.

Food.

Matthew waited and then followed the girls hoping to trail them to the food station that was producing those marvelous smelling tube steaks. He had been at the concert for less than an hour and a half and he was lost inside the concert hall and within his own mind.

Karl got off the hotel room phone, looking distraught.

"Well, that's it. We are officially screwed. Swigert confirmed he can't attend the goddamn parade. Something personal came up. We now have to go public with the news and announce that R2 Hunt will be the Bicentennial marshal for the parade."

"Oh, honey, I'm sorry. There officially is no God!" Susie declared with empathetic conviction. She rubbed Karl's back and glanced at the boys reading their books on their rollaway beds. She loved the refugee camp feel of close-quarter vacation travel. Unfortunately, the requested Matterhorn room at the Madonna Inn had been taken and they were now bedded down in the Carousel junior suite with its huge wooden horse that grinned angrily and tossed its head against the reins.

The sinister-looking stallion had at one time been part of a real merry-go-round on the Santa Cruz boardwalk. John and George already had convinced Freddie that the carousel had been part of a tragic carnival accident in 1929 and that all the people riding it had died. The only survivor of the freak catastrophe was the single demonic horse, carved by a disaffected woodworker who had committed suicide after being fired from his job. He had vowed revenge on the community in his suicide note and had placed a curse on the horse he had created for the Grand Carousel.

Freddie glanced over his shoulder and met the stallion's frantic eye and shivered, turning his back to the animal. Susie chuckled to herself and then returned to her vacation reading: local newspapers she had brought with her to catch up on the daily rhythms of her community. She sneered as she saw a picture of Janine Randall and one of her baby-faced male escorts at a summer fundraiser for the Los Angeles Symphony Orchestra. Janine wore a crème colored Halston dress slit suggestively high on her thigh. She was perfectly posed with her slight tilt and hand resting just above her generous hips. A Cartier necklace complimented a low-cut neckline.

Susie knew the smile was a terrorist's list of demands. Janine's face-lift surgery most certainly included the removal of her dorsal fin. Susie realized how lucky Don Randall had been to escape his marriage to Janine with the clothes on his back, let alone the Balboa house. *She's a man-eater.* The last time she had seen Janine was at Hunt's market. Susie had been filling up the Impala at Junior's Mobil station when she spied Janine looking bored as Ralph Hunt worked to strike up a conversation with the aloof divorcee.

She sighed and looked up at her husband feeling blessed for having married for love rather than money. She was suddenly struck with an idea.

"Karl, I just had an inspiration. I don't know if it will help you and Russ, but I think I have a perfect candidate for your parade."

Kitty sat at the bar of Woody's Tiki Lounge and exhaled. Woody's was a nexus for the over-forty crowd. The lounge's garish interior was adorned with tiki torches, a bamboo bar, and grass skirt booths, and was frequented by a predictable diaspora of disaster survivors hopelessly scanning the horizon for a human life preserver.

Melissa Storms was talking to Kitty about her own divorce when she noticed a handsome man staring at her from across the horseshoe-shaped bar. Titillated by the attention, she created an excuse to use the ladies' room to be sure everything was in its place should he approach her to make conversation.

The Tiki Lounge was a favorite late-night haunt for predators like Ralph Hunt the Younger, who enjoyed patrolling the bar for vulnerable women in search of younger men and companionship. It was a permanent twilight of raw need and desperate, empty liaisons.

Kitty had never been to Woody's before but had heard that it was a place where old divorcees went to die. She despised cocktail bars but her damaged self-esteem and the persistent badgering from her friend to go out for a drink weakened her resolve. She agreed to meet Melissa for "just one" Mai Tai to celebrate her emancipation.

The notion of rejoicing in the deconstruction of her marriage seemed macabre to Kitty. A part of her had died and she was profaning its passing at a lounge for lonely-hearts. The divorce was in motion. The hostilities had now escalated to a point of no return. There would be no détente or reconciliation. If her mother were alive, she would have told Kitty that it was a Southerner's responsibility to secede from any corrupt union.

After his arrest, Garrett had been released on his own recognizance, but had been issued a restraining order by both Diane and Kitty. She had not heard from him nor had the children. Cliff had spoken to his attorney – an attractive young, west side divorce counsel. Kitty assumed that Garrett had interviewed counsel until he found his next mark – someone willing to accept emotional promissory notes and the delusion that this man was merely misunderstood.

A booming voice disbursed the gloom of her self-pity.

"Kitty? We have not met, although I've seen you at my market. I'm Ralph Hunt. Everyone calls me R2. So, how are you holding up?"

"Holding up?" She glanced dismissively at the man dressed in an open white linen shirt and cotton slacks. He was wearing a thin gold chain, linked bracelet, and a garish alumni ring with a massive ruby. She suffocated a laugh as the chubby lothario plopped down on the adjacent barstool.

"Well, this is a small town and we tend to take care of our own. Most of us hear about it when a good person has been through a trauma. From what I have gathered, you handled your situation with impeccable grace."

Kitty caught herself feeling flattered by the superficial praise but knew she couldn't trust a single statement spoken in a bar. She felt disheartened as she caught Hunt's bloodshot eyes darting down her body to her long, slender legs.

Kitty made distressed eye contact with Melissa, who had returned but now stopped behind Hunt and began making faces, causing Kitty to smirk. As Melissa aped R2, the handsome older man moved in behind her, inviting her to join him for a drink. Melissa slipped easily into conversation with the slender stranger, who was dressed as if he had just gotten off the eighteenth green at Pebble Beach.

Hunt was getting the impression Kitty was warming to him. Across the bar, Kitty watched over Hunt's shoulder as Melissa's eyes darted back to Kitty as she suddenly blew out her cheeks to mock the fat, bearded man and his mannerisms.

"I have never seen you here before," Hunt remarked as he lifted his finger to order another gimlet.

Kitty was trapped. She could offend the young man by dismissing him or allow herself to have a drink and relax. It was a pathetic moment, but she had learned that God gave her only the things she could handle. She should not be offended by the overtures of a sanguine, cock-sure bachelor. Even against her will, his attentions seemed to stitch up a portion of her shredded self-esteem. "Well, Master Hunt. Tell me about yourself. I understand you are one of the guardians of commerce in Huntington Hills and that you and your family are as essential to this town as its roads, schools, and jewelry stores."

Hunt smiled and peered into her glass, which was three-quarters full. He once again caught the bartender's eye and flicked a forefinger down toward Kitty's drink. He quickly followed with two fingers like a baseball manager signaling the bullpen. The bartender added an extra shot and mixed her a double.

Matthew wandered over to the left of the stage, sweating profusely and feeling faint. He spied an exit door and opened it to a rush of fresh air. His head had stopped swelling, but now his eardrums felt damaged, and he was afraid he'd gone deaf. He yelled and barely heard his own voice. He wondered if he would be able to master how to sign.

He could not register the million thoughts that raced around his head like Formula One race cars, but then in a sudden surge of focus, he fixated on the progress of a black carpenter ant as it traveled up the wall of the auditorium.

The music was still pounding relentlessly inside the Paramount. He leaned against the alleyway wall that ran parallel to the theatre and heard a click as the side door snapped shut, leaving him stuck outside. Matthew could not stomach the idea of working his way through the security guards to get back into the building. He had left his ticket inside his shirt pocket and was now frowning as a cold June mist descended on to a Friday night in Portland.

It was suddenly eleven o'clock and Matthew found himself shirtless walking east along a residential street. He remembered that Steve, Billy, and Libby wanted to leave at six a.m. to drive back to Marin, where his parents would be waiting. Matthew panicked when he didn't recognize the darkened houses or storefronts. He walked to the edge of a grass lawn and found himself overlooking the Willamette River.

Fear rose in his chest as some homeless men passed him, laughing and drinking in the shadows. He thought he heard one of the derelicts say, "Let's get him." Although Matthew had a good fifty pounds on the inebriated skeletons, he had very little experience with homeless people, and his father had warned him that any indigent could be dangerous. "Anyone who has less to lose than you do is a threat, at work or in a fight."

Matthew felt himself to be in extreme danger. He turned north and started to jog and then to run. He was in good shape, and a strange calming sensation overcame him as he ran. Jogging along the bluff that looked out over the river, he spotted a broken path that led down to a riverfront trail. As he zigzagged down the hillside toward the footpath, he fell forward and gained speed, his momentum carrying him out and on to the river path at a full sprint.

Running once again, he felt the intoxication of exercise beginning to moderate his frayed brain chemistry. He felt more in control as the pulsing in his legs pushed him farther and farther up the trail.

A light mist had softened everything to muted watercolor gray. Matthew could see the outlines of jagged pines and the ebony expanse of the river. He imagined he was a muscular white-tailed deer running through the forest, bolting between brambles and low-hanging branches. He gained speed and soon found himself sprinting.

He passed another shadow running in the opposite direction. Perhaps it was another deer-man like himself, racing in the shadows and moving with a strong heart deeper into the wilderness to find a safe, warm place to bed for the night.

Across the river, Billy Montague, Libby Robinson and Steve Ashmore were screaming Matthew's name outside the Paramount as stragglers, roadies, and cops milled and cleaned up.

"Hey," Billy said to a group of strangers, "did you guys see a dude with long dark hair and no tee shirt tripping out inside near the stage?"

A cop turned to Billy Montague and looked incredulous, "You're kidding, right?"

Susie squealed with delight as the car crunched into the driveway of the O'Reilly family compound. The headlights threw a beam of light across the chest and chin of a scarecrow of a man with silver hair and a long, dour face. Just as quickly, Freddie saw the man disappear from view. He was like the swamp creature from the movie the *Legend of Boggy Creek*.

"There it is again!" Freddie said out loud, as the walking man darted across the parking area with what looked like a wheelbarrow.

Susie barked in the back at her son. "That thing, Frederick Mark Patton, is your grand-uncle Seamus. Don't you go falling to pieces and seeing a monster in every shadow of this wonderful place. It is full of my happiest memories."

George offered reassurance. "Freddie, Seamus hasn't killed anyone in years. A few years back, he ate a kid to see if his brain would make him smarter. The Indians believed if you ate the vital organs of the things you killed that it would give you their power, so Seamus ate the kid's brain."

Freddie made a nervous sound as Susie slapped George's arm in reprisal. She ran across the gravel and jumped into her uncle's arms. Karl said nothing. Normally, he would chastise George and reassure Freddie, but he had neither the energy nor the inclination. He just wanted a little knock of gin and a soft pillow. He knew that Susie would be up half the night in the kitchen with her cousins, aunts, uncles, and her mother and father. Susie loved family, and this den of testosterone offered more men per square foot than a YMCA.

It was four a.m. when the police car eased alongside Matthew, who was now jogging along a stretch of highway. He was drenched from rain and sweat. He had been heading north, mistakenly thinking that he was progressing south toward Portland.

"You know it's still a good sixty miles to Seattle, son. Only you and black bears out at this hour. Why don't you get in and let me give you a ride wherever it is you're going."

Matthew stopped and waited while the patrolman parked his car. After a brief conversation and sharing his driver's license, he climbed in the squad car and lay down in the back seat. He immediately fell asleep as the officer called into headquarters on his radio.

"Yeah, it's him. I got his ID. Long black hair, no shirt, blue jeans… Negative, he's sawin' logs in the backseat. On my way. Ten-four."

Fifteen minutes later, Matthew woke up and bolted upright to the sound of the squad car's turn indicator. As the officer edged into the station parking place, Matthew could make out the thin chrome line of an approaching summer morning and the wild hair of Libby Robinson inside the foyer of the police station as she chatted up the night shift desk sergeant.

"Oh, my God, you're all right!" Libby screamed as she rushed to Matthew and grabbed his face with both hands. She planted a huge kiss right on his lips. It both electrified and resuscitated him.

"He was running to Canada. I told him the war was over and there's a no vacancy sign up for conscientious objectors." The officer laughed and moved over to pour himself some coffee.

The desk sergeant kept a somber expression, glaring at Matthew. "Son, I do not know what you took tonight, but I hoped you learned your lesson. My guess is staying sober beats dying of hypothermia on some Oregon logging road. Now get your ass back home to California."

"Yes, sir," Matthew said sheepishly as he inched closer to Libby. "Where are Billy and Steve?"

"Steve is hanging out near the park and Billy is driving around with another patrolman who offered to look for you." She punched Matthew hard in the shoulder. "You are such a buzz kill. We were so worried."

Libby slipped her hand into Matthew's arm and hugged him again. Matthew glanced at the amber-skinned pixie from Santa Cruz. A single daisy dangled from her hair as it fell down around her shoulders. Matthew reached up and gently pulled the flower and presented it to her. "Thanks for worrying."

He was angry at himself for being so stupid. He had been trying to make a statement about his coolness and ended up almost losing his mind. Why was it that he cared more about impressing people who disapproved of him than those who offered unconditional support?

Matthew suddenly worried about the long-term effects of LSD. Would he and his future wife have babies with big heads? Would he have a flashback ten years from now and jump out a hotel window like the guy in *Pit of Despair*? Had he changed his DNA forever like the Incredible Hulk? He felt the panic rising again, and then he smelled the freshness of Libby Robinson.

For some bizarre reason, he found himself wondering if she liked white-tailed deer.

CHAPTER 16

"Never look down on anybody unless you're helping him up."

~**Unknown**

The phones had stopped ringing for Junior Riggs. The peanut gallery of parasites, politicians, and media seemed to have lost his number. The *Tribune* article had reached the Army as well, and he was informed that his medal would be unceremoniously presented at the VFW post on the Monday before the Fourth of July. The medal already had been devalued, so it was only fitting that the ceremony be brief.

He felt the antipathy rising again, an emotional ulcer that would not go away, like that first cherry you get sliding in baseball at the beginning of every season. You spend the rest of the spring and summer, diving on the rough red dirt of a cement infield ripping that damn scab open, again and again. Junior could remember the burning sting and then the warm blood oozing into his pants with its burgundy bloom. It would discolor everything—his sheets, his slacks and his uniform. That scab never healed.

Junior switched on a fan and activated the hydraulic lift to elevate a gold-colored Toyota Corolla. Asian cars were piles of shit. He could not understand why people would buy them. Yes, they got better mileage, but they were four- and six-cylinder tin cans. Shit, if you wanted economy get a 60-horsepower VW bug. Say what you want about the Germans, those Nazi boys knew something about engineering.

He removed the spark plugs and was cleaning them when he heard a rumble in the back alley. He knew that sound. Eight cylinders and an eight point two liter engine. Wiping his hands, he peeked out the back door. There it was again - the Deville belonging to that crazy mother-fucker Thomas. No mistake about it this time. The dude was watching the back door of the loading dock. Junior's eyes squinted as if he was trying to solve a problem. The solution came quickly. *That mother is casing the market.*

A car honked and the service bell rang as a Mercedes entered the station. Junior pretended to be Redd Foxx, clutching his chest in shock. "Mr. Quintana. Oh my, God, Elizabeth. It's the big one. I'm coming."

Russ laughed out loud.

"Now what can a man like me do for a man like you?" Junior said. "You must be slumming over here. It is my understanding that you are strictly a Mission Street Shell man."

Russ removed his sunglasses and extended his hand. "Now, Junior, you know I could never buy gasoline from anyone but you—and a million Arabs."

"From your mouth to God's ears," Junior said as he watched Ronnie turn on his ignition and drive slowly up the alleyway to El Molino Road. Their eyes met and Junior flipped his head up, acknowledging Ronnie. Ronnie gave him a cold, empty stare. Junior had seen that gaze before. In his neighborhood, it meant only one thing: something was about to go down.

"Thanks, Russ. You are a champ."

Karl hung up the phone. He was feeling much better. Susie's idea had been a masterstroke. Russ had loved it and acted immediately. Quintana had volunteered to get to the editor of the local newspaper and to Hunt Senior before anyone had proceeded with ratifying plan B. Russ assured Karl that he would not allow R2 to submarine the idea.

The final full committee meeting was next Tuesday night and if the plenary session approved their recommendation, the parade would have its Grand Marshal.

Kitty was a bit tipsy. She was trying her best to be a good wing-man for Melissa, who was now in full flirtation mode, touching the arm of the man Kitty had labeled Mr. Silver. Attracting the opposite sex was like breathing for Kitty, but true flirtation was an adult game played with wit. Everything was perfumed and disguised. The sexual tension arose out of the innuendo. Verbal foreplay was a prerequisite to unlocking the hearts of true Southern belles. Yet, the game tonight was all about surviving her obsequious stalker while her partner determined her next move.

However, it was hard not to be a little annoyed by her predicament. The women had driven together. She was stuck, and now Ralph Hunt had cornered her. Kitty knew lots of men like Hunt—mean, self-centered meat-eaters. His empathy did not extend beyond his own self-interested pack of one. She kicked herself for agreeing to come to Woody's and now chastised herself for initially flirting with this young ox.

Hunt had tossed back five gimlets and was beginning to show signs of mild intoxication. He was getting rather loose with his words and his hands, making increasingly inappropriate remarks and touching Kitty's arms and shoulders, which made her skin crawl.

"We're going to have a hell of a Fourth of July parade coming in a few weeks. You should come as my guest. It looks like I am going to be the Grand Marshal this year."

"I read in the paper that the astronaut fellow from the Apollo mission was going to be joining our festivities." Kitty asked.

Hunt let out an annoyed guttural chuckle. "Yeah, those guys are flakes. I knew all along that it was not likely to happen. Patton and his band of conspirators almost did a number on this town but could not pull it off. What an asshole."

Kitty looked suddenly very innocent. "Who?"

"Karl Patton. I don't know if you know him. He has eight thousand boys. He's a stiff, conservative asshole like my old man. He's the kind of guy that wanted to send all of us to Vietnam and believes there's a Russian spy hiding behind every rock.

"The son of a bitch is working for me on a subcommittee and signed up this astronaut without consulting with me. I would have told him the whole thing had a low probability of happening. You know his kid's a drug dealer. Sells pills, aphrodisiacs, whatever he can lay his hands on."

"The astronaut?" Kitty said flippantly.

"Noooo," R2 mooed with chubby pursed lips. "John Patton. I caught the kid trying to sell some drugs out of the store the other day. I fired him. The other Patton kids are delinquents, too. Keep your kids away from that family. I hear his wife thinks she is some kind of witch. It's fucked up, I tell you. Oh, excuse my French." Hunt raised his hand to the bartender and ordered two more gimlets.

"Actually, the etymology of the 'f' word is Germanic, most likely from the word fokken, which means to breed. But I am sure you already knew that." Kitty smiled. She was beginning to enjoy toying with the besotted man-child.

Hunt narrowed his eyes. "Yeah, well, I got even with that jackass. Next week, the committee will vote for the changes that I have endorsed for the parade. We met last night in a special emergency session." He looked at Kitty with adoring eyes, which were now no more than watery slits balanced on two fat cheeks. "I'm sure this is boring the hell out of you. It's all BS and politics."

"Oh, no," Kitty lied. She touched R2's arm. "My father was a small-town mayor in Alabama. I find political affairs fascinating. Do tell me more."

Katie O'Reilly was in heaven. Her daughter had arrived, and her grandchildren were once again roaming Forest Knolls. This evening at the family reunion there would be three O'Reilly and Patton men for every woman, but it was clear that the women wore the overalls in this clan. The after-dinner kitchen patrol was a cacophony of laughter, insults, and jokes as dishwashers and helping hands crowded the massive basin and counter. Howls of amusement erupted from the dining room as the women gathered up dishes while maligning their men for obvious shortcomings. The house was a mélange of reassuring smells—cedar, apple pie, fresh-baked bread, cigar smoke, and rich coffee.

Karl was finally relaxing. He was normally wary around Susie's relatives. Years before, his first meeting with Seamus had ended with Karl laid out in a North Beach jail after a barroom brawl in a Tenderloin jazz club.

Seamus O'Reilly was a sinewy man with massive hands and stubborn muscle built over a lifetime of hard labor and hard living. He had a heart the size of San Francisco Bay, but the judgment of a sardine. Susie had learned many of her techniques for raising boys over an adolescence of helping her uncle and cousins dig out of their own self-inflicted circumstances.

Susie was raised to mobilize in times of crisis and to subordinate her own needs to the greater good of the tribe. In a strange way, she enjoyed the chaos and had long ago found her raison d'être in healing, stitching, bailing out, and chastising her clan of hapless and hearty O'Reilly men. She seemed to be most certain of herself in times of tempest and would secretly feel melancholy during the mud seasons of life. She thrived on calamity.

Earlier in the evening, Freddie and his cousin, Jonathon O'Reilly, had walked into the kitchen with Susie's uncle Declan. Declan grabbed Susie's shoulders and gently turned her to see the boys who were grinning and holding up four large trout. "Missy, most of the San Geronimo has been fished out. However, we have a secret place, and look at what these boys did with a little cheddar and treble hooks. Brilliant!"

Outside, John and George were playing horseshoes with their grandfather, Thomas, who was belittling their technique. "What do you young ladies do all day in that hoity-toity town of yours? Let me see those hands!" He examined their palms and shook his head. "Not a callus among your twenty fingers. We have some fence posts that need to be dug tomorrow near the road. I'll make sure you go home with some blisters to show your friends."

"Damn right, Thomas," Karl yelled without lifting his head from his paper as he sat on the front porch. "Give 'em as much work as you want.

They don't do a goddamn thing at home anymore. You'd think they were a two-man labor union."

"Now, Karl," Thomas said, as he leaned down to determine if his shoe was close enough to the stake. "There is nothing wrong with the notion of a union, especially if it helps protect the workers from being exploited."

"Oh, fuck. Here we go," Karl muttered.

"Dad does not believe in worker's rights, Grandpa Thom," Matthew said as he walked outside and broke into the conversation. "He believes in the benevolence of the boss man and finds nothing wrong with owing your soul to the company store."

Karl rolled his eyes. "Thomas, you would be very proud of your grandson. In the O'Reilly tradition, he is studying to be a communist across the bay at Berkeley and has great designs to tax and spend this country into the ground. What's even more exciting is that I am financing this transformation, and then perhaps when he becomes an elected official, I will pay again."

"Ah, but Karl, if a boy is not a liberal by the time he is twenty he has no soul."

"Yes, but Churchill promised that he would become conservative by forty or he had no head. I'm surprised you would quote the feisty patrician given that he was not well-liked by the Irish."

Thomas focused on Karl. "Personally, I found the man refreshing. He made some grave errors early in his political life, but he showed resilience during the Blitz." His countenance suddenly went gloomy. "War makes men do terrible things and sometimes, the least likely people do awful or extraordinary things."

Thomas bent slowly to measure John's horseshoe throw. He shook his head at his two grandsons in feigned disgust. John and George both laughed.

Ronnie slumped in his car and waited. The neighborhood was a rundown string of tiny stucco cottages separated by waist-high chain link fences and barred windows. Laundry was strung across back and side yards along stretches of wires. Although it was after eleven at night, people lingered everywhere, sitting, watching and resting, emotionless, hollow faces buried alive in a community that had lost its soul. A police air support helicopter circled overhead with a piercing spotlight. People did not live here. They rotted.

The front door opened slightly. Gonzales peered out and motioned with his head for Ronnie to come inside. Ronnie stepped out of the car and immediately sensed the eyes of an entire block fall upon him. He felt the hatred and contempt every time he entered a 'ville. He was an outsider and he understood their resentment. He wished he was carrying a weapon. In Hue, he called his M-16 "my baby blanket." As long as he had his "blankie", he could walk through the devil's fucking master bedroom.

In about five minutes, he would purchase a .44. He would transform into a Dirty Harry and once again become Doc Ronnie, the baddest motherfucker in the land.

After dinner, Matthew plopped down on the front porch of the house at Forrest Knolls and watched as the men played horseshoes under an outdoor spotlight. A confusion of moths swirled in erratic circles around the solitary beam.

Susie sat down next to her eldest son and put her arm around his shoulder. "Well, you have been too quiet since you got back from your concert. What's bugging you, Matthew? You are so irritable, just burning to pick a fight with your father, who, by the way, is on a vacation he does not want to be on. He would rather be sitting on the beach in Balboa. I think he is being a pretty good sport, but you, sir, are a surly ball of unpleasantness."

"I don't know. Everything just bugs me. Nothing has turned out like it was supposed to, and all I know is what I *don't* want to be and what I *don't* like."

Susie ran her fingernails up and down her son's back, scratching it like she used to when he was six years old. He immediately arched his back as he had when he was growing up and smiled.

"You missed that spot in the middle of my back. You always miss that spot."

Susie scratched the middle of his back furiously with an evil grin. "Matthew, you are in between two worlds—the order of men and the universe of boys. My guess is you have tasted some of life's forbidden fruits and are suffering from the letdown that always follows one's loss of innocence. A man in transition tends not to always feel good about himself. We raised you to work hard, know right from wrong, and it's not always such a bad thing if you offend yourself. It means you are building your own moral guardrails."

She looked over as Seamus O'Reilly was showing Freddie how to throw an axe into a eucalyptus tree. The first throw caromed hard off the wood, barely missing Freddie's foot.

"Watch it over there, Injun Joe. That child has to make it to the eighth grade."

Still keeping an eye on Seamus, she spoke quietly. "Some of us did not get the same life training and have a harder time exercising good judgment. The point is that when people are unhappy, they are usually unhappy with themselves. This is a Catholic compound. Do you need confession?"

"I mistakenly took some acid when I went to the Dead concert and I kind of freaked out," Matthew blurted.

Susie didn't blink. "So what happened?"

"You're not mad?" Matthew said, surprised at Susie's composure.

"It doesn't matter whether I am angry or not," she said. "You're an adult now and making your own choices. I'm curious about what you thought about the experience."

"There was a time when I was sure it was never going to end. It was a really bad trip," Matthew said, shuddering. "I just wanted to run and run. There were flying bats and melting faces. It's like my brain just went completely haywire."

"So, what did you learn? Did you have some great spiritual awakening and become one with the universe?"

"I hated the lack of control, and I know I'll never do something like that again. I do remember how much I liked the running part. I thought I was a deer. It was the only thing that made me feel, you know, right."

"Then consider it a good life lesson."

You're not going to tell Dad?"

Susie laughed loud enough to have Karl glance over at mother and son. "I think your dad has had all he can take for one month. He can't really handle information like that. It's too foreign and too frightening. You know when the Old Man gets scared…"

"He gets pissed."

"Right. My job is to protect all of you from yourselves and each other." She shifted her gaze back to Seamus as he tossed the hand axe. This time it actually sparked as it hit something in the dark and ricocheted back with the blunt head of the axe hitting Seamus in the knee cap. The gangly older man started to leap up and down howling in pain. Freddie and his cousin John fell to the ground, buckled up in hysterical laughter.

"And occasionally from a well-intentioned uncle."

Kitty saw Melissa writing down her number for Mr. Silver. She glanced at her watch. It was late. "Ralph, it's been wonderful making your acquaintance. I have hope for the future if the next generation is led by such urbane and articulate young men."

"You make me sound like I am twelve years old."

"Sugar, I was fifteen when you were getting your nappies changed."

Hunt lost his smile. "I have managed to catch the attention of women a lot older than you."

Kitty smiled. "If they get much older than me, you'll be changing *their* nappies."

"At least let me walk you to your car," Hunt insisted.

Kitty's eyes darted toward Melissa, who was whispering in Mr. Silver's ear. Kitty was sure Melissa would be leaving with her; her friend would never consent to a one-night stand.

Kitty was exhausted and wanted to leave. Besides, she had extracted what she had needed from Hunt. "Well, there is no harm in that in your escorting me. I am glad to see that chivalry is not dead in this lugubrious part of the world."

Hunt brightened and moved with amazing dexterity for a man legally drunk three times over. Kitty met Melissa's eye and pointed to the parking lot. Melissa nodded a half-centimeter and broke into an affected laugh as Silver said something close to her ear.

The parking area was still warm from the day's heat. The lot was relatively empty as cars sped along the San Gabriel Avenue, a busy thoroughfare that marked the eastern boundary of Huntington Hills.

Kitty turned to find Ralph Hunt literally in her face. Instinctively, she held out her arms and gently backed off, the way a startled hiker might retreat slowly from a bear.

"Oh, that's just about close enough, Gentle Ben. Thank you for a nice night, and I wish you luck as you take over for your father."

Hunt smiled and stared drunkenly at Kitty. "You're a sexy woman. Have you ever been with a younger man?"

"Well, I do drive my sixteen-year-old son to school at times. And there was the ninth grade when I had a beau who was in middle school but he had been held back twice because he could not seem to master his calculations."

"Quit playing around with me. You were in there talking German about breeding and shit," Hunt growled.

"My, Mr. Hunt. You *are* a charmer. Look, my good friend Melissa will be here any minute. I appreciate your animalistic attraction to me, but I am old enough to be your mother. A young mother, but nevertheless, your mother. I suggest you go home and sleep off your vodka gimlets, and I am sure we will cross paths in the aisles of your supermarket."

"You have a nice ass. Let me see it." Hunt moved quickly and clutched Kitty by the waist. Sliding his hands down her dress, he quickly found its hem and moved his fat fingers up her hamstrings and on to her panties.

Kitty slapped Hunt's face. He grinned.

"I met a lot of girls like you at school. They say 'no, no, no' but they mean 'yes, yes, yes." He grabbed her left bottom cheek and squeezed it hard enough to hurt.

"Please stop. You don't know what you're doing."

"Oh, I know. I'm taming a tart and getting into her knickers."

Hunt reached his right hand over and roughly shoved it into her blouse, tearing the fabric. Kitty squirmed but could not escape his powerful grasp.

"You bastard. Release me this instance or I'll scream."

"What the hell is going on here?" yelled Melissa. "You get your fat paws off her, you spoiled little shit, or we'll call the police and report a rape."

Hunt laughed. "Rape, schmape. You can't rape a whore."

Mr. Silver, who was accompanying Melissa to the car, made an effort to intervene.

"Hey, pal, let the lady alone and watch you mouth."

Hunt considered the thinner, older man and grinned. "I would stay out of this, grandpa. If those are your real teeth, you are going to want to keep them."

Melissa went ballistic. "You go to hell and if you ever touch another woman, I will call your father and Norm Pinsky. Go home and try to locate your manhood under all that fat. Get out of here! Now! Leave!"

Hunt remained remarkably composed as we walked away. He turned one last time.

"Pinsky is a family friend. Hell, I helped get him his last promotion. I think he would take the word of a Hunt over the word of a …"

"You are pathetic," Melissa shouted.

"It's the last name that matters most in life. Ladies, you have a splendid evening removing all that make up."

"Fuck you!" Melissa shouted.

Kitty gave Melissa a sick smile. "This is what I get for dancing on the grave of my marriage."

"Honey, I am so sorry this happened to you. It's my fault. Let's go down to the police station and report that bastard."

Kitty readjusted her dress, pulling down the skirt and tugging at the shredded bodice. "No, my guess is it would not go very far."

"You're not going to let him get away with it?"

Slipping into the passenger seat, Kitty remained somber.

"I think it was Gandhi who said, 'An eye for an eye would make the whole world blind.' Just take me home."

CHAPTER 17

Revenge is the act of passion; vengeance is an act of justice.

~**Samuel Johnson**

Russ Quintana was frantic. "Karl, we got a big problem. When you guys were up north, Hunt called a special emergency session to deal with the Swigert thing. He elected himself parade marshal and the committee voted. It was a two to one vote. Since we did not know about the meeting, we couldn't cast a ballot. We were set up, and now this thing is off the rails. What's even worse is I feel bad for Junior Riggs. He's thinking he is finally going to have his day.

"Tonight's the final meeting. We can go in there and protest this decision, although I'm not sure what good it will do. The deck is stacked against us." Karl listened, rubbing his eyes.

Russ sounded defeated. "Look, buddy. I respect what you tried to do, but I'll be honest. It's a goddamn parade in a pissant town on the Fourth of July. Get over it. Let's move on. Let the little shit have his day in the sun."

Karl hung up the phone dejectedly and went downstairs to tell Susie. He hated to lose at anything and felt like he was betraying some basic moral law by allowing corruption and self-interest to prevail because good men did nothing. As he shared the disappointing news, he could see his wife growing more furious.

"You look like you want to say something."

"Karl, I just got off the phone with Kitty, and she told me a story. Apparently, she had a run-in with Hunt last weekend. I will flatten the tire of every float in the parade before that fat butt rides anywhere on behalf of our town."

The boys had been riding back and forth from the Red Devil Fireworks stand all week. Each year, Red Devil would erect a makeshift farmer's market of combustibles along Huntington Hills Drive to satisfy the latent male need to play with fire. A kid might save up enough money for the basic $4.99 *Black Cat* package, the larger $19.99 *Demon* family pack or the granddaddy of all ordnance, a cornucopia of pyromania called *Cauldron,* priced at $199.99. Assembled in a three-foot by two-foot crate with an exterior painted with skulls and crossbones, *Cauldron* was the Pandora's box of fire.

Each year, some well-to-do Hills family was rumored to have purchased *Cauldron,* although no Patton boy had ever seen the insides of the massive box of missiles. The firework collection was a multicolored profusion of sparklers, smoke bombs, cones, Roman candles, Piccolo Petes, and pinwheels. Having access to so much gunpowder and saltpeter was heaven for an advanced arsonist who could deconstruct each missile only to use its contents to create an even deadlier and more destructive weapon of mass destruction.

Bruce Hegarty's back yard had become an anthill of activity as the boys constructed forts in anticipation of their upcoming battle. To clueless Jane Hegarty, the frenetic construction was a reassuring sign that her son was not growing up too fast. "Look, Dan, Bruce, Sean and the Patton boys are building club houses. Isn't that cute?"

Dan Hegarty lowered his reading glasses and made a face. "Why in the hell are they building four of them?"

The Hegartys were set to depart for an annual Santa Barbara Fourth of July vacation. Although he had made the Senior Babe Ruth all-star team, Bruce was the youngest of the five kids and his parents were now well past the point of sacrificing a family holiday to broil in the midsummer purgatory of a July baseball tournament.

"Been there, done that," was Dan Hegarty's standard response to a neighbor asking if he was going to cancel his summer break vacation plans to watch Bruce pitch. Bruce would remain behind to play baseball and stay with his grandparents. With no parents at home, The Towering Inferno '76 would take place as planned at the Hegarty house.

George had procured his explosives from buddy Glenn "Plums" Plumdon, a fellow baseball player who spent the last two weeks of each June camping with his family at Rosarita Beach. Given that Mexico was only three hours south of Huntington Hills, there was a healthy black market in illegal fireworks as teens moved across the border with their families on annual beach vacations.

Plums controlled the pre-Fourth of July market for M-80's, M-40's, firecrackers, skyrockets and smoke bombs. George was short of money and had to turn to Freddie to finance the purchase of his ammunition. Once Freddie heard the details of the upcoming firefight, he demanded to be included, agreeing to lend George the funds only if he could join the Independence Day battle.

The firebases were fashioned from scrap wood, cardboard, tarpaper and discarded corrugated metal. The rules of engagement were simple: combatants could assault each man's citadel only from the front or sides. Firecrackers, Roman candles and bottle rockets could be used to repulse attackers. The half- and quarter-sticks of dynamite could be tossed at the outside of forts to weaken their structural integrity. Forts must be open in the back to afford their occupants an avenue of escape. Each soldier of fortune was required to fill a bucket of water and have it handy in the event that a fire got out of hand. Participants would be required to wear goggles, gloves, tin foil and football helmets. Last man standing won.

Freddie could hardly contain himself as he stood in the bathroom creating a highly flammable bottle of homemade napalm. He planned to create a wall of fire around the forts of his opponents and then disable them like the fixed fortifications along the Maginot line. He might be the youngest enlisted man in this battle, but he was the most experienced in understanding the wild and unpredictable properties of combustion.

Ralph Hunt II called the final meeting of the 1975-1976 Huntington Hills Bicentennial Committee to order at the community center.

"Miss Saunders has distributed the minutes from our session last week. Motion to approve?"

"Mr. Chairman, I would like to call for a recount of last week's vote." Karl was now standing.

Miss Saunders looked uncomfortable and glanced up at Hunt, who shook his head in disgust and glowered at the other committee members. "Karl, it was because of your unilateral and reckless recruitment of a celebrity who probably had no intention of ever actually showing up to our town's parade that we were forced to meet in emergency session to appoint a replacement Grand Marshal. A few of you were unavailable, while others took time from our jobs and families to meet and move forward. I'm honored to serve. I also do not think our rules of order require a recount."

"You never allowed our committee to offer our alternative candidate, Raymond Riggs, Junior. Ray has just been awarded a Bronze Star for heroism. He is a business owner. He's a veteran who deserves our thanks for his heroism and duty to our country. He would be honored to be our Grand Marshal, and although he does not live in our town, he is part of the fabric of our community."

The doors opened up and Susie walked into the back of the room and sat down.

"Excuse me, this is a private meeting," Hunt growled.

"Actually, Mr. Hunt, given that this is a public committee, I believe it is open to any taxpayer in the community. I thought it would be good for me to improve my understanding of civics in our town."

Hunt looked at Miss Saunders, who was smiling at Susie's confident response. "Well?" he said to the homely secretary.

"She's correct, Mr. Hunt."

Karl continued. "Actually, my subcommittee could have been represented at last week's meeting. Mr. Myers was in town. It is true that two of us were on vacation. However, Russell Quintana was also in town and was home all evening. No one attempted to reach him. Parliamentary procedure requires a quorum. Our committee, which was responsible for this event planning, was not even consulted."

"So you want another vote?" Hunt said. We have four subcommittees. If we end up deadlocked, it falls to the chairman to break the tie."

"We understand."

The chair for the Rose Park festivities, the cantankerous Len Downer, immediately spoke up. "The Rose Park committee votes for Corporal Raymond Riggs as our Bicentennial Grand Marshal." He smiled at Karl and then gazed fixedly at Hunt.

Russ Quintana spoke up, "We second the nomination recommending Junior Riggs."

R2 peered at ancient Freeman Dewitt. "We would like to nominate Ralph Hunt, Junior," he said.

Malcolm McDonald, the owner of the Huntington Hills Hardware stood up like a broken beanpole. "We second that vote for Ralph Hunt, Junior."

This was his moment. Hunt beamed with triumph looking like a pig that had found the rarest of white truffles. "Well, I guess it falls to the chairman to break the tie."

The door to the meeting hall opened again. Melissa Storms, Kitty Erickson, and Police Chief Pinsky walked in. The women pointed at R2, who, drained of color, suddenly resembled an albino walrus.

The phone rang and Seamus O'Reilly called upstairs, "Comrade, a call from the Kremlin!"

Matthew groaned and sat up in his bed, assuming it was a call from his mother, or even worse, his father. He felt a sudden surge of dread, wondering if Susie had had second thoughts and decided to share the LSD episode with Karl. He could not imagine his mother reneging on a promise to insulate him from his father.

"Matthew?"

"Yeah, who's this?"

"It's Libby. How's it going?"

"Hey, how'd you get my number?" He hit his forehead, immediately regretting sounding like he was put out by her call.

"Oh, is it okay to call here? I spoke to your parents to find your number in Marin. Your mom's really cool. She talked my ear off. I now know all about your aunts and uncles and your questionable Irish heritage."

"Great. Did she tell you that I am trapped in the middle of nowhere with no television and insane relatives?"

"It actually sounds kind of fun. It's just my parents, brother and I here in Santa Cruz. It gets boring. Dad teaches at City College and mom runs a boutique and is a dog trainer."

"Dog trainer?"

"Oh yeah, she takes all the hard cases. The biters, the howlers and the whizzers."

"Whizzers?"

"The ones that pee everywhere."

"My little brother Freddie is like that."

"Oh, he's a baby?"

"No, he's eleven, but it is easy to scare the piss out of him."

Libby seemed to be biding her time. "You recovered from your mind marathon at the Dead concert?"

Matthew sounded embarrassed. "Yup. I don't think I'll ever do that again. Somehow Dr. Billy didn't prepare me well for melting faces and people who resembled storks."

Libby laughed. "I tried something like that once and thought I was a rabbit. I had been reading *Watership Down*. Everything was going cool until we started hiking by a river and then we saw some real rabbits and a black rabbit appeared. In the book, the black rabbit is like a symbol for death, and I flipped out. I spent the next four hours hiding in the back seat of the car."

"*Wow*, that sound's *really* fun, like my evening. My mom's take is anything that causes you to lose control can't be good for you."

"You told your mother?"

"Shit, I tell her everything. Beats confession and she's pretty cool about rationing information to Dad."

"Wow. That's very cool."

"So, how's Stevie?"

"Oh, we broke up right after the concert. We just like different things. He wants to be serious, and I want to see other people."

Matthew's chest suddenly tightened and his mouth felt dry. There was a long pause.

She spoke slowly. "You're making this kind of difficult. Are you doing anything on the Fourth?"

Matthew was relieved. "Well, if you call watching a dozen Irishmen get drunk, play cards, and get in trouble with their wives for *doing anything*, then, yes. Otherwise, no. I'm not heading home to L.A. It's too far and I have to work on Tuesday."

"Well, we have a Democratic fundraiser for our local representative, Congressman McFall. He's an old friend of Dad's from Manteca. We have a big bonfire, hang out by the beach and light fireworks. I figured you might be a little lonely."

Matthew clenched his fist and silently pumped it into the air. "Let me check my trusty Karl Patton Fireman's Fund Weekly Planner." He waited a beat. "Hmm. No appointments that weekend. Yes, I think I can attend. Actually, it would be very cool."

"Bring your surfboard. My brother knows some good breaks near Capitola."

"Got it. Can I bring anything else?"

"Nope. Well, actually, bring a sleeping bag. There will be lots of bodies sleeping around the house. You can show up any time on Saturday morning, and then you can hit the road Monday after the traffic dies down."

"Cool."

"Any problems, call me. I left my number with your uncle yesterday when I called."

"Yesterday? I didn't get any message. Wait a minute." He ran back up to his bedroom and looked on his floor. A thin cigarette paper was discarded on the floor near his bed. Turning it over it read: *Liberty 4087815717*. It appeared to have been written by a three-year-old. Matthew groaned and ran downstairs.

"Let me guess, 408-781-5717?"

"You got it."

"My uncle doesn't have all his oars in the water. Next time, ask for Mrs. O'Reilly or Comrade Matthew."

"Oh, he was very funny. He kept calling me Liberty and asked me if I was excited for my birthday on the Fourth of July. Look, I got to go. Dad wants to use the phone. I will see you Saturday."

Matthew hung up and fell back on to the couch.

Katie and Thomas O'Reilly were reading the paper and heard a war whoop from the hallway.

"Is your grandson drunk?" Thomas asked.

"In love, I suspect, Thomas. It's a form of intoxication except the hangover takes years to hit."

Thomas lowered his paper, "And what the hell is that supposed to mean?"

"I'm marrying Don, Ronnie."

Diane stood at her son's door. "Baby, we're moving down to Newport. I got an offer on the house today, and I'm going to take it. I want you and Joanie to have the money from the sale. It will give you both a chance for a fresh start."

Ronnie rose and hugged his mother. "Hey, I'm happy for you. Did you tell Joanie?"

"Yes. She is going to be my maid of honor, and Don would like you to be his best man."

Ronnie smiled. "Best man? It's been a long time since anyone has used the term 'best' in the same sentence with my name."

"Baby, it's time we all forgive ourselves. We aren't perfect, but we have a right to be happy."

Ronnie hugged his mother again and rested his chin on top of her head. He had already decided to leave. He could always come back for the wedding. With the money from the house, he would have enough to make a life for himself somewhere in the Northwest. But he still had a score to settle. He had the mission mapped out down to the minute. At eleven hundred hours, he would enter Hunt's Market through the open loading dock door and hide in the back supply room. At twelve hundred, the store would close early, with a week's worth of holiday cash in the safe. If R2 Hunt got in his way, he would teach him what it really meant to go dinky dau.

R2 hesitated and watched the newcomers in the back of the room. Melissa smiled a vindictive grin. Pinsky was hesitant but kept whispering into Kitty's ear. Kitty looked up and caught R2's eye and waggled her finger in an admonishing way. She shook her finger and mouthed very clearly, "No, no, no."

Karl was not sure what was going on and Russ Quintana was equally clueless.

"Hunt, what's it going to be?" barked Downer.

"Well, as chairman, I need to recuse myself from the vote since I have a conflict of interest. I would like to suggest we defer the vote and ask a third party to break the tie."

"No need," said a voice from the corridor.

Ralph Hunt Senior wheeled himself in the room and was immediately surrounded by committee members. He was smiling and excited to be back among his friends.

"Son," he said, disappointment in his voice, "You have to make this decision."

R2 surveyed the room, taking in the expressions on every face, especially those of the women standing at the back of the room with the chief of police. "Folks, I have decided to remove myself from the running. I vote we move forward with Junior Riggs as our Grand Marshal for the Bicentennial parade. May I get a motion to adjourn this committee?"

"So moved," shouted Russ Quintana

"Second?" Hunt said, sounding deflated.

"Second," shouted Kitty.

Outside, in the parking lot, Karl looked incredulously at his wife. "What the hell were Kitty, Pinsky, Hunt and Melissa doing here tonight?"

"I think Melissa asked Ralph Senior to dinner. The girls gave me a ride here so I could support you. They also wanted to see how the wheels of city politics work. We are all *so, so* insulated as stay-at-home moms. Then Kitty called Norm and told him she though Garrett had followed her to the community center. Norm came right over to make sure Garrett wasn't lurking nearby."

Karl smirked. "When you women walked in, R2 looked like he had just seen The Exorcist. You are a devious creature, aren't you? He should have known better than to screw with the first wives."

"Well, in a way, you could say we were helping exorcise a bad spirit. Congratulations honey. I'm proud of you - even if you didn't have a plan." Before he could protest Susie kissed Karl and he hugged her waist.

"Woman, I think when God made you, he used Adam's rib and two of his testicles."

"But that would have left Adam a eunuch."

"Exactly."

Will Crane couldn't take his eyes off Rebecca. "You look beautiful. I did not think it was possible, but since you became president, you seem to have let go of a ghost."

Rebecca smiled and looked out into the darkness of the horizon line. They sat on the deck at the newly opened Ventana Inn in Big Sur. The central coast spread out across a vast canvas of ebony night. There was little light pollution in this part of California, and the summer constellations were arching overhead as the cool fog laid a bed of soft cotton at the foot of redwoods and scrub brush.

Will pointed toward the southwest. "That's Vega. To the bottom and right is Altair. The bright star there is called Aquila the eagle. Deneb is the third star of the constellation triangle. Deneb is supposed to be a swan. Personally, I don't see it. Now the Milky Way, like you, is miraculous and gorgeous, but difficult to see unless you are away from the lights of big cities. When you have dark skies, you can see her running north to south, curling through the summer triad. Always trailing at the hem of the Milky Way's evening gown is Scorpius. His heart burns red with love in the form of the crimson constellation Antares. He is always there following her, his mother galaxy."

Rebecca sighed and reached out for Will's hand. "You are the most debonair man I have ever met. Why do you put up with my selfishness?"

He raised his glass of champagne and smiled. "I am your Scorpius and you are my Milky Way."

Rebecca smiled contentedly and sipped the final finger of Bollinger. As she tipped her glass, something struck her upper lip. Her eyes darted to Will. She held the glass up to the light of the fire. The engagement ring, a ruby encrusted in a constellation of diamonds, glowed. Her eyes widened, and she turned to Will, whose eyes never left her face.

"Rebecca, please marry me. I need you and you need me. Between the two of us, we make up the most complete human being on the planet. We are here on this earth for such a short time, and I want to be with you for every tiny milestone. I want to wake up next to you and I want you to be the last thing I see at night. I will never leave you. In my family, we mate for life."

"Oh, Will," she whispered. "I'm not sure what to say anymore."

He looked dejected. "Well, I tried. I checked the Guinness Book of World Records and the number of declined proposals before yes was one thousand times by some guy in England. She finally consented and he died of surprise."

"Darling, I don't want you to die of shock but I accept."

Will bolted up from his seat. "You mean it? God, are you serious?"

"Yes, I love you. I could not find a more perfect man. I just had to realize that any success I have means nothing unless I can share it with someone, and that someone is you."

Will knelt by her Adirondack chair and leaned in to kiss her. Off in the distance, Antares flickered, a ruby red sparkler in the midsummer sky.

CHAPTER 18

You have to love a nation that celebrates its independence every July 4, not with a parade of guns, tanks, and soldiers who file by the White House in a show of strength and muscle, but with family picnics where kids throw Frisbees, the potato salad gets iffy, and the flies die from happiness. You may think you have overeaten, but it is patriotism.

~Erma Bombeck

The Fourth of July reveals much about a small town. In its preparation, one can measure the populace's capacity to work together and subordinate their differences. In celebrating any birthday, people reveal their commitment, apathy, excess, and parsimony. The nucleus of any community is its volunteers—those that show up to staff the concession stands, decorate the floats, drive the ancient fire truck, dust off the old trombone to play Dixieland jazz, and lose themselves entertaining children and the elderly.

The Bicentennial festivities of Huntington Hills were intended to remind everyone that freedom is earned and its privileges are worth defending. In a town of sixteen-thousand souls, freedom meant the opportunity to move in any direction, chart your own trajectory, conform to society, or rub against its grain.

Karl felt the flutter of happy anticipation for the first time in several months. The following week, he and Rebecca were pitching a big construction client that had been with A&A for twenty years. Together, they were focusing on the bigger accounts of larger competitors and were pleased with the receptivity they were getting from prospects that liked OB&T's intimacy, diversity, and their specialized risk expertise. One insurer started referring to Karl and Rebecca as Sonny and Cher, and the sobriquet stuck.

Karl was comfortable with Rebecca as president and saw a logical succession plan that had him becoming president when she succeeded Bob as CEO. Susie had convinced him that the risk of starting over with no safety net and four boys on a conveyor belt toward college was not a good idea. She trusted Rebecca and encouraged Karl to support her. Rebecca had promised to enlarge his equity stake in the firm and give him an ironclad contract that protected him in the event of a change in control. Though they had known one another less than a year, he found that he trusted Rebecca more than he did Bob.

Karl was looking forward to the parade and picnic. He had spilled a little blood protecting the integrity of the parade and was proud of his civilian Purple Heart. The entire Riggs family would be at the festivities, and it would be good for his town to see the pride that Pops Riggs had in his son. Junior was everything Karl believed in—hardworking, self-sufficient, and a man who defended his country by putting himself in harm's way.

Karl had barely missed Korea and had heard stories of the heroism and sacrifice at places like Pork Chop Hill, the Hook and Frozen Chosin. He wondered, like all men, what he would do if faced with a life-and-death situation. His favorite book had always been *Les Miserables*. He understood and sympathized with Jean Valjean. In the suburban splendor of America, a man did not get up each day wondering if someone was going to knock on his door and take him away because of his religion or political affiliation. He was not forced to choose between crime or starvation. He had never had to test his own values to know whether he was a sunshine patriot or a man for all seasons.

It was eleven-thirty, and he was due at city hall with Susie to prepare for the parade. The procession would start at three o'clock and conclude at the park at four. Most of the town would be spread across a patchwork quilt of blankets and lawn chairs at the destination, Roses Park.

From ten thousand feet, the community park now looked like a pair of discarded plaid pants. The greenbelt of property that had been donated to the town in the 1920s by a wealthy industrialist had served as a gathering place for families more than a half-century. Many residents identified with the thirty-acre sanctuary as a monument to personal firsts: the wobbly fifteen feet of a bike without training wheels, an awkward stolen kiss, a disgusting sip of forbidden beer, or the first chance to watch a sky illuminated with a thousand floral bursts of Fourth of July fireworks. Roses Park smelled of summer grass and endless possibility. Like the town itself, it was virtually impossible not to encounter a friend or acquaintance while walking your dog or jogging. It was a sacred setting made special because of the people and their understanding that once a year, they would celebrate being part of something bigger than themselves.

Freddie had fashioned his dugout from discarded corrugated tin found behind a building undergoing construction. The round fort had narrow slits near the roofline. The wooden roof was fashioned from square plywood and tarpaper. Freddie had cheated and infiltrated Bruce's back garden the previous evening, burying plastic milk cartons of his homemade liquid napalm in front of Bruce and Sean's forts. Once a rocket or firecracker ignited his dark fire liquid, he would be able to charge their burning buildings from the front and flush them into submission with a barrage of pyrotechnics and smoke bombs.

George's fort was rudimentary. He did not plan on remaining inside but on the offensive with brown bags loaded with quarter-bricks of firecrackers tied with fuses. The homemade satchel bombs would create enough distraction that he could charge Freddie's fortress, take his supplies, and then roll up the other enemy pillboxes. He had studied Roble's fort and was certain he could blow up the left side and collapse the structure. Roble had been more consumed with his interior design, spending time finding carpet, assembling a small table and a shelf that held a transistor radio.

George smiled. Sean was building his hooch as if he were expecting a month-long siege like Khe Sanh. If George had anything to do with it, this would be no war of attrition. Roble did not know it, but he was a plantation French colonialist who was about to drink the bitter dregs of his own vintage Dien Ben Phu.

Hegarty aka "Higgs" was going to be a problem. He was a military history fanatic and had studied defensive strategy. He had built a sloped defensive berm to cover the front of his dugout fort with two sides protected by large metal plates, the kind that road works crews often laid over potholes and asphalt under construction. How he dragged those 250-pound armored rectangles to his back yard was beyond anyone's comprehension.

The fort looked impregnable, with slits in three locations that offered Higgs a complete field of fire. He had drilled three holes below each slit where he would presumably launch his bottle rockets and Roman candles. Higgs would be the deepest weed to root out. His metallic Masada reeked of stubborn home field advantage and was going to require a firestorm of ordnance culminated by a direct hit by the flare gun.

Ronnie got out of the Deville and opened the trunk. He was still surprised at how heavy the .44 felt in his hands. The large-bore cartridges could do some serious damage to anything that got in his way. He knew the weight and heavy recoil could make the gun less reliable beyond a few yards. Hollywood made Dirty Harry look like a pistol marksman. The fact was you could miss a target as close as five feet if you forgot to make concessions for weight, speed, and distance.

In country, he knew guys who had carried .37 pump-action shotguns and Colt M199s but he had never used a .44. He did not anticipate using the gun, but wasn't afraid to shoot. He'd already capped seven people. The Corps never told you that the real problem wasn't killing; it was that your victims never stayed dead. They come back every night to visit you when you close your eyes.

He was dressed in camouflage pants, army boots, and a black sweatshirt. He stuffed work gloves and ski mask into the waist pocket of the sweatshirt. He had stashed a plain canvas satchel in a trunk that he had found while rummaging through his father's old clothes closet. Glancing at his watch, he saw that it was eleven forty-five and the dock door was open. He jumped up on the loading platform, pulled his ski mask over his face, and tucked his hair under a hair net. Easing open the door, he slipped inside the back storage area and entered the bathroom door, keeping it open only a crack so he could observe any movement inside.

Gert Spitz peered through the slats of her garden gate and waited until the young man with the mask had gone inside the market through the loading dock door. Armed with a push broom, she scurried across the alleyway to peer into the bins, removing a case of spoiled oranges and two moldy cantaloupes. A sudden burst of noise that sounded like the backfiring of a car caused her to dart across the alley and back into her yard, shutting the postern behind her.

Junior Riggs was keyed up about the parade. It helped to be at work that morning. It had been a long time since he had felt anything other than resentment or empty relief. He had remained true to his commitment to be one of the few gas stations open on the holiday and given the fact that the Fourth fell on Sunday, he was certain his Mobil and Hunt's Market were the only retailers open along Huntington Hills Drive from South Pasadena to San Gabriel. He glanced at the clock inside the station office. It was already quarter to twelve.

Perhaps it was an old habit dying hard or that manic sixth sense that beleaguered him during search and destroy missions, but Junior felt compelled to check out the alleyway behind his business one last time to ensure his perimeter was safe. He had a full safe, and ninety percent of the town's cops were regulating activities in and around the parade route and in Roses Park. He was going to close at two o'clock and drive over to the park, where he would change into the olive drab he'd sworn he would never put on again.

He locked the station door and circled north before slipping into the alley and the shadows of an ivy-covered wall. As he walked toward Hunt's Market, he heard movement across the alley and smiled as the Crab Lady peeked at him through the fence.

It sent him into a flashback: walking down some Central Highlands blood red dirt road. People watching – numb and dumb – just staring from the other side of walls, fences, and rice paddy levees. The sun was at 1200 hours. The Crab Lady's furtive eyes locked on him. In the old days, you could not shake that sense of dread when you were stepping into a hostile 'ville.

On S&D missions, every villager was assumed guilty. You had to expect that every door was rigged with claymores, that everyone was a friend of Charlie, and that the VC were watching the entire ballet of incompetence from nearby tree lines that afforded them perfect lines of sight. Vietnam had been part of some old white man's genocidal vision of a Caucasian world order. He could almost hear Norman whooping and screaming fanatically as he did during firefights. "Kill those injuns, boys. The only good injun's a dead injun."

The loading dock door was open. He stuck his head into the market. "Mr. Hunt, you around?"

He looked inside and could hear mindless elevator music playing as a skeleton crew of workers prepared to lock up and return to their families for the afternoon festivities. Turning to leave, he shielded his eyes from the sun, once again adjusting to the light outside. He looked down the alley to Oak Knoll Road that ran perpendicular to Huntington Hills Drive. Everything seemed tranquil.

Junior was satisfied. He stood with his hands on his hips and glanced up at the sun. Lowering his eyes without moving his head, he saw the old lady still watching him from the fence. He smiled and strolled back toward the station when he froze. It was Ronnie's Deville, parked to the northwest of the Mobil.

The staccato pop of firecrackers splattered off in the distance sounding like a firefight. Junior felt an overwhelming urge to fall to the ground but resisted. Five years later, he still felt naked without the weight of his M16 and the uneven tug of a half dozen M61's fragmentation grenades. Out of the corner of his eye, he saw movement inside the store as the loading dock door suddenly eased shut. Something was not right. He circled back to take one last look.

George had not expected the initial assault from his flanks, and his ears were ringing. Roble had fashioned some kind of circular rope that he had tossed like an explosive Frisbee. The throw had been perfect, with four M40's tied to each end of a long interlocking strand of rope and homemade fuses. They had landed on George's roof and exploded in succession. Smoke bombs now ignited in the open yard that separated all the forts. There was a crackle of firecrackers outside his defensive positions. Suddenly, five bottle rockets streamed out of the smoke and struck the front of his fort, with one managing to thread the narrow slits of his observation ports, exploding inside near his head.

Freddie launched five M-40's in succession at George's fort and leveled a dozen skyrockets at Roble's hooch. Freddie had conspired with Higgs that they would take out George and Roble first and then wage a final fight to the death once they had eliminated the two weaker foes. Freddie had predictably reneged on his treaty and embedded enough napalm at the base of Hegarty's fort to ignite Lake Superior.

George covered his head and struggled to light his own bombs. He managed to ignite an M40 but dropped it next to his foot. The bomb went off and his foot felt as though a sledgehammer had hit it. He stood up as three smoke bombs penetrated his fort, making it impossible to see. He could sense someone moving toward him and off to his left. He decided to get out into the open. As he hopped into the clear area, he was hit with a half-brick of firecrackers that stung him like a thousand bees. He could hear Freddie laughing as he flailed and swiped at the exploding air. Pulling the flare gun from his belt, George wildly pointed and fired the flare in the direction of Hegarty's redoubt. There was an explosion and ensuing mushroom cloud that climbed over eight feet into the air.

He could hear Sean Roble laughing, "Oh, my God! Look at that!"

A scream tore the air. Through the smoke, George saw a flaming figure running across the back garden.

"Help me! Jesus, put it out!"

It was person—on fire. Instead of dropping to the ground to extinguish the flames engulfing his body, Bruce staggered through the yard and out the back gate into the alleyway. The boys were frozen, immediately aware of the repercussions and consequences of their stupid decision to play with fire.

George watched as the flaming figure disappeared through the ivy-covered portal. "He's going to die," he muttered.

Choking on the shock of the explosion and the rush of toxic smoke, he finally found his voice and screamed out, a frightened primal call for someone to intervene. "He's dying! Somebody help him!"

An arm swung around Junior's neck in a combat chokehold and he felt the cold pressure of a gun muzzle under his chin. "What the fuck are you doing here?"

His larynx compressed, Junior spoke in a high pitch. "I thought someone was breaking into the store, man. We can't have crime in this area. It's bad for business."

"You don't know shit, motherfucker."

"I know it's you, Ronnie, and I know what's going on with you. I know what it's like to hear thunder and have to dive to the ground. I know that sick feeling in the pit in your stomach that makes you want to scream. The terror, man, I know it. It wraps around my neck like a goddamn hangman's noose. No matter how many times I say it, I can't just drive on, man. The dudes I capped won't let me forget. I can't outrun the bullets. My old man says that for every fucking month a man spends in combat, it's takes a year to mend his mind."

Junior felt the hold loosen but not release. Ronnie drew close to Junior's ear.

"You don't know shit about me. I just want to get the fuck out of this town and be around grunts who understand what it's like."

"Hey, man, I know what that's like, but you don't need to do this."

A massive explosion suddenly detonated and both men fell to the floor out of instinct. Ronnie looked outside the dock door and saw a plume of fire rising out of an adjacent back yard. "What the fuck?" he said.

Suddenly a flaming figure of a youth stumbled into the alleyway. Ronnie dropped his gun and leapt off the loading dock. In a flash, he tackled the human torch and rolled over him to extinguish the flames.

Behind the man and singed crying boy, three kids ran into the alleyway and stood watching. "Higgs, are you okay?"

Ronnie screamed at them. "Call a medevac, you idiots."

George saw it was Ronnie and couldn't believe it. The psycho had saved Bruce Hegarty's life.

Freddie ran up to the market doors and pounded furiously, yelling for someone to call the fire department.

Junior dashed back to the alleyway, grabbed the handgun, tossed it into the garbage bin, and sprinted back to help Ronnie. Ronnie had stripped off his own sweatshirt and wrapped the boy's second-degree burns. He barked orders at Junior and the boys. "You guys get into that market and get me several bottles of cold water. Run! And see if they have any sterile gauze. We can't remove his burned clothing."

Bruce was coughing and moaning as Ronnie grabbed the boy's wrist for a pulse check and yelled at Roble to get a blanket. "We need to elevate his legs to keep him from going into shock."

Ronnie could hear the police sirens now as Junior returned with Andy Haskell from the market. "We called an ambulance." Andy said. "What the hell happened?"

Ronnie was not listening. He was inventorying all the steps he must take to stabilize his wounded comrade. "Cover the area of the burn. Use sterile bandages. It's mostly first- and second-degree burns. The blisters need to be left alone. No signs of milky white skin."

He held Bruce Hegarty tightly and started to cry. "You're going to be okay, grunt. You got the million dollar wound. You're one lucky little motherfucker."

The ambulance arrived and police interviewed the kids. Freddie and George were in the back of one squad car, while Roble was tucked in the back of another, crying. Everyone's parents were being contacted. The fire department had extinguished the blazing fort and confiscated the fireworks.

A young firefighter walked over to Junior, Ronnie, and Officer Mitch Walsh. "Those little radicals had enough quarter-sticks of dynamite to blow up this block. Jesus!"

"So, Ronnie, what were you doing when the youngster ran out into the alley?" Walsh was writing notes for his report.

Ronnie hesitated.

"The man came by to congratulate me on being the Grand Marshal of the goddamn parade," Junior said. "You know Ronnie was a doc up in Hue. Made my time look like R&R in Bangkok."

Walsh looked up at Officer Bob Maddox. "Well, it looks like we have a couple of heroes here."

Engine Company 926 rolled up its last hose and secured its equipment. A handsome young fireman ran around the passenger side of the vehicle, jumped on an elevated step, and pounded on side of the truck. The engine revved reverberating like a locomotive as it lurched unevenly over speed bumps, splashing pools of brackish water against the heaps of blackened wood now piled next to the market's trash bins.

East of the market, an entire town was congregating along the parade route, gathering near backyards pools, lighting barbeques, and staking out their picnic perimeters at Roses Park. The town had closed its eyes and made a wish, ready to blow out the candles of the nation's birthday cake.

The white worn gate creaked open. Gertrude Spitz moved with her broom over to the garbage bins. She lived alone in a simple one-story home, close to her son who would come over each week to maintain her property and make sure that she had the food and medicine she required. Gert rarely changed out of her morning clothes or dementia, but was active inside her shaded, hydrangea-filled garden, where she compulsively hoarded the odds and ends she uncovered while rummaging through the large industrial bins behind the stores along Huntington Hills Drive.

The Hunt's Market refuse containers were overflowing with pieces of burned, wet wood, and a double load of Fourth of July cardboard that had arrived on Thursday as families descended on Hunt's to purchase grilling meats, potato salad, coleslaw, beverages and watermelon.

As Gert poked the containers aside with her broom handle, her sharp eyes caught the glimmer of something inside a produce box. Leaning against the filthy container, she eased the broom handle into the loop of the silver object and strained to lift it from the box. After it slid off the smooth handle several times, she pinned it to the side of the metal dumpster and dragged it to the top. A massive handgun dropped with a thud on the wet asphalt. Scrambling off her box, she scuttled over to the handgun and picked up the .44 magnum. It was heavy in her hands but she sensed this weapon could help protect her and the lifetime of treasures she had accumulated in her garden.

Karl and Susie were enjoying a conversation with Vin Nobalski. His son, Ed, had come to help his father enforce parade security and seemed to be a terrific young man. Vin excused himself when he heard the sirens and fire trucks racing down Huntington Hills Drive. He waited, listening to status reports about the fire and any possible injuries. Ten minutes later, he interrupted Karl and Susie as they threaded red, white, and blue paper streamers through the slats of a 1930s Hunt's Grocery Store delivery truck. "Karl, could we have a word?" he said.

Eddie watched his father from across the parking lot as Karl's expression changed from carefree to apoplectic.

"Are you shitting me? Is anyone hurt? Vin, you better call Pierce Brothers and order two coffins, because those boys are as good as dead."

Vin laughed and put his hand on Karl's shoulder. "Karl, it's the Fourth of July. We expect this sort of thing. It's just lucky that we caught it in time. Apparently, Ronnie Thomas, of all people, was over with Junior at the Mobil, saw the whole thing, and saved the Hegarty boy. He field-dressed the wounds better than an EMT. He was a medic in Vietnam. The kid's a goddamn hero."

Russ walked over and smiled at the group.

"Anything wrong?"

"That is a rhetorical question, right?" Karl replied.

Matthew had spent the day surfing with Sean Robinson, south of Santa Cruz. The marine layer had bled off early, leaving warm sun and feathery conditions for smaller three-to-four-foot sets. Matthew loved surfing and the surge of adrenaline he got from using every muscle in his body to catch and control a wave. He was sure-footed and strong, preferring the larger Northern California waves to the smaller southwest swells that often rolled into Southern California beaches. The surfing culture was accepting and mellow. No one shouted except when they were stoked with excitement. The only conflicts arose over girls, territory, or the lack of surfing etiquette. Everyone was generally in the same economic bracket—young and poor—and often lived at home or out of the backs of their vans.

Libby greeted him at the shore and wrapped a towel around his neck as he unzipped his wetsuit. Wearing a bathing suit top with a short tie-dyed skirt and flip-flops, she seemed to be floating on the soft morning breeze. Matthew had only seen her wearing loose dresses and jackets and had not appreciated her figure. She took him in with her large eyes and unusually long lashes. She had a slight build, with the short powerful legs of a gymnast and skin that reminded him of maple syrup. Restless tresses of golden sienna hair that resembled the Northern California hills in August fell around her shoulders.

Catching him peeking up at her as he dried his hair, she shivered and pulled his towel around her shoulders drawing him in and purring as he touched her. A few hours later they were dressed and sharing a beer as their back yard filled with friends and fellow Democrats.

The Robinson's political fundraiser was unlike anything Matthew had ever seen. Congressman McFall was a handsome and confident presence. When Matthew met the congressman, he was awed by his laser stare and firm handshake. He asked Matthew several questions about Cal and his opinions on the upcoming election.

McFall was impressed with Matthew's grasp of the issues facing the American electorate. "I know Mo Udall. He is a tremendous thinker. But I think Carter has a better chance. People see him as an outsider, and he can really offer an alternative to the stumbling policies of the GOP. I am certain we can take the White House. Matthew, we have inherited a real mess. Interest rates are climbing. The nation's reputation is in tatters. The Middle East has us addicted to fossil fuels, and we have no renewable energy strategy. The Republicans want to only help the wealthy, cut taxes, and deregulate industries and then blame others when deregulated markets cause prices to increase. The middle class and poor will continue to take it on the chin as long as these brutes are in power."

Matthew was enthralled with McFall and the eclectic gathering of Northern California Democrats and Santa Cruz socialists. It was strange but it seemed like Republicans all looked alike. Democrats seemed a more diverse group, with everyone genuinely looking to government to play a more influential role in ensuring social equilibrium.

As twilight fell, the first coils of a distant fog bag floated closer to shore, a steady marine breeze picked up off the ocean and drove most of the guests away from the beach. Libby and Matthew sat by the bonfire as sparks and smoke twisted and swirled in invisible currents. He leaned in and kissed her. She slipped her arm around his neck and returned his energy and passion. After a few minutes, she stood up and silently took his hand.

"Where's your sleeping bag?" she said.

"Sean's room."

"Get it. I'm freezing."

Matthew bolted up the wooden stairs to Sean's room in two energized leaps. The stereo was playing the soundtrack to *Five Summer Stories* by Honk. He knocked on the door and turned the handle hoping he was not interrupting an amorous liaison.

"Sean?"

He poked his nose slowly through the crack of the door and saw the reflection of an empty bedroom on the sliding closet door mirrors. The room was a shrine to surfing with three boards standing in the corner. Apart from a "Keep On Trucking" placard, the walls were plastered with surfing shots and posters of Gerry Lopez and Shaun Tomson attacking massive winter swells on the Hawaiian north shore at Makaha, Waimea and the Bonzai pipeline.

He lingered for a moment, thinking about Libby while staring at a bumper sticker that read "Reelect Congressman McFall." Matthew knew he was a traitor, a modern Montague fraternizing with his father's sworn enemies—the Liberal Order of Capulet, a house his father avowed would always collapse because it was fashioned out of rice paper altruism and built on the landfill of rotting good intentions.

Screw the Republicans, Matthew thought, suddenly remembering his purpose. People like Ford and his father had had their chance and fucked it up; besides, liberal girls were a hell of a lot better looking. He grabbed his sleeping bag, ran down the stairs and into the dark of the Independence Day evening.

Plate 4

The Basic evasion techniques utilized when egging motor vehicles full of hostile teenagers, or law enforcement, include achieving diffilade positioning to avoid detection and to facilitate a counterattack or cover for confederates' escape. In the end, every technique must address the angle of pursuit. Any pursuit angle over 90 degrees guarantees a successful escape, assuming a positive combination of aerodynamics and the geometry of pursuit with the physics of managing one's energy-to-weight ratio (i.e. you don't fall down). After Hours Grab Ass (AHGA) has launched the career of many a fighter pilot.

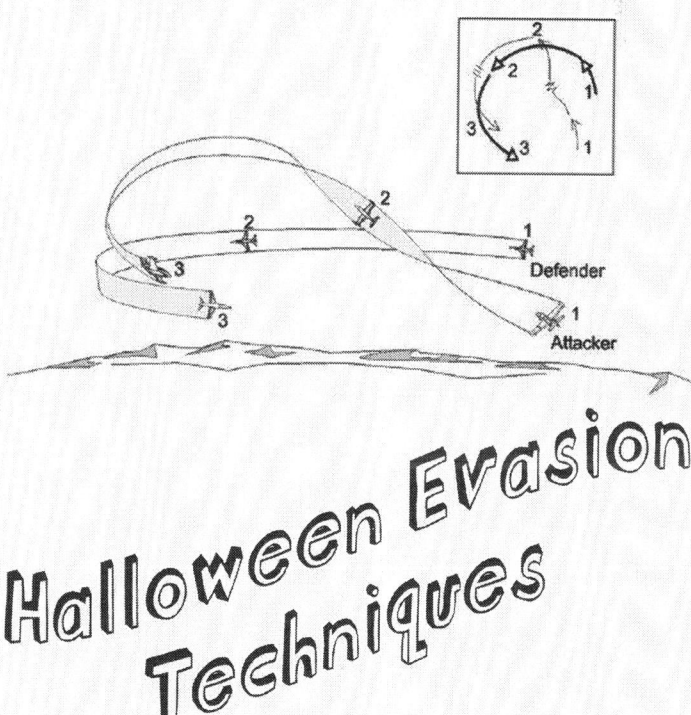

Defender

Attacker

Halloween Evasion Techniques

AUTUMN

Fall

CHAPTER 19

"I know but one freedom and that is the freedom of the mind."

~Antoine de Saint-Exupery

Fall in Southern California arrived on the end of a red-hot iron. Summer seemed to stall in the LA basin and linger like an unwanted guest for weeks beyond Labor Day. While the rest of America enjoyed Indian summer days, temperate open window nights and a palette of changing colors, autumn seemed to consist of a single large sycamore tree that would unceremoniously drop its brown leaves as it succumbed to the withering dry heat and smog that erased the mountains from view. In Huntington Hills, air conditioners, swamp coolers and fans rattled and groaned, pleading for a change in temperature. For those less fortunate, nights were endless equatorial hours of sweaty sheets and discomfort until the cool autumn dawn would creep into their homes through open screen doors and windows.

With her boys safely through another summer and firmly chained to classroom desks, Susie felt as though a life-threatening illness was now in complete remission. Nothing fazed her—not the hundred-degree heat wave, the poor air quality of the San Gabriel Valley, or chaotic evening routines filled with school forms, bike bags, books, homework assignments, and back-to-school nights. The dog days of desultory men had ended.

This particular September 1st, she had informed her platoon of men that the days of free breakfasts and fights over when one should leave for school were officially over. She had declared her own self-rule - no more rising at dawn, no more thankless debates or ungrateful men grabbing toast and bacon as they left a house full of dishes and grease smoke. She would sleep in and leave breakfast, dirty dishes, lunches and punctuality to the boys and Karl.

It was the first day of his sophomore year, and George was feeling the loss of identity that comes from being a high-school middle child. Two classes of older kids towered above him, and a new class of freshman had arrived, wet behind the ears and eager to assimilate. George needed to distinguish himself – to wear something that made a statement about who he was. Perhaps a new freshman girl would notice him or an upper-class cougar would choose to toy with his affections.

As he looked at his pathetically worn out periwinkle Hang Ten tee shirt with its signature footprints, he knew he must take a calculated risk. He considered the suicidal thought of borrowing John's Carlos Santana tee shirt but decided it was too perilous a risk since he and John shared the same high school hallway.

George was desperate. He needed to showcase that the freshman caterpillar had emerged from his summer chrysalis to become a teen-aged Tiger Tail. He had noticed how upper classmen wore nicer clothes to school. He surveyed his depleted hand-me-down wardrobe of faded iZods, surfer shirts and striped rugby pullovers that made him feel like an Easter egg, and realized that his clothing spoke clearly to the public that nothing about George Patton had changed. In this dark moment of self-centered doubt, he made the fatal decision to borrow one of his father's pinpoint Oxford cloth dress shirts.

Karl was a hoarder. He possessed and stored every piece of clothing he had ever owned. His dress shirts filled multiple dressers and several bureaus. Each drawer was stuffed with a rainbow-colored palette of neatly folded and bagged dress shirts that easily accommodated George's starved adolescent build.

Susie stirred softly as George tiptoed into their bedroom to survey the treasure trove of Brooks Brother Oxfords. George considered it a very low probability that Karl would notice that one of his sixty shirts was even missing.

Karl had been the only boy and youngest child in a family of girls. He took little interest in his sisters and considered himself to be an only child. He inherited midwestern frugality and understood the need to care for possessions to ensure they would last. In his youth, the shadow of the Great Depression had only recently receded, and the goal in any family of modest means was to get maximum utility out of any apparel, appliance, toy or equipment. When your shirt collars frayed, you reversed them and squeezed another two years out of the garment. Depression-era frugality was tough but at least as the only boy, Karl never had to share.

When Karl married and had four boys, he had no notion of how his organized, rational world would come unhinged. Life became a permanent freeway on which he occupied the middle lane. He now understood why men died earlier than their spouses.

Karl's home office was his castle and its door his portcullis. A boy could not enter this sacred chamber without knocking. At times, the door would be locked. One was forbidden to borrow a pencil, piece of paper, tape, scissors, or any other item from this eight by eight man cave. Susie accepted his periodic self-exile as a way for the "only child" to cope with the fact that he must now share everything. Karl loved his family, but needed some place where he could work, protect his sanity and preserve a few precious possessions from the dirty, destructive fingers of thoughtless simians.

Weekends would find him justifiably ballistic as tools that he had wire brushed and lubricated after each use were left to rust outside by a teenager trying to fix a flat tire. He would lose control when encountering paintbrushes that were not cleaned with turpentine but returned to their milk carton home, and left to harden like punk-rock Mohawks.

Bikes were routinely left on the front lawn and sometimes stolen. He could not fathom how this spoiled generation had so little regard for precious possessions. The Baby Boomers were pampered, sloppy, and undisciplined ingrates who had perfected the art of consumption but did not honor the notion of restraint.

Karl's biggest peeve was how George and Freddie treated their Sunday clothes. He would turn five shades of purple when entering the boys' closets to see blue blazers and neckties tossed on the floor with their grey slacks crushed under items that had been tossed into the closet when they had been ordered to clean their rooms. For an ex-Army officer, disrespect for clothes signified disregard for work, authority, and responsibility.

To add insult to injury, Susie had once again gone on strike, refusing to press anyone's clothes. She had done the math and realized that her domestic obligations were paying her less than minimum wage. Karl was convinced that some local neighborhood organizer had undermined her commitment to ironing and home economics.

"Karl, I do a lot of things around this house, but you make enough money now that you can take your shirts to Chung's. The boys will wash and iron their own shirts."

Karl grumbled but knew he was outranked. Nonetheless, relying on someone outside the family to handle something as intimate as the care of his clothing—and then paying him an exorbitant fifty cents per shirt—was irritating. The local drycleaner, Mr. Chung, might as well be wearing pantyhose over his face and wielding a gun.

Chung did not like Karl, who intimidated him. George and Freddie would laugh, telling their friends stories about the legendary cat-and-mouse games between Karl and Mr. Chung. It was not uncommon to enter the cavernous cleaners and find the front counter unattended. Karl would pound on the visitor's bell as the drone of rotating dryers and the hot breath of steam made it difficult for the proprietor to hear a customer.

With a frozen grin, Chung would appear from behind a mechanized clothesline of hanging garments and plastic bags. As soon as he saw Karl, his manufactured smile would drop to a scowl and his pace would slow, the way a dog moves once he has been ordered out of doors. Chung endured a detailed list of Karl's demands and specific requests for mending, spot repairs, and pressing.

Susie's edict that George and John once again wash and iron their own dress shirts led to unintended consequences. As his own supply of shirts dwindled, George procrastinated about washing and ironing. He soon found himself wading through his dirty clothes and reusing shirts until the wrinkles and smell required action.

Given Karl's surfeit of shirts, George's initial pilfering of his father's clothes became a habit. He wore the shirts during the hours his father was at work and then slipped the soiled garments back into Karl's laundry hamper. In a few instances, George forgot to return a shirt to the hamper or left it in his locker at school – but there were so many shirts. Karl could barely keep track of his car keys.

On this particular October Saturday, Karl and George were buying some new cleats for football and had made an unexpected stop at the cleaners. A striking young Asian girl with black silk hair came to the counter. "Is your father here?" Karl asked with patronizing enunciation.

She glanced nervously behind her. "He's busy in the back. Can I help you?"

To the rear of the building, hiding behind an endlessly rotating line of hanging garments, Karl spied two legs in polished cotton slacks.

"I know you're back there, Chung!" he shouted over the girl and the thrum of dryers. The slacks were frozen in place. Karl flashed a disingenuous smile at the young teenager and spoke loudly over her shoulder. "Please tell your father when he's no longer hiding that he needs to call me. I am now missing *five* of my best shirts!"

Chung finally came out to the front counter, but he was now angry. "I no have your shirts!" he shouted at Karl. "I count each one. See tags and clips?" Chung held up the hem of a shirt which had a unique customer marking number ironed on to the shirt and a safety pin with a colored piece of paper.

"I want my shirts, Chung!" Karl yelled and stormed out to the car. As he turned the ignition, he yelled. "I'm missing five Oxfords and that goddamn guy is probably supplying the Red Army with them!"

George's heart nearly exploded in his chest. Five shirts? He hadn't realized he had been so reckless in keeping track of the borrowed button downs. Terrified that Karl would retaliate against the timid immigrant proprietor and be arrested for suffocating him in an industrial dryer, George went to Susie.

"You know those shirts of Dad's that are missing?"

Susie stopped paying bills and glanced up at George.

"I think I know where they are," George said, gaining confidence as if somehow he might get credit for locating the missing pinpoints.

"You *think*? Do you care to share with me what you *think* happened to Dad's shirts?" she said, stifling a smile.

George confessed his misdemeanors and gathered up three of the shirts that had been stuffed under his mattress, promising to recover the other two from school. Susie tried to look disappointed as she took the shirts and shoved them into a canvas bag on the back porch.

"Listen, it can't be a surprise to you that your Dad is very meticulous about his things. He considers it a personal violation if you take something without his knowledge. Think of him as a country – a very territorial nation. You don't want to fly into his airspace or cross his borders without permission. I don't care if it is socks, underwear, or an undershirt. He counts everything. For God's sake, do your own wash and fold your laundry."

George later heard his mother sharing with Karl that she had "miraculously" discovered the missing shirts. Karl's inventory was returned to normal. However, he still suspected that he was being insulated from the truth.

After years of broken buttons, misplaced garments and high prices, Karl would never bring himself to apologize to the dry cleaner. Chung would continue to wage his own covert war on Karl by putting too much starch on his shirts or keeping the occasional five dollar bill that he might find in a pair of Karl's gabardines; and while Karl could have patronized any other cleaners, he seemed to delight in this strange game of spy versus spy with elusive Mr. Chung.

John had gained weight over the course of the summer and was now more man than boy, evocative of any number of leading men of Hollywood. His deep brown eyes, dimpled chin and unselfish charm made him a favorite of every woman and girl between the ages of fifteen and fifty. Still a straight-A student, he was now holding down honors Calculus, Biology and History. He had joined a fall basketball league in nearby Pasadena, where he had his first exposure to the athleticism of the predominantly black high schools that competed in higher divisions in the L.A. county school district. In his first game as point guard for the Hastings Ranch Indians, John scored twenty-four points, pulled down eight rebounds, and had eleven assists. Karl had made a rare appearance at John's game and could not stop deconstructing his performance as they drove home.

Having played basketball in college and spent hours under a driveway spotlight he had wired to the garage to illuminate the kid's basketball court, Karl considered himself the majority stakeholder in his son's success.

John's game had significantly improved in less than a year and he was now a candidate for all-CIF honors. He was a dutiful and talented player, listening to his father and trying to apply the principles of Karl's idol, John Wooden, to his game. Father and son would periodically attend UCLA basketball games and watch as the Wizard of Westwood led his teams to a record eighty-eight consecutive wins and four thirty win undefeated seasons. Wooden had retired the previous year after winning ten straight national championships and was replaced by Gene Bartow, a nice but hapless changeling that Karl said could never step into the old man's high tops.

"So, on that give and go in the third quarter, why did you try to force the pass? You could have pivoted to the right and then drove left, dumping in a left-handed hook. They were double teaming Bobby, and that guard was too quick for him."

"I don't know. Coach called the play and I sorta forced it. Bobby didn't get a good jump on the guy after he dished it to me, and I tried to lead him, but the other guy got his hand on it and tipped it to their center."

"John, there is a reason why they call the point guard the general on the court. He has to make the calls. Remember what Wooden said, 'relentless repetition leads to rehearsed excellence'. Jesus, you're better than that."

John was tired. He wanted to be somewhere else. His team had just won sixty-six to twenty-eight. He had been the leading scorer and had dominated every facet of the game. But, unlike his brothers, he found it easier just to mollify his father.

"Got it, Dad."

George and Freddie had been under house arrest for at least four of the last twelve months. In that period of incarceration, Freddie became obsessed with a new television show, *In Search Of,* hosted by actor Leonard Nimoy. The weekly series explored the shadowed glens and dark recesses of the modern world where the paranormal rustled. Freddie's need for temporal certainty often collided with his fascination with the unexplained. He could not resist stories of disappearances, alien encounters, hauntings and unsolved mysteries. Freddie was, at his core, a fear junkie. He was preoccupied with anything that could harm, kill, or maim. His propensity to project when he was afraid was leading him toward a life as a compulsive hypochondriac.

Earlier in the year, he had been consumed with the swine flu epidemic that had started with the death of a soldier at Fort Dix, New Jersey. He had followed the newspaper articles as epidemiologists narrowed the culprit to Swine Origin Influenza, a cousin to the deadly pandemic of 1918 that had killed an estimated one hundred million people across the globe. The Ford administration had been caught off guard by the lack of resources necessary to vaccinate an estimated two hundred fifty million citizens.

Freddie pestered Susie daily to get an appointment with the family pediatrician, Dr. Gildersleeve, to be inoculated. Susie was reticent to be among the first movers to get a swine flu shot after reading about side effects and complications from an early set of immunizations that purportedly killed more than two hundred fifty people after infecting them with Guillain-Barré syndrome. Freddie was more than willing to risk Guillain-Barré for the sake of his own salvation. He had seen Charlton Heston in *The Omega Man* five times and understood what would be required if he ended up as the last man on earth following a pandemic.

Freddie carefully followed newspaper heat maps that tracked the virus, and warned everyone that if 1918 was any indication, the whole family would soon be laid out in a make shift morgue at the Middle School under white sheets next to their neighbor, Mr. Gilmore. In recent weeks, the link between Guillain-Barré and deadly immunizations had been discredited, making it harder for Susie to deflect Freddie's frantic pleas for the family to be vaccinated.

Kitty was on the phone laughing uproariously as Susie shared her youngest son's latest obsession. "I'm inclined to call the damn doctor and have him give us all placebo shots just to shut him up."

"Susie, I am nominating you as the patron saint of boys—Saint Suzanne. I still may join you as a martyr, although I have not seen signs of stigmata."

Susie paused and turned to see if any kids were in the room. "So when are you leaving us?"

"January. Seth and Candace are actually excited. They have not heard a word from their father in more than six months. He's stopped paying alimony. Cliff is working on seeing what we can do to garnish his wages, but I understand the rapscallion has gotten himself terminated from his agency. My little sister Jane loves Charleston and has three children. Two of them are Seth and Candy's age. Arriving during the school year is better for new children. You are a novelty and more likely to stand out. It's so hard when you try to break into a new place. Kids and adults, for that matter, can be so cruel. You can spend your entire life never really fitting in.

"I'm finally going home, Susie," she continued, her voice quivering a bit. "The West is not the proper climate this orchid. I require the heat and humidity of Southern pretense and the fertilizer of genteel lies. I am an old soul living in the new world. It's time to go home, but I am leaving on my terms."

"Kitten, you are what I call instant gentrification. All anyone needs to do is add you to the mix, and the quality of the neighborhood improves. We love you, dear."

"Et toi, amour. Kiss that grumpy old Republican of yours and those fabulous boys, especially Jonathon, and make sure he knows that in a past life he was Lancelot du Lac. He has a keen sense of honor."

"They are all diamonds in the rough, and it takes a skilled hand to contour any stone into a gem. Will we see you before Thanksgiving?"

"Definitely. I believe the first wives need one last assembly like Macbeth's witches."

"Bubble, bubble, toil and trouble. Ooh, I like the sound of that. "

The television was loud. Freddie lay on the ground doing his homework while Karl swore out loud. "Listen to this goddamned buck-toothed cretin. He'd make a better can opener than a president."

ABC's Frank Reynolds had just asked Governor Carter to elaborate on his plan for making job creation his highest priority. As Carter was giving his answer, Karl continued to talk to himself.

Freddie scrutinized Carter as the earnest Southern upstart smoothly answered, "*Another very important aspect of our economy would be to increase production in every way possible, to hold down taxes on individuals, and to shift the tax burdens on to those who have avoided paying taxes in the past.*

"*These kinds of specific things, none of which are being done now, would be a great help in reducing unemployment. There is an additional factor that needs to be done and covered very succinctly, and that is to make sure that we have a good relationship between management, business on the one hand and labor on the other. In a lot of places where unemployment is very high, we might channel specific, targeted job opportunities by paying part of the salary of unemployed people and also sharing with local governments the payment of salaries, which would let us cut down the unemployment rate much lower before we hit the inflationary level.*

"*But I believe that by the end of the first four years of the next term, we could have the unemployment rate down to three percent—adult unemployment—which is about eight percent overall, a controlled inflation rate, and have a balanced growth of about four to six percent, around five percent, which would give us a balanced budget.*"

Karl groaned out loud. "Look at Ford. He looks drugged. This guy Carter will drive this nation into a ditch. He does not know shit about monetary policy or how to get things through in Washington."

Ford responded, "*In my judgment, Frank, the best way to get jobs is to expand the private sector, where five out of six jobs today exist in our economy. We can do that by reducing federal taxes, as I proposed about a year ago when I called for a tax reduction of twenty-eight billion, three-quarters of it to go to private taxpayers and one-quarter to the business sector. We could add to jobs in the major metropolitan areas by a proposal that I recommended that would give tax incentives to business to move into the inner city and to expand or to build new plants so that they would take a plant or expand a plant where people are and people are currently unemployed."*

"Dad," Freddie interrupted as Ford concluded his response, "Ford seems kind of stupid. He couldn't get the swine flu vaccine out for ten months. America could have all died. Carter looks smarter."

Karl listened infuriated as Ford concluded his remarks. He turned and nudged Freddie softly in the butt with his foot. "Carter? You little pinko! You don't know what the hell you're talking about."

Freddie stood up gathering up his books and papers. He shuffled towards the den door and then hesitated. "Ford's stupid and he's going to lose!" He slammed the den door and Karl could hear him sprinting up the stairs to his room.

Karl did not take his eyes off the television as he muttered, "You're probably right, you weird little man."

CHAPTER 20

"Where there is no imagination, there is no horror."

~**Arthur Conan Doyle, Sr.**

Ronnie guided his Harley Davidson FXE Super Glide into the Mobil station and slowed to a stop, revving the engine. Junior came out of the office sporting a huge grin.

"Man, look at that hog. Looks like that beast could take you all the way to the North Pole."

"Just need to get as far as Sand Point before the snow flies."

Junior walked around the new motorcycle admiring its clean lines and engineering. "Seventy-four cubic inch Shovelhead, polished cases, rocker boxes." He stopped and peered at the engine. "Ten to one pistons, ceramic coated cylinders, ported and polished heads, and ooh, lookie at that big-ass cam, and twelve-inch z bar. My, my, I see you only got a single seat. Not planning on taking me with?"

"Didn't figure you for a cold weather guy," Ronnie smirked.

Junior looked to the east. The heat wave had been pushing late October temperatures over 80 degrees. Smog choked the eastern horizon and obscured Mount Wilson from view. It was the kind of afternoon that hurt to breathe if you made the mistake of running or exercising.

"A little snow would be a nice change, although my people don't seem to know what to do when it's all white out. Kind of makes us nervous."

Ronnie held out his hand. "I owe you, brother."

"You know, man, you're a true hero. You saved that kid, got your name in the newspaper. And old man Hunt went and bought you that hog. Best of all, you got a place to go. More than I can say for most people."

Ronnie revved his engine and put his pilot glasses back on. "Drive on, you Air Cav pussy!"

"Keep moving, Ronnie T. You the baddest ass in the valley."

As Ronnie accelerated the 1200cc engine, the doors to Hunt's Market opened and R2 struggled out loaded with groceries. An elderly woman dressed in a hat moved slowly as Hunt shuffled behind her. Inside the store, Junior could make out the outline of Ralph Hunt Senior's wheelchair. It appeared that the old man was back in the saddle.

Ronnie nodded toward the market and flew through the intersection toward his future.

Rebecca stood up from the restaurant table and waved as Karl made his way toward her, grinning.

"Well?" he said.

"We got them! You were the clincher. The way you described how you would have handled that builder's risk claim won over the CFO. The guys at A&A are going to freak out. I can't believe we just took their largest account. They have had Timmons & Company for over 25 years! Revenge is sweet."

Karl hugged Rebecca and then caught himself. "Now that I know you are *not* a lesbian, I have to be careful about hugging and overtures of affection that could be misinterpreted."

She smiled and kissed him on the cheek. "You don't know how incredible this all feels."

Karl was red-faced but elated. Life was back in balance and both work and family were trending upward. To round out his early Christmas wish list, his Bears were playing a rare televised game against the Vikings in two days on Halloween. The Bears were stumbling, but it would be fun to finally spend a Sunday cursing Fran Tarkenton instead of bad luck.

As they ordered lunch, Karl realized he'd never had such a candid conversation with a woman aside from Susie. He had grown up viewing women as sexual objects to be conquered or pains in the ass to be tolerated. He had never been close with his sisters and did not know how to be friends with a woman, especially one that was his boss.

He noticed the ruby and diamond engagement ring on her finger. "That's quite a rock. Does this mean you and Will have decided on a merger?"

Rebecca looked radiant. "Yes, I finally saw the errors of my ways. I guess I do want what you and Susie have."

"Really? Chaos? Teenage terrorism? I can lend you one until you grow another of your own. You can choose between a liberal idiot, an enigma, a smart ass, or the most ancient twelve-year-old on the planet."

"I think we will stick to cats. They have better hygiene."

Karl raised his hand to catch the eye of their waitress. "This calls for a drink. Will is a lucky man and I am a fortunate to have two great women in my life. One that runs my days and another that runs my nights and weekends."

The champagne arrived and they tipped their glasses together. Karl gave Rebecca a sheepish grin. "I was wrong about you. You are a hell of a visionary. It's clear that you understand where this business is going. I am happy to ride shotgun for you."

"Thank you, sir. I would love it if you would consider becoming president of the firm when I succeed Bob. I think we will make a hell of a team."

"It would be an honor." Karl said as he poured them another glass. "But, I do have one last admission for you since we are now partners in crime."

Rebecca her glass down prepared to absorb Karl's confession.

"I realize it now. *I'm* the lesbian."

Rebecca howled with laughter.

"I mean it. It finally makes sense. I am hopelessly attracted to women."

It was All Hallows Night in Huntington Hills—a holiday that awakened the latent delinquent within every kid. What some parents called vandalism was tolerated as "boys being boys" by Susie. October 31st marked the first pearl in a delicious string of holidays, spaced thankfully over two months, allowing just enough time for a kid to recover from overindulgence or regain privileges that were perhaps lost for some silly misunderstanding such as conducting a firefight with quarter-sticks of dynamite or throwing a party while parents were out on business. Halloween was a night fueled by sugar and poor judgment.

At the age of twelve, Freddie had declared Halloween costumes "stupid," opting instead to don Karl's oversized, olive-green army jacket with its deep pockets and durable, double stitched woolen lining. The coat was a talisman of good fortune for Karl who, having missed the Korean War, endured two years of Officers Candidate School, and survived one angry gunnery NCO from Alabama who hated ROTC-trained second lieutenants. The green canvas overcoat was warm, twilight camouflage when one needed to elude a parent, a patrol car, or an older kid with dark intentions. It also carried the surname "PATTON" tattooed in indelible military font on its white cloth lapel.

Karl was in a good mood after watching his Bears upset the Vikings. He considered Freddie as he prepared to go out into the night, "That's not much of a costume! You need some fake blood and bullet holes."

Freddie looked offended.

"I'm a soldier."

"You look more like a conscientious objector. You need a gun. I have this old Makarov from the war that I could probably…"

From the other room, Karl heard Susie yell, "Leave him alone, honey. He's just going to a few houses with a friend."

"Well, he should go over to Sherwood Road. There are all commies over there. They give away a lot of free stuff and won't mind a pacifist ringing their bells." Karl barked. He pointed at Freddie and looked stern.

"No grab-ass tonight!" He slapped his son on the shoulder and closed his office door.

Freddie and Tommy DeSantis had begun discussing Halloween since early September. The boys were filled with bravado as they meticulously planned a mission whose success would be measured in pounds of candy and shattered pumpkins. To venture into a Halloween night was a risky business. A kid must be armed and ready to rumble at a moment's notice.

The standard issue weapon of choice for an All Hallows infantryman was shaving cream. The boys started by purchasing several cans of highly pressurized Gillette's "The Hot One" self-heating cream. It was the closest thing one could get to canned napalm. Many nighttime soldiers modified their weapons, creatively improving their accuracy and reach by inserting a sewing needle into the inch-high nozzle and melting plastic around the needle, waiting to remove the attachment once the nozzle's tip had cooled. The result was a microscopic hole from which the high-pressure shaving cream would release, producing a powerful stream of heat that could reach as far as ten feet.

When doused with The Hot One, the victim would experience a gradual burning sensation as the shaving cream rose in temperature. A larger assailant intent on pilfering your booty would perhaps think twice when confronted with the prospects of writhing on the ground in pain.

Freddie was determined this year to prove himself the most reckless prankster—the crazy guy willing to throw the smoke bomb into the police station or pump three eggs into the side of a bus. Yet, Freddie had seen his brothers get into trouble so many times and he was more afraid of Karl's belt than peer humiliation. Like Stephen Crane's young protagonist, Henry Fleming, Freddie wondered what he would do when faced with the elephant of combat: would he run or man up?

Halloween evening was ushered in by a cool, purple twilight. The heat of the Indian summer day was receding and the autumn air rushed down the residential streets. Daylight Savings had run its course, and early evening was the safest time to move openly from house to house. Freddie and Tommy were being typical smart alecks grabbing handfuls of bite sized candy and stuffing them into pillow cases as an elderly neighbor urged them to just take one piece.

"Leave some for the other children, boys." Behind her, her curmudgeonly husband scowled. He was most likely a WWII veteran and was disgusted that a boy was defiling an U.S. Army officer's coat.

"So, what are you, a soldier?" the vet asked sarcastically.

"No, he's a beekeeper," said Tommy, sniggering. The older man shook his head as he confirmed the decline of America's youth and returned to Mort Dean and the CBS Sunday news.

As twilight yielded to a more adult, sinister night, jack-o-lantern candles dimmed and the manicured lawns and sidewalks emptied of all but a few shadowy stragglers rushing toward a warm fire and a candy feeding frenzy. Freddie and Tommy now moved into deeper waters of consequence. They had become a submarine wolf pack searching for quarry, perhaps a bloated merchant Cadillac or a defenseless station wagon.

A van pulsating with loud music suddenly broke the silence, skirting around a corner and splashing the boys with an uneven slash of halogen headlights. Gratefully, the suspicious vehicle raced past them, revving its oversized three hundred horsepower engine. Someone inside the van yelled something unintelligible at the boys. For some incomprehensible reason, Tommy felt the need to verbally retaliate. "Assholes!" he screamed.

"What the heck are you doing?" Freddie whispered. He often wondered if Tommy had maybe been hit in the head too many times by his twelve siblings. An explosion of adrenaline rose in Freddie's torso as he watched the brake lights of the van illuminate, followed by menacing screech of rubber as the vehicle snapped a U-turn.

The boys had the good fortune of being next to a long private driveway and retreated into the dark, while an adjacent group of innocent bystanders also scattered in a burst of panic. The van sped past Freddie, chasing two of the more slovenly members of the other group. The doors and windows of the car were now open and Freddie and Tommy could see teens hanging out manically whooping and throwing eggs. Nowhere in Freddie's meticulous planning had he made provisions for this scenario.

Freddie suddenly remembered the eggs he had resting like pinned grenades in Karl's coat. He turned to Tommy, motioned to his pocket and mimicked the tossing of a baseball. Tommy nodded, understanding that their hiding place gave them perfect cover and that a direct hit with the eggs would appear as if it were coming from the other kids.

In rapid-fire succession, the boys launched five eggs, two of which thumped against the back of the van. The driver slammed on the brakes. There was a moment of confused debate. The van was a raging bull uncertain where to charge. As Freddie and Tommy hesitated and ducked behind the safety of a high wall, a pair of floodlights flashed on from the adjacent garage. A large raccoon wandering underneath a motion sensing light had revealed their hiding place.

The boys bolted out onto the asphalt road where the van gave chase. They stopped, gasping for air, and stood perfectly still inside a tangled juniper bush. The vehicle slowly moved down the street and idled like a Tiger tank. They could overhear arguing from the back seat, when the van suddenly revved its engine and peeled off into the night. The smell of burned rubber and the prospects of being beaten to death by upperclassmen suffocated what little flame of mischief still burned within the boys. It was time to call it a night.

As Tommy ran ahead and melted into the darkness, Freddie beamed triumphantly and peered inside his pillow case to inventory his take from the evening. He opened tore open a Milky Way bar and moved out into the weak street light, attempting to cling to the shadows. As he prepared to cross Huntington Hills Drive, the van from hell suddenly reappeared. Freddie heard someone yell, "Get that kid!"

Freddie tore across the asphalt, avoiding light traffic. He made it to the south side of the Drive and ran down to Roses Road, a stretch of thoroughfare that offered access to an assortment of backyards and dark hiding places. He wheeled to the west and made a dash across a wide front lawn, forgetting about a metal cable that had been anchored in the ground to brace an ancient live oak tree. The wire rose out of the lawn at a forty-five-degree angle and reached ten feet up to the middle trunk of the oak. The cable was exactly the height of Freddie's head, and as he turned the corner to sprint across the wet grass, the half-inch thick wire struck him directly in the face.

From the road, it must have looked as if he'd been hit by a high-powered rifle; his legs flew out in front of him and his head jerked backwards. Horizontal when he hit the grass, he lay motionless and moaning. The van pulled up and he could hear the teens inside the darkened cab talking in low tones.

"Dude, I think he's dead. Let's get out of here. Someone might say we killed him.

"Kid, you okay? Hey kid?"

Freddie groaned on his back. "I don't know."

"See, dude. He's alive. Seriously, let's bolt."

The van door shut and the vehicle sped off into the night.

The bridge of Freddie's nose was now bleeding, and he had a diagonal gash that ran from his left eyebrow down to the right of his chin. Staggering home the two final blocks, he had decided to give up his life of crime and grab-ass. Halloween was hazardous duty. He would have preferred to be at home, eating candy and watching *It's The Great Pumpkin, Charlie Brown.*

He pushed the front door so hard it bashed into the wall, announcing his arrival. Karl, working in his study, glanced up, irritated. Outside, a van rumbled slowly past the Patton house like a Mekong Delta patrol boat. Karl took in Freddie's bloody face, mud-stained jacket and massive diagonal welt.

He smiled at his son, seemingly oblivious to the injuries. "Now *that*" he said, "is a goddamn costume!"

CHAPTER 21

"Humility is greatness in plain clothes"

— **Spencer W. Kimball**

"Rebecca, do you have a minute?"
Bob O'Brien stuck his head inside her office and then retreated to his own space. Rebecca followed him. The office was immaculate, with no papers on a massive glass desk. The bureau was decorated with color photographs and Asian and African artifacts—all mementos of Bob's second shot at life with his new, younger bride. As the agency had become more successful, he seemed to be taking more money out of it and spending less time with clients. Beyond social activities that offered only a fringe benefit to the firm, Bob was slowing down at work while engaging more at home.

"Connie and I are going to the Lesser Antilles for Thanksgiving," Bob said. "The kids are with their mother or off on their own junkets. We have some friends from France who have a home there and have invited us."

Rebecca did not even know where the Lesser Antilles were. She suspected they were somewhere in the Caribbean, but that sounded too pedestrian for Bob. She was surprised he would vacation anywhere that incorporated the adjective "lesser" into its name.

"What's up, Bob? We're prepping for the Timmons meeting tomorrow. We just picked up the builder's risk and the workers compensation on their casino project in Vegas. We figure with contingents, supps, and fees, we could book two hundred thousand."

Bob raised his eyebrows and started fiddling with a dark figurine of an animal. "That's mighty impressive. I'll admit I'm surprised at how you and Karl have taken to each other. Someone told me they are starting to refer to you guys as 'Sonny and Cher'. I wouldn't have agreed to any bet that had the two of you working so well together."

"You almost sound disappointed, Bob. I distinctly recall your saying my success hinged upon two things: winning clients and winning over Karl. Mission accomplished."

Bob was silent, continuing to stare at the ebony statuette.

"Bob, seriously, what's going on?" Rebecca asked, impatience in her tone.

"I've decided to extend my contract another four years. Connie and I are talking about starting a family. There's lot's going on. My oldest, Ginny, now wants to go to med school. All I know, is this job keeps me feeling young, and well, I'm not ready to give it all up to hang out in a park with a two-year-old or accompany my wife as she spikes old growth redwoods to save the environment.

"Look, I've spoken to the board and everyone has agreed that the firm could use all hands on deck given our recent successes. Besides, with Carter taking office, the political winds are changing, and our business environment could get tougher. It might help to have a CEO with strong ties to the Democratic Party in California."

"Remain as CEO, Bob? I was under the impression that I was already doing that job. Remember, I just made Karl the offer to become president."

"Well, you can un-offer it. He's a big boy. Rebecca, I'm fifty-seven years old. I have a lot of gas left in the engine. Connie is used to entertaining. She'll be a good partner for me when I am out with younger clients. Besides, I'm not ready to retire. The board ..."

"Bob, cut the shit about Connie and the board. The board is you, your college roommate, Steve Richardson, and Chancellor Orlando from Caltech." She placed her hands on his desk, leaning across only inches from his face.

"Well, I've given it a lot of thought and I'm not ready to step down. Hell, Rebecca, you're getting married. You don't need the added hassle right now. It's a time for you and Will to enjoy one another. You're not spring chickens yourselves anymore."

"Bob, don't presume to tell me what I need or want. I joined this firm to become CEO. I have done everything you asked. If you're afraid to stay home with your flower-child trophy wife, that's your problem. If you're telling me I am not going to be CEO this January, then you are constructively terminating me. Please accept my resignation, effective immediately."

She was not going to cry, even though she had made the mistake of letting her guard down and believing that things could actually work out as she had hoped. Bob would now immediately call Karl and offer him equity and the president's title, and she would be stuck trying to pull clients into her third employer in as many years. *Well, I guess this fairy tale ends really well for everyone but me,* she said to herself.

George had been starting at linebacker on the junior varsity football team and performing well. He had a game-saving tackle in their heated rivalry against South Pasadena that cemented a 6-0 heart stopper and got him a rare compliment from Varsity coach Coombs.

Barrett Coombs had played football at UCLA and was a bear of a man with massive hands and forearms. He waddled unsteadily on knees that had long since lost their cartilage to a half-dozen surgeries, and would most likely be eligible for a handicap parking place had he been willing to accept his circumstances. Coombs was beloved by every boy who ever donned a helmet at Huntington Hills. He was a hard man, accustomed to screaming at players when they made stupid mistakes. He also had a signature way of referring to any mistake by using the offending kid's last name.

"What kind of Patton was that, George? You let your man get outside of you!"

"Two Carrolls in a row, Mark. That could cost us a game if you choose to do that in the fourth quarter."

Coombs took George aside. "George, we're bringing a few sophs up for the Temple City game. You up for it?"

"Coach, I would kill to get into that game," George said, sitting shirt-less in the locker room.

"We'll see about that, son. Just want to make sure my future play-ers get a taste of the present. The best education is experience. You'll be doing two-a-days, practicing with the JV and the varsity. You have to give me everything."

"Coach, you'll get it."

Coombs shuffled off to his office and George felt his heart swell five sizes. He was getting a shot at the big-time. As he rode his bike home from practice, all he could think about was which girls would be in the stands to see him suit up for the varsity game. Perhaps Kelly Reed would be there. For a year, the cosmos had conspired to preclude the couple from following up on their mutual attraction. Tim Irwin had broken up their first two dates. Now that the oversized fool had graduated, other guys had been expressing interest in Kelly. George hated the idea of being a bridesmaid. It would be too embarrassing and it made him wonder whether she was worth the hassle. The risk of rejection seemed worse than the reward of the girl, which was some pretty sick thinking.

Jimmy Carter's margin of victory was wider than the political gadflies had imagined it would be. Karl stared in churlish disbelief at *The Wall Street Journal* article that forecast escalating inflation and a slowdown in the economy. His eyes darted to the electoral vote count that showed Carter, the unqualified hayseed with the razor thin resume winning 297 to 240, with only a tenth of a percent over one-half the popular vote.

Tossing the Friday paper across the table, Karl could not find a sil-ver lining in this outcome. The economic indicators were not good, and the wrong kind of fiscal policy could tank the nascent GDP recovery of five percent that had followed the severe recession of 1973 to 1975. If the Democratic president-elect went on a spending spree, the soaring costs of borrowing would clamp down on construction, middle market financing, and many of his clients.

Ford and his GOP had made too many physical and foreign policy gaffes during his ill-fated campaign. When he downplayed the influence

of the Soviet Union in Eastern Europe and suggested that Poland was comfortable with oversight by the Soviets, the media depicted him as a neophyte.

Karl had studied monetary policy and understood what was now likely to happen once a Democratic Congress and Democratic President finally clasped hands. He spoke into the newspaper although he was talking to Susie. "Carter says he is going to focus on the nine percent unemployment rate through a bull shit Federal jobs programs. You watch, the Democrats will bloat the deficit and create a lot of unnecessary grab-ass public sector jobs. Then they'll make things worse with wage and price controls. Neither works. By the end of next year, I bet you twenty bucks that we still have high unemployment and higher interest rates."

Susie looked up from her magazine. "Were you speaking to me, dear?"

"Yes. Let's be sure we are socking some money away," Karl said. "I'm going to be making more money as the agency grows and my guess is that bastard Carter will raise our taxes as he loses control of the economy. The S&P went up seventeen percent under Ford. I don't see that continuing. Tell Ted Bullock to put the kids' college money into some tax-free municipal bonds and value-based stocks that throw off some dividends. We need hard assets if inflation goes up and we need to bring down our effective tax rates."

Susie had been playing the stock market with Freddie for the last two years and had become fairly adroit with the money Karl had staked her. Even though he was a middle man by trade, Karl hated paying commission to stock brokers like Ted Bullock and went out of his way to avoid the scores of fathers on the sidelines who tried to give him investment advice or induce him to open a brokerage account with Dean Witter or EF Hutton.

The phone rang in the breakfast room and Susie left the dining room table to answer it. "Hi, Bob. Yes, he's here. As you might suspect, he's mourning the death of the GOP. I hope you can say something that can cheer him up." She smiled into the phone. "Good. Here he is. Say hi to Connie."

Karl grabbed the receiver. "Bob, are you calling to gloat over Mr. Peanut?"

Karl listened. Susie watched his face as it went grim. "That's strange. She seemed pretty committed. I have not thought about it since she got the nod. Sure, I'm flattered. Yep. Okay, great. See you tomorrow."

Karl got off the phone, clearly perplexed. Susie's violet blue eyes were riveted on him.

"Rebecca resigned today. Bob asked me to be her successor. Given her decision, he wants us to circle the wagons on her accounts tomorrow. Jesus, we just had lunch and she seemed so happy. I wonder what the hell happened."

"Have you spoken to her?" Susie asked.

"No. I just don't get it. Bob sounded almost relieved when he told me. He didn't give a hint of panic like he normally does if anything goes wrong. He seemed ready to move on. No counter offer, no pleading or stopgap changes to accommodate Rebecca. That's just not Bob's style. I don't want to get between the two of them and have this thing bleed all over me. But this is goddamn strange."

Susie frowned. She was happy for Karl, but she had grown fond of Rebecca. She glanced at her watch. "Goodness. It's seven o'clock. We have to get to the high school for George's game."

"You go ahead. I'll meet you over there. I need to do something."

Friday night stadium lights glowed in the distance like a Hollywood movie premiere. George had played only in JV games, which were usually during the afternoon and in the middle of the week. To be on the sidelines and suited against a Rio Hondo league rival was more than his senses could take. Checking out the sidelines, he saw the copper-toned legs of cheerleaders and pep reps.

The band was playing "Louie, Louie" as students swayed and hurled creative insults at the opposing student body. Off in the distance, the equipment-shed window was now open and doubling as a concession stand.

He spotted the long blond hair and athletic legs of Kelly Reed. She was at the base of a pyramid of cheerleaders that had just launched petite

Debbie Lawlor into the air. The crowd cheered as the ensemble of girls caught the petite cheerleader.

George had arrived. This was the big-time. There would most certainly be a team party after the game where all the upper classmen would congregate. Coach Coombs had allowed George entry into the elite company of Varsity football. Not even ever-popular John Patton would be allowed admittance into this private party.

The lights cast an odd glow, and George felt a sudden surge of nerves as he watched massive lineman pounding each other's shoulder pads, screaming and shaking their heads like carnivores tearing flesh from a recent kill. George got caught up in the moment and looked for a partner to engage in this violent pre-game ritual.

He turned to the man next to him and screamed, bringing both of his hands down hard on his shoulder pads. Instead of hitting hard plastic, his fists came down on the bony shoulders of all-CIF kicker Blake Kramer. Kramer had just been cleared to play after suffering a shoulder injury during a blocked field goal attempt. As George pounded on his shoulder, the slight kicker fell to the ground in agony.

The trainer, Bill Udell, glanced over and saw his star kicker on the ground next to George. "Jesus Christ, Patton, what the hell happened?"

"I, I, I..." George stuttered, trying to form words.

"Mr. Udell, I think my shoulder is separated again. Aw, Jesus, it hurts like hell."

Udell rushed over to Coombs who, seconds later, threw his clipboard to the ground. He waved the trainer away. "Well, Patton," he said, "if we lose this goddamn game, I'm going to recommend that you transfer to Temple City."

Karl went into his office and closed the door. He was conflicted. He had won. He had gotten to the mountaintop. Bob had promised him a significant equity stake and the title of president. He would run the entire operating company. Yet, he felt the way a silver medalist finisher might feel after winning gold because the winner was disqualified on a technicality. He wanted to succeed, but not this way, not without knowing why Rebecca had given up on the firm. He dialed her number.

"Hi Karl," she said, her voice subdued. "Congratulations. I'm sure Bob has told you the news. I guess he believes staying as CEO will allow him to play Peter Pan a little longer. It's funny how things turn out. I sort of blame myself. I guess I am suffering from a form of serial feminine hubris, believing that I can fly near the sun with the big boys. It was a mistake coming to OB&T and thinking that I could run this agency."

"What the hell are you talking about? We just celebrated a record quarter. Why would you resign? I thought we were a team."

"Is that what Bob told you? That I resigned? Did he tell you that he is staying for another four years as CEO and that he wanted me to demote you and remain president until he decides to maybe retire in ten more years?"

"That little bastard! Listen, Rebecca. Bob may have the equity but we have control of the people and the clients. It pains me to say this, but one of the few advantages of living in a liberal fucking state run by Jerry Brown is that the employment law makes it impossible for an employer to enforce non competition contracts. We can't be restrained from engaging in our trade, and if clients and people choose to follow us, there is not a goddamn thing that little silver-haired prick can do about it.

"Meet me at my house in an hour and we can draft our proposal to Bob. He will learn to like the role of non-executive Chairman of the Board. We can ask a few people to join our Board and create a real business. And it will be a privilege carrying your bag for however long you care to lead this company."

Karl waited for her response, but nothing was forthcoming. "Can you be here in an hour?" he said.

Rebecca had not cried once since her resignation. Now, she released a torrent of relieved tears and smiled as she wiped them away. "Yes, I can."

Susie had not left for the game yet. She sat quietly in the den, ostensibly waiting for Karl, with the television on mute so she could eavesdrop on his call through the heater. After he hung up, she walked into his study. He was organizing papers and pulling client files from his own filing cabinet.

"Hey, I just talked to Rebecca and she's coming over. Looks like old Bob tried to screw her over. Go ahead to George's game. Okay if we use the dining room?" he said.

"You never cease to astonish me." She hugged his neck and gave him a big kiss.

CHAPTER 22

"What we're really talking about is a wonderful day set aside on the fourth Thursday of November when no one diets. I mean, why else would they call it Thanksgiving?"

~Erma Bombeck

Thanksgiving arrived unceremoniously on a warm desert wind sweeping down across uncongested freeways and empty school yards. Karl was still in mourning over the election, but had shifted gears, focusing his anger into a toxic resolve to criticize the new president, his cabinet, Congress and their doomed liberal policies at every possible turn.

Susie secretly celebrated the Carter victory, hoping that humanism might, for once, prevail over partisanship. However, she also trusted Karl's pragmatic instincts about the economy and knew that as an upper middle-class family they were not all that well insulated from the ravages of high interest rates that might undermine their standard of living.

She was pleased that her parents had arrived for the holiday. Thomas and Katie O'Reilly added old-country charm and always seemed to leaven mythology and humor into each family meal.

There was plenty for which to give thanks, and a lifetime of political, social and economic issues to debate. Close-quarter holidays meant four days of conservative versus liberal dogma and the testosterone of three generations of men who grew restless at the percussion of chopping knives and deaf to appeals for someone to help peel the potatoes and string the beans. Susie looked forward to preparing meals; she loved being in the kitchen with her mother and easily yielded the right of way to the matriarch of the O'Reilly clan.

Karl was in his office considering some organizational changes that Rebecca had proposed. They all made sense. He had grown very fond of her personally and felt fortunate that things had worked out so well. He stopped and listened. The low, dulcet tones of multiple conversations and soft laughter mixed with the reassuring aroma of sautéed onions and roasting turkey. A football suddenly bounced off the side of the house. Startled, he stood up and darted to the window. Outside, a boy in sweats had appeared, grinning, but now retreated from the terrifying visage of Karl Patton.

"Sorry, Mr. Patton. Uh, are the guys inside?"

Aaron Doney stood in a tear-away shirt, sweat pants and cleats. There was a sudden rush of motion in the front hallway outside Karl's office as Matthew, John, George, and Freddie mustered to pull muddy cleats, balls and jerseys from the front hall closet and walk the two blocks to Hills Junior High, where a scrum of boys argued over the balance of talent and rules of engagement for this year's football game.

The annual Turkey Bowl was a rare opening for a younger kid to run with the larger dogs of the neighborhood—siblings home from college and older teens that would normally look right past a younger kid as if he were an insect. Yet, on this day, a hard tackle or timely body block might win a rare encomium from an elderly icon, creating a moment that could be deposited in one's shoebox of memorabilia and taken out many times over a lifetime of self-reflection.

There was the occasional broken bone or cut requiring stitches, the badges of honor and fodder for the exaggerated legends and bragging rite debates that would persist longer than the gridiron dirt stains. As in life, there were failed plays, personal fouls, selfless acts, winners, and losers. There was instant acceptance when one was picked on a team. It was a Christmas-morning thrill for Freddie to watch as an older teenager opened his huge, muddy palm and designed a play especially for him.

"Little Patton, go five yards out and turn around." It was the old buttonhook, and it was his play, designed exclusively for a rabbit-sized kid and awarded like a jewel-encrusted Faberge egg. Freddie hated power sports but wanted to prove that he could physically compete. Building respect with older kids was essential. It limited the potential for bullying and created critical connectivity to a broader base of future customers. Having older brothers made him always feel like everyone knew his name.

Here he was—a twelve-year old paramecium deemed worthy of possibly receiving a forward pass from this multi-celled nineteen-year-old quarterbacking god, Cary Rebstock. There was just one problem. Freddie was being guarded by JR Spitler, a sixteen-year-old simian with bad acne, mood swings and suborbital ridges whose lineage could most likely be traced back to Dr. Leakey's discovery of the missing link.

"Ready, set, you bet, go Charlie go, hike!"

Before Freddie could sprint to his designated spot, Spitler shoved him roughly to the ground like a rag doll, stepping on his hand as he rushed toward the quarterback. .

"Stay down, wiener,"

Back in the huddle, everyone was complaining that they had been open. Freddie was busy rubbing his stinging fingers and blinking the dirt out of his eyes. With each down, history cruelly repeated itself with Spitler slamming Freddie to the grass, making it impossible for him to complete his assigned buttonhook. By the fourth quarter, the youngest Patton had eaten more mud than an earthworm. The score was tied at 49. Matthew had scored twice, John had intercepted two passes, and George had sacked the quarterback four times. Freddie had not touched the ball.

Lisa Doney rode up on her bike and yelled to her brothers. "Todd, mom says get your butts home now before Grandpa and Grandma get here."

Every kid looked up. The first summons from home was a two-minute warning indicating other siblings or parents would soon be arriving, extracting players and creating an imbalance of power. There was immediate talk of ending this year's grudge match in a tie.

"Screw your sister, keep playing!" yelled one of the ten thousand wolf faced cousins who visited the DeSantises each year from the East Coast. The feral-looking kid had not closed his mouth all day and resembled a yeti with buckteeth and hailed from some town called, Wehawkem.

"Well, Jersey," said George sarcastically. "I have never met your sister. Does she have your single eyebrow?"

Larry DeSantis laughed. "Don't mind Georgie. Lui è finocchio."

The buck-toothed Bigfoot let out an unintelligent laugh.

Mikey DeSantis shouted, "One more play!"

In the huddle, Rebstock spoke in a hushed yell, "Shut up, you idiots. Look, everybody go out. John, I'll toss it to you on the option. You run or pass. I'll hang on the left sideline if you want to throw it back to me."

Freddie lined up for the last play. He was once again across from Spitler, who was grinning with ominous intent. "Just lie down you little turd and save me the energy."

Rebstock called for the snap. Instead of running his inside button-hook, Freddie juked right and then suddenly spun left, sprinting toward an increasingly crowded end zone. He screamed and waved his hands. John spotted the knot of receivers and let the ball fly. The spiral soared in Freddie's direction and his heart leapt as he stumbled through the muddy, churned grass, never taking his eye off the pigskin. Spitler had fallen down when Freddie made his spinning cut, and Freddie was now alone behind a riot of teenagers grasping for the ball.

The pass hung in the autumn air for an eternity as larger defensive players scrambled trying to intercept the ball. The throw tipped off Matthew's hands and caromed off Mikey DeSantis' right shoulder flying just beyond the outstretched arms of several defenders. There was a flash of brown as Freddie dove forward, his miniature arms straining for the deflection. Muddy fingers clawed under the ball preventing it from hitting the dirt. He fell awkwardly, feeling a white flash of pain in his knee. But he held on. Celebratory screams from down field confirmed the reception as Freddie spiked the ball. With the final score, the tie was broken and the game disintegrated. Team Rebstock, Doney and Patton had won.

As he limped to the sidelines, he heard the deep baritone of Rebstock, the nineteen-year old super-hero quarterback. "Freddie, you're a mini Terry Metcalf."

Freddie blushed and limped to the street with his brothers, tossing the ball to John and George and playing catch all the way home.

"Hey Georgie, who the heck is Terry Metcalf?"

Dressed in pressed linen, Rebecca and Will walked down a bougain-villea-lined path to a beachside restaurant. Thanksgiving in Puerto Val-larta had been Rebecca's suggestion. She had fallen in love with the film *Night of The Iguana* and had always fashioned herself the business ver-sion of Deborah Kerr, a dignified woman plagued by conflicted burning desires. Will was not the defrocked, alcoholic priest played by Richard Burton, but in many ways, the irony of coming here to celebrate her commitment to a life of balanced passion between work and Will was unmistakable.

They were two souls mending under the warmth and solitude of the Bahia de Las Banderas—the Bay of Flags. God was not Tennessee Wil-liams' "senile delinquent," but instead a patient silent partner who had waited to reward her for finally letting go of her fear of needing other people.

She watched as a flock of pelicans flew just inches above the calm azure bay. Yes, this was just what the doctor ordered. It was not the Lesser Antilles, but it was tropical and a perfect place for someone who did not want to be found.

Rebecca's first official act as CEO of OB&T was to declare the office closed for Thanksgiving week, giving all the employees paid vacation. Karl was initially opposed to the decision, asserting that the holiday was something a Democrat might do to curry favor from their constituency. She had expected his reaction and had savored showing Karl the quar-terly financials that indicated a remarkable spike in growth. Karl was amazed at the surge in revenue and profit improvement. He laughed at the terrific numbers. "Lady, you are one of the few people I have met who actually lived up to their billing."

Rebecca's second executive fiat was to order Karl to take the holiday week off. Karl looked surprised. "It's the busiest time of the year and Susie doesn't like having me around the house."

"Well, she'll have to tolerate you the way I do. The teams have every-thing covered. Go spend some time with those boys of yours."

"They like it even less when I am around. Dad is the antonym for fun."

Rebecca beamed and returned to her moment with Will, lifting her crystal glass to his champagne flute and touching it. "Here's to a long life and here's to Karl. They broke the mold when they made that man."

Will looked at her adoringly from across the table. "You know, Rebecca, I think I am going to enjoy being a housewife."

Ralph Hunt the Younger was drunk again. His father was making remarkable progress recovering from a small stroke and had decided to reinsert himself into the business. R2 had spent the morning in the cooler drinking eggnog laced with rum and was now staggering toward the bathroom to pee. The toilet door was locked. As he wrestled with the handle, he heard Andy Haskell's cough from inside.

He opened the loading dock door and covered his eyes, peering in each direction down the alley. There was no traffic and that crazy old witch was not scrounging around in the trash. He unzipped his pants and began to pee on the store's brick façade with his back to the alleyway. He wavered back and forth, spraying the wall with a wide, looping stream.

He heard a click as the gate behind him opened and Gert Spitz skittered into the alley. "Go drink yourself to sleep, you old Nazi bitch," he yelled, still concentrating on his urine designs.

"You're a bad man," she shouted in a thick accent and disappeared back into her garden.

Hunt laughed and began zipping his pants when he heard the metallic click. The gunshot was deafening and felt like a mule's kick. Hunt slammed forward and smashed his face into the side of the building. The recoil of the firearm threw Gert Spitz back into the fence, knocking her unconscious as the gun flew out of her hands, over the trellis, and into her hydrangeas.

Andy Haskell thought he heard a car backfire. Checking the storage room, he noticed that someone had once again left the loading dock door open. Irritated, he slid the bar down across the door but thought better of it after the incident over the summer. Maybe one of the box boys was emptying trash or breaking down cardboard on the back platform. Haskell poked his head outside the loading dock door, taking in the fresh air and strengthening morning sun. He spotted what appeared to be a pile of clothes in the shadows across the narrow cement road and felt his heart sink when he noticed it was the old crazy lady from across the alleyway unconscious on the ground. *Heart attack*, he thought.

As he moved toward the edge of the dock, he discovered another body. It was R2, his pants soaked with blood from a wound on the wallet side of his trousers.

"Holy shit!" Haskell said as he bolted into the market yelling for someone to call an ambulance and the police.

Freddie donned his normally dreaded church clothes for Thanksgiving dinner. He was flush with self-esteem. Somehow the shirt collar did not feel so tight, and the gray wool slacks didn't itch so much. The hand-me-down loafers did not bite his heels. On this night, his turkey would retain the rich taste of the hunt. The mashed potatoes would melt on his tongue like butter on a hot skillet. The pumpkin pie would finally appeal to his more mature palette, tasting like fresh pastry snatched from the windowsill of an Amish farmhouse. That was, of course, if Freddie could penetrate the swarm of adult locusts who always preceded him at every holiday meal.

It was three p.m. The dining room had been transformed into a New England harvest celebration, with a holiday centerpiece with husks of amber and yellow corn, gourds, miniature pumpkins, and fresh autumn-colored flowers. The sideboard was crowded with steaming dishes of yams, mashed potatoes, green beans, Brussels sprouts, two kinds of stuffing, cornbread and a bizarre paste called bread sauce that was an old-country favorite of Thomas O'Reilly's.

Karl and his father-in-law were first through the Thanksgiving Day food line. Chivalry died each Thanksgiving at one minute past three, when the lords of the manor exercised their prerogative to initiate the cavalcade of consumption. The men moved slowly, like bull elephants, surveying each dish like discriminating judges at a Midwestern bake-off. To Susie's horror, they heaped massive portions on their plates, amassing a Mount Everest of food.

Thomas was feeling no pain after several screwdrivers. He ate as he walked through the line, stuffing a roll in his mouth as he turned to ask

Matthew a question. Spraying breadcrumbs on every Patton child, he uttered something completely incomprehensible. Max was swimming under Thomas O'Reilly like a pilot fish, darting in between legs and chairs to lick up the bread.

Susie scolded her father. "Dad, don't talk with your mouth full." She was also quietly doing the math on food portions and realized that it was now unlikely that anyone under six feet tall would be eating anything other than dark meat, yams and a couple of string beans.

Off in the distance, CBS sports announcers Pat Summerall and Tom Brookshier were overheard discussing the pathetic Detroit Lions, who were 5-6 headed into this year's game. Karl hated any team from the NFC Central that competed with his Bears. He was rooting for the Bills since they had drafted USC graduate O.J. Simpson.

Despite the chaos of the holiday, Susie understood that Thanksgiving was the one holiday likely to be celebrated by everyone irrespective of religious affiliation. A baking turkey blended with the aroma of sautéed onions, sausage, stuffing and celery created the most reassuring of all moods. It was a time for family—no distractions, gifts, holiday cards, competing social obligations, religious services, or pressured traditions. It was about eating and talking with your mouth was full.

Thanksgiving also heralded the beginning of the season of family dysfunction where age-old scars could tear open and disagreements could flare. It invariably started with the Thanksgiving prayer. Once a year, the entire Patton family would hold hands across generations and Karl would christen the family feast.

"Lord, thank you for blessing us this year and for providing us this generous bounty. Please bless all those in our family who cannot be with us today. Watch over those who are less fortunate and please help those in Washington to not become corrupted by the self interest of their own need for reelection but instead to act with integrity and decisiveness to protect the interests of our free market, our democracy and our society where there are no social, educational or financial barriers to success if one is willing to work hard enough. Lord, please safeguard the greatest nation in the world and allow us to stand firmly as a formidable alternative to the corrupt, long shadows of communism."

Matthew sighed and Susie looked up at her oldest son with furrowed eyebrows.

Karl leered at Matthew. "And please help to improve the education and perspective of those too blind to see the obvious shortcomings of charlatans disguised as giveaway artists…"

Susie spoke up. "Karl, my beautiful feast is getting cold and I am certain God gets your point."

"Of course he does. He's a Republican" Karl said defiantly.

Susie looked over and saw that her father had fallen asleep with his mouth open. She nudged her mother who in turn, sharply elbowed Thomas Riley in the ribs.

"What?" He spurted, looking surprised. "Ah, amen."

Dinner was a collision of diagonal conversations, laughter, gilded nostalgia and good-natured insults. Yet, there were lots of issues to be anxious about in November of 1976. "Liberal" and "Shit for Brains" were common pejorative pronouns ascribed to anyone who opposed Karl's reasonable and well-informed views on domestic and foreign policy. As Susie and Katie cleared the plates, Karl lamented the recent plans for a high occupancy traffic lane, known as the Diamond Lane, through Los Angeles,

"The goddamn thing was created by some liberal do-gooder who wanted to reward people who have more children. It's another incentive to get more money from welfare."

Matthew could stand the vitriol no longer. "Dad, how can you possibly impute the creation of a multi-passenger lane to reduce carbon emissions so we might breathe our air and occasionally see our mountains to a liberal conspiracy to promote more welfare mothers?"

In the soft gray of his intoxication, Thomas Reilly was proud of his grandson for standing up to his father, but was also pondering Karl's theory on rewarding promiscuity. Thomas was a big proponent of personal responsibility and felt people were too reckless sexually today. Kids these days favored sexual promiscuity, as long as it was with someone you loved or someone willing to split the hotel bill.

"The boy's got a point, Karl. You Southern Californians steal our water and have no rapid transit. You drive your damn cars everywhere. You are less than half the state's population, but you consume three-quarters of its resources."

"When did this become a local 1166 meeting?" Karl said.

"By the way, the last person that ever made income redistribution work was Jesus fucking Christ when he turned loaves and fishes into food to feed the masses. He was probably a liberal. Face it, Jesus was mortal and it was really his father, God, the Republican, who helped make the miracle happen. And note how I said 'miracle'. Trying to feed more mouths than you have food for is not humanly impossible. You need a goddamn miracle. Yet, every day in Washington, we see those idiots trying to do just that; Give away what we don't have. In the real world, we do that, we go into debt and then we all starve."

Matthew stared at his father with his mouth open.

Karl smirked realizing he had his son's full attention.

"Everyone knows God is a Republican. The whole goddamn Old Testament is a rulebook for how to kick ass, take names and manage those who are too stupid to think for themselves. You mess up? Boom! A plague upon your house! You worship the wrong God? Splat! You're fly shit on a Egyptian chariot windshield!"

"Are you really serious? How did we get from The Diamond Lane to God being a Republican?"

Freddie sat under the dining room table listening to the debate. He never really thought about God being a member of the Grand Ole Party. His mother had secretly told him once that God was really a woman. As for the Diamond Lane, he assumed Catholics and Mormons would be driving the majority of cars in this special lane reserved for fertile families. He was not sure what welfare was, but he began to suspect that having more than four kids was a great financial burden. Why else would you need financial assistance?

Karl advanced his attack on the left. "When Reagan was governor, we had a balanced budget and business was growing. The GOP chose Ford over Reagan. No wonder we lost. Reagan is the guy you want to give the ball to on the last play of the game because somehow you know he will score."

"Dad," Matthew responded, "You're reading too many John Birch pamphlets. Reagan ratted out his friends during blacklisting while at the same time he was representing them as the head of the Screen Actors Guild. He was a Democrat, but then got a little money and switched to the GOP because he wanted to keep it. He speaks for General Electric and learned all his capitalist tricks from them."

Thomas O'Reilly chuckled. "Karl, looks like your tuition is going to good use. The boy knows his history and is learning to speak his mind."

"Capitalist tricks?" Karl bellowed. "Jesus Christ. Those capitalist tricks are paying for his Commie education. When he graduates with a degree in poly-bullshit, what's he going to do? Build huts in Africa with all the crap that comes out of his mouth? He could start his own political party—The Mental Masturbators. I suspect he will want to marry someone from another country, have little commies, and send them to the University of Moscow."

As the political gloves came off, the tenor and tone grew sharper. Susie pretended not to hear, while Katie, being from a generation that had long since abandoned personal views that differed from her husband's, hummed as she did the dishes. It was now six p.m. and Thomas was pickled and ready to pour another glass of wine. Thanksgiving at the Pattons was a more realistic depiction of Norman Rockwell's iconic *Freedom from Want*. Yet, the debate seemed to center not on having too little; it was about having too much.

As the voices rose and the barometric pressure dropped, the women melted away, ostensibly to clean up, but really to escape the oncoming political storm of opinions. It was a domestic version of dine and dash. George and John loitered near the table, torn by boredom, but hoping to overhear one of Karl's infamous blue streaks of profanity. No amount of pumpkin, pecan, or apple pie could sweeten his dislike for liberals. His passion and his deep conviction could not be restrained. Thanksgiving was a time to be grateful, and gratitude included appreciating those people who that kept our economy chugging, our country safe from foreign interests, and our minds out of the gutter.

While Karl's ethos was born out of wholesome midwestern values, it was protected by barbed wire views, political landmines and shoot first and ask questions later guard towers. His views were not shared so much as they were released like water from a high-pressure fire hose. They were intelligent, rational, and totally devoid of compassion.

"No one ever gave me a goddamn thing!" he sputtered.

Finally, Susie could take no more and came back into the room as men were finishing their desserts. "Honey, don't talk with your mouth full."

Later in the evening, the bodies were discarded around the house like accident victims. The Thanksgiving topics had shifted to more benign subjects like sports and the upcoming holidays. Thomas O'Reilly was passed out on the couch, and Freddie had fallen asleep under the dining room table, dreaming about his game-winning catch.

Susie loved this day. It was a time when everyone was reminded that life's epicenter was family. It was the chance to fill rooms with the voices of generations, laughing, debating, wrestling, struggling, rising and falling. The spirit of Thanksgiving was still all about "us." Their extended family was a unit—a team that looked out for one another, tolerated each other's eccentric foibles and diverse political views, but remained deeply bonded by the fact that no one on earth knew them better than they knew one another.

On this day, there was much for which to be thankful. Freddie woke up and glanced at the thin ankles and bare feet of his mother and grandmother as they rearranged the dining room. He was content. Freddie Patton, a single-cell amoeba had entered the pantheon of Turkey Bowl heroes. Perhaps, he was on his way to evolving into something bigger, and more accomplished. He frowned realizing that he must wait until next Thanksgiving for his chance to show that this year was not a fluke.

Only 364 days to go.

Vin Nobalski thought he had heard it all. He was late for Thanksgiving dinner because he'd been pulled into a possible attempted armed robbery at Hunt's Market. Criminals got desperate this time of year and often assumed that cops were either on vacation, asleep in their squad cars, or shorthanded.

Having taken a page from Junior Riggs' retail playbook, Ralph Hunt Sr. had decided to keep the store open for the morning of the holiday hoping to capture any last minute business from families needing last minute items. The emergency call had come into the police earlier that morning. Apparently, an intruder had attempted to break into Hunt's Market from the loading dock when an elderly neighbor interrupted him. From this point, things were fuzzy, and there had been no witnesses. It seemed Ralph Hunt Jr. had been working on the dock when the assailant fired his weapon, taking a huge chunk out of Hunt's right buttocks and knocking him unconscious. The treating EMT had written in his report that Hunt was highly intoxicated. The neighbor, a confused octogenarian named Gertrude Spitz, apparently had been assaulted and knocked unconscious, but was recovering well at Pasadena Memorial Hospital.

There was no assailant and no weapon, and neither Hunt nor Spitz seemed to be able to recall anything. Vin finished typing his report and ripped it out of the Corolla, dropping the carbon paper into the waste can and the second copy into his out box to be filed. Snatching his jacket, he turned out the lights in his office. He patrolled one last time down the silent corridor and stopped at the front desk to see if he could catch the desk officer napping.

Vin Nobalski smiled. "Happy Thanksgiving, Jimmy. Try to stay awake until I get back Monday."

Jimmy looked up from his *True Crime* magazine and nodded. "Don't worry, Sarge. Small towns like these have shots fired about once every fifty years. My guess is it will be 2016 before we need to write another firearms report."

"That's what I want to hear, Jimmy."

Vin grinned as he walked out into the cool November afternoon.

R2 Hunt shot in the ass. Couldn't have happened to a nicer guy.

Plate 5

Using three metal tennis ball cans with lids (no pop-tops), take the top off of all the lids. Next take the bottom off of two of the cans. Take the only can with a bottom and punch a pencil sized hole in the side of the can near the bottom. Duct tape all of the cans together. Make sure the only can with a bottom is on the bottom. Put a small amount of lighter fluid in the hole in the bottom can. Add some lighter fluid on the inside of the top two cans. Put a tennis ball in the top of the top can. Pointing the top of the open can away from yourself and others, hold a lit match to the hole in the bottom can. The immediate explosion will shoot your tennis ball from 50 to 100 yards in the air. The cannon shot makes a great 'bang' noise, too.

Making your own
TENNIS BALL CANNON!

ABOUT THE AUTHOR

Michael Turpin received his B.A. in Literature from Claremont McKenna College and is a native of San Marino, California. He has lived in Los Angeles, San Francisco, London and New York. A healthcare consultant by day, he is a contributing columnist for magazines, newspapers as well as a popular blog that covers a range of topics from popular culture to the travails of modern day parents. His first novel, T-Rex By The Tail, is an anthem to the alpha fathers of the Silent Generation and their take-no-prisoners Jurassic parenting styles. Turpin lives in New Canaan, CT with his wife and three teenaged children.